D1267226

CURRENT ISSUES IN
AGRICULTURAL ECONOMICS

CURRENT ISSUES IN ECONOMICS

General Editor: David Greenaway, University of Nottingham

Current Issues in Agricultural Economics

Edited by

A. J. Rayner

Professor of Agricultural Economics
University of Nottingham

and

David Colman

Professor of Agricultural Economics
University of Manchester

St. Martin's Press   New York

 For information, write:
Scholarly and Reference Division,
St. Martin's Press, Inc., 175 Fifth Avenue,
New York, N.Y. 10010

First published in the United States of America in 1993

Printed in Hong Kong

ISBN 0–312–09091–9

Library of Congress Cataloging-in-Publication Data
Current issues in agricultural economics / edited by A. J. Rayner and
David Colman.
p. cm. — (Current issues in economics)
Includes bibliographical references and index.
ISBN 0–312–09091–9
1. Agriculture and state—United States. 2. Agriculture—Economic
aspects—United States. 3. Produce trade—Government policy—United
States. 4. Agriculture and state. 5. Agriculture—Economic
aspects. 6. Produce trade—Government policy. 7. International
economic relations. I. Rayner, A. J. II. Colman, David.
III. Series.
HD1761.C87 1993
338.1'0973—dc20 92–30623
CIP

Contents

List of Figures

List of Tables

Series Editor's Preface

The *Current Issues* series has slightly unusual origins. *Current Issues in International Trade,* which Macmillan published in 1987 and which turned out to be the pilot for the series, was in fact 'conceived' in the Horton Hospital, Banbury, and 'delivered' (in the sense of completed) in the Hilton International in Nicosia! The reader may be struck by the thought that a more worthwhile and enjoyable production process would start and finish the other way around. I agree! Be that as it may, that is how the series started.

As I said in the Preface to *Current Issues in International Trade* the reason for its creation was the difficulty of finding suitable references on 'frontier' subjects for undergraduate students. Many of the issues which excite professional economists and which dominate the journal literature take quite a time to percolate down into texts; hence the need for a volume of Current Issues. The reception which *Current Issues in International Trade* received persuaded me that it may be worth doing something similar for the other subject areas we teach. Macmillan agreed with my judgement, hence the series. Thus each volume in this series is intended to take readers to the 'frontier' of the particular subject area. Each volume contains nine or ten essays, one of which provides a general overview whilst the remainder are devoted to current issues.

As series editor the main challenge I faced was finding suitable editors for each of the volumes – the best people are generally the busiest! I believe, however, that I have been fortunate in having such an impressive and experienced team of editors with the necessary skills and reputation to persuade first-class authors to participate. I would like to thank all of them for their cooperation and assistance in the development of the series. Like me, all of them will, I am sure, hope that this series provides a useful service to undergraduate and postgraduate students as well as faculty.

Current Issues in Agricultural Economics is the ninth in the series. Agricultural economics is one of the oldest branches of economic analysis. It is an area of considerable controversy – in industrialised, developing and erstwhile centrally planned economies. In this volume, Tony Rayner and David Colman have selected papers which have a topical and current policy focus, including the political economy of agricultural policy, agricultural policy reform in the US and the EC, agricultural trade and the GATT, transformation in Eastern Europe and in China, and environmental economics and policy. Certain complementary topics are also covered – macroeconomics and agriculture, agricultural research and biotechnology, and the rural economy and less favoured areas. These are interesting and exciting issues both to specialist students of agricultural economics as well as students in other sub-areas of the discipline. The editors have persuaded a group of distinguished authors from three different countries to contribute in order to give a balanced and international perspective to the subject matter. I am grateful that they have cooperated to produce such a useful addition to the series.

University of Nottingham   DAVID GREENAWAY

Notes on the Contributors

David Colman is Professor of Agricultural Economics, Universi of Manchester.

Csaba Csáki is Professor of Agricultural Economics, Budapest University of Economic Sciences, and President of the International Association of Agricultural Economists.

R. C. Hine is Lecturer in Economics, University of Nottingham.

K. A. Ingersent is Senior Research Fellow in the Centre for Research in Economic Development and International Trade (CREDIT), University of Nottingham.

Tim Josling is Professor of Agricultural Economics, Food Research Institute, Stanford University.

D. Lee is Professor of Agricultural Economics, Cornell University.

W. Lesser is Professor of Agricultural Economics, Cornell University.

P. Midmore is Lecturer in Agricultural Economics, University College of Wales, Aberystwyth.

D. A. Peel is Professor of Economics, University College of Wales, Aberystwyth

A. J. Rayner is Professor of Agricultural Economics and Assistant Director of CREDIT, University of Nottingham.

Terry Sicular is Associate Professor of Economics, Harvard University.

K. J. Thomson is Professor of Rural Economics, University of Aberdeen.

L. Alan Winters is Professor of Economics, University of Birmingham.

1 Current Issues in Agricultural Economics: Introduction and Overview

A. J. RAYNER and DAVID COLMAN

The post-war period of the 1950s and 1960s was a comparatively stable one in terms of agricultural policy. It was a time of reconstruction based on the agricultural price support measures put in place by the developed countries in the 1930s during the Great Depression. International trade in agriculture was influenced by the colonial structures still in place over much of the third world, the first and second worlds were locked by the cold war into mutual trade isolation, and the USA's overwhelming economic power led to policies whereby it effectively stabilised international grain and many other markets besides.

Processes of change starting in the 1960s began to undermine the conditions for stability. The successful rebuilding of the economies of Western Europe and Japan gave them more autonomy of action, and the expansion of their agricultural sectors behind protective barriers began to change the pattern of agricultural trade. The budgetary costs of the USA's agricultural policies, whereby it in effect held the free world's grain stocks, became too burdensome, so that in 1970, in the presidency of Richard Nixon, decisions were taken to reduce stocks by emphasising acreage diversion and promoting cereal exports. Many countries in Asia and Africa became independent, and with their rapidly growing populations placed new demands upon the trading order, not least because of their needs for additional food imports. The system of exchange rate stability, which had been created following the Bretton Woods Conference of 1944, came to an end in 1971. The resultant freeing of exchange rates added significantly to the other sources of uncertainty ushered in by the 1970s which were intensified by the extreme inflationary conditions of 1973 to 1975. Many of the issues which are considered in this book can be seen as agricultural policy contributions to an ongoing process necessary to restore stability to world trade and the economic system generally.

Indeed, agricultural policy issues are at the centre of the current international political agenda. In the Uruguay Round of global trade liberalisation talks which have taken place since September 1986 under the auspices of the GATT (General Agreement on Tariffs and Trade), the most intractable area of negotiation has been the attempt to reform agricultural policy in key countries in order to reduce agricultural protectionism. Agricultural policy reform has played a key role in the economic transformation of China since the late 1970s, and it represents one of the most critical sets of policy issues for the future of Eastern Europe. Rapid developments in agricultural technology have underpinned the dramatic population and economic growth of the twentieth century. The processes of intensification and specialisation in production have had major impacts upon rural communities and upon the environment. Conservation and 'green' concerns have consequently gained increasing prominence on the political agenda and are fascinating as well as important areas for economic analysis. All these and other complementary issues are taken up in the volume in a manner designed to be accessible to final year undergraduates.

Chapters 2, 3 and 4 address various facets of agricultural protectionism in the industrialised world. There is a tradition of agricultural protectionism in Western Europe reaching back to the nineteenth century, whilst government intervention into agricultural markets in the USA stems from the depression period of the 1930s. The levels of protection and agricultural price support and the complexity of intervention have generally increased over time although there have been exceptions, as in Britain where the repeal of the Corn Laws led to free trade until the 1930s, and as in certain small- to medium-sized agricultural exporters such as New Zealand, Australia and Argentina.[1]

Domestic agricultural policies provide financial support to producers by way of monetary transfers from consumers through higher prices for agricultural products, and from taxpayers, via government budget outlays. The extent of this support in the major industrialised countries has increased substantially over the last decade according to Producer Subsidy Equivalent (PSE) estimates made by the OECD.[2] Specifically, the average net percentage PSEs for twelve major agricultural product categories across eleven important OECD member countries (including the EC as one 'country'),[3] increased from 28 per cent in 1980 to 50 per cent in 1987 and was 44 per cent in 1990. These average figures conceal considerable inter-country variation so that, for example, net percentage PSEs in 1990 were estimated to be 68 per cent in Japan, 48 per cent in the EC, 41 per cent in Canada, 30 per cent in the USA, 11 per cent in Australia and 5 per cent in New Zealand. Overall, the monetary value of net subsidies received by agricultural producers in these OECD countries amounted to some $176 billion in 1990,[4] equivalent to $15 000 per full-time farmer equivalent or $171 per hectare farmed (OECD, 1991, p. 133). Approximately 75 per cent of subsidies was provided by market price support and 12 per cent via direct payments from governments to producers.

In general, the assistance provided to producers through government policy is not production neutral. Rather, the higher prices and direct payments generated by intervention provide incentives to expand commodity output, unless accompanied by output quota, or input restrictions. Producers increase the purchase of inputs from other sectors of the economy and retain resources which might otherwise have shifted elsewhere. As a result, costs of production increase and the increase in welfare of producers is only a proportion of the monetary transfers made to the agricultural sector. For example, it has been estimated that producers benefited by $1 for each $1.5 transferred from consumers and taxpayers in the mid-1980s.[5] The costs of transfer are also raised by (i) the substantial administrative expenditures incurred in implementing and policing subsidy measures and curtailing fraud, and (ii) the socially unproductive lobbying expenses generated by farm groups seeking increased support and non-farm groups seeking to counter agricultural protectionism. Furthermore, typical farm support mechanisms are not only inefficient at transferring welfare to agricultural products but they are also inequitable. Thus, under a system of non-selective market price support, larger farmers benefit more than smaller producers and the transfer is via an implicit regressive expenditure tax imposing a proportionately greater burden on the poorer non-farm households. Other undesirable effects also follow from domestic support programmes. For example, transfers become capitalised into the value of assets in inelastic supply such as land or quotas, enriching their first generation recipients but giving their successors higher entry barriers and a burdensome cost structure. Finally, intervention leads to domestic resource misallocation and a drag on economic growth.

The growth in support to domestic agricultural sectors has led to disarray in agricultural trade, increased instability on international food markets and misallocation of resources in world agriculture.[6] The impact of support policies on international markets generated acute conflicts in the 1980s between the major players – the USA, the EC and Japan – and caused considerable economic damage to smaller agricultural exporters such as Australia and New Zealand, and developing countries like Argentina. The declaration launching the Uruguay Round of multilateral trade negotiations in 1986 recognised that agricultural trade was severely distorted by government policies and aimed to liberalise this trade through the reform of domestic agricultural policies.

In short, economic analysis points to a substantial social dividend that would be realised from a reduction/withdrawal of agricultural support and protectionism in the industrialised countries. Furthermore, recent political indicators have been favourable to the lowering of agricultural protection and the tightening of disciplines concerning the conduct of agricultural trade. However, in seeking to reform public policy, all governments are 'prisoners of the past'. Agricultural protectionism is entrenched in domestic policy legislation which has proved difficult to dismantle. Alan Winters, by means of a political science approach, examines how this situation has arisen and why it has been allowed to continue in Chapter 2 on 'The Political Economy of Industrial Countries' Agricultural Policies'. The goals of agricultural policy, as espoused in official documents, might at first sight,be viewed as non-economic or social in nature. However, Winters asserts that they are rightly considered as SNOs (so-called non-economic objectives) and shows how they are amenable to economic analysis. He then examines the interaction between goals and the economic environment surrounding policy making; the latter constraining the extent and form of possible intervention. Actual policy is shaped and implemented by the major actors – politicians, bureaucrats and the farm lobbies – Winters draws on relevant theory in providing insights into their behaviour and influence. Finally, he offers two models of the making of agricultural policy: 'the political market place' and 'policy as a process'. Together they help to explain the prevalence of the costly tangle of potentially conflicting instruments that currently constitutes agricultural policy in most industrial countries.

One conclusion drawn by Winters is that policy innovation occurs only at times of crises. Tim Josling expands on this theme in Chapter 3 in considering 'Agricultural Policy Reform in the USA and the EC'. His central premise is that agricultural policy reform is a response to a confluence of events or pressures such that the benefits from change outweigh the benefits to retaining the status quo. He identifies three events which combined to exert pressure for reform in the 1980s. The first of these was disillusionment with the efficacy of government intervention into agricultural markets and a growing realisation of the costs entailed by such intervention. Second, was the growing linkage of agriculture to the macroeconomy and its increased vulnerability to macroeconomic shocks (see also Midmore and Peel, Chapter 7) such that the traditional policy instruments have declining effectiveness. Third, was the growing interdependence of the US and EC economies both among themselves and with other countries; not only did this increase the importance of trade influences on the outcomes of agricultural policies and on farm incomes, it also led directly to agricultural policy offsets such that some fraction of price support in one country is used to offset the impact of support in other countries (see also Rayner *et al.,* Chapter 4). Josling chronicles the history of agricultural policy changes before detailing policy shifts in the 1980s within the context of his central thesis . He then attempts to ascertain if policies have been improved in the sense of becoming less costly and employing more consistent instruments. Finally, he considers factors influencing the future direction of agricultural policy.

Taken together, the chapters by Winters and Josling provide the reader with both analytical insights and a historical perspective on the current state of domestic agricultural policies in the industrialised world; particularly in the USA and the EC. The evident resistance to agricultural policy reform so clearly enunciated in these essays has led to mounting agricultural trade tensions. Agricultural trade policies are largely an adjunct of domestic commodity programmes; as a consequence it has been difficult, if not impossible, to foster agricultural trade liberalisation in the period since the Second World War despite significant reductions in barriers to trade in manufactures.

Tony Rayner, Ken Ingersent and Robert Hine provide a perspective on agricultural trade issues in Chapter 4 on 'Agricultural Trade and the GATT'. They start by noting that agricultural trade has not been governed by the institutional framework for international trade relations that has been provided by the GATT since its inception in 1947. Rather international trade rules have been adapted to conform with domestic agricultural programmes. After noting the structure of world agricultural trade, they then discuss the trade distortions and disputes, and the increased instability of international commodity markets induced by the interventionist agricultural policies that are the norm in OECD countries. In the 1980s, there were pressures for reform of agricultural policies (as discussed by Josling in Chapter 3) and the Uruguay Round of Trade Negotiations included the liberalisation of agricultural trade as a major item on its agenda. The authors discuss the potential for trade negotiations to promote the reform of farm support policy before going on to detail the protracted nature of the negotiations between the launch of the Uruguay Round in 1986 and the position arrived at in January 1992. They conclude that there is a gradual ongoing reform of agricultural policies in the industrialised countries (note that Josling in Chapter 3 is less sanguine), that this reform will tend to reduce distortions imposed on international food markets and that the international agricultural trade negotiations can assist policy change by locking governments into the reform path.

Chapters 5 and 6 deal with issues of agricultural policy reform in Eastern Europe and China respectively. In both regions, reform is directed towards reducing administrative intervention in the rural economy, increasing reliance on economic levers, decentralising decision-making on farms and rural enterprises and expanding the role of markets.

Chapter 5 by Csabi Csáki discusses agricultural policy in the context of the ongoing transformation of the economies of the countries of central and Eastern Europe. Authoritarian regimes employing central planning have been replaced by pluralist democracies which are committed to a transition to a predominantly market based economic system. The reform of agriculture represents a major challenge in this transition given the importance of agriculture in these economies: agriculture contributes between 8 and 20 per cent to national product and employs 9 to 22 per cent of the population depending on the country under consideration. Csáki discusses some of the major problems arising from the legacy of the past; for example, retail food prices have been heavily subsidised, there is an inefficient dualistic structure of agriculture with large high cost state and collective farms coexisting with small-scale private plot production, an absence of markets in land and a pervasive monopoly in food processing and distribution. Csáki then provides a 'manifesto for change', detailing the economic and institutional innovations that he believes are required to develop a market-oriented and competitive agriculture. These include, legislating for the reprivatisation of landed property and implementing changes in the structure of agriculture, bringing in price reform and introducing competition into agro-industries. Finally, he outlines possible scenarios for the future course of agriculture in the medium term. One important factor affecting the potential for development is future agricultural trade relations with Western nations; in particular, the extent to which the latter reduce agricultural protectionism (see also Josling, Chapter 3).

In Chapter 6, Terry Sicular discusses agricultural policy in China in the period of economic reform initiated from the late 1970s. China's reform process has led to dramatic improvements in economic performance, albeit from a low base. Agriculture has been a leading sector with emphasis placed on decollectivisation, so shifting the basic decision unit in agriculture from the collective farm to the household, on price incentives and on a move away from mandatory production planning and procurement. Sicular notes that whilst the measures taken were undeniably successful in raising agricultural output, productivity and farm incomes, performance in the agricultural sector slackened from 1985 onwards. In discussing reasons for the slowdown, she finds previous explanations wanting and places emphasis on policy measures enacted in 1983–5 that had negative effects on agriculture. Specifically, she directs attention to agricultural policies that reduced incentives to farmers and to non-agricultural policies that induced a flow of resources out of farming and into private rural enterprises. In particular, Sicular concludes that reform policies should be coordinated such that the linkages between agriculture and other sectors of the economy are recognised and so that 'balanced' growth is achieved. If this is done, she is optimistic about the potential for sustainable agricultural growth.

The remaining four chapters of this volume address themes that are complementary to the previous analyses of agricultural policy reform in diverse institutional settings. Specifically, they deal, respectively, with macroeconomics and the agricultural sector, agricultural research, environmental issues, and less favoured agricultural areas and the rural economy.

Josling in Chapter 3 notes the growing dependence of the agricultural sector on developments in the non-farm economy and its increased vulnerability to macroeconomic shocks. Midmore and Peel elaborate on this theme (Chapter 7). They begin by examining links between changes in exchange rates and the behaviour of commodity prices and agricultural profitability in the US context. They then present two hypotheses which underpin much of the new 'classical' macroeconomics: namely the rational expectations hypothesis and the efficient market hypothesis. These hypotheses are next combined into a model which is used to explore the proposition that agricultural prices 'overshoot' in response to macroeconomic policy shifts. This is a

controversial area, where as the authors note, the available econometric evidence does not provide a clear cut conclusion as to the
relevance and importance of the overshooting proposition. However,
the potential sensitivity of the agricultural sector to macroeconomic
policy is not just a field for academic debate; it is suggested that
agricultural policy directed at reducing instability in the farm sector
needs to be reassessed in the light of linkages with the macroeconomy.

The chapters by Winters, Josling, and Rayner *et al.* note that
agricultural protectionism is often justified on the grounds of providing assistance for adjustment to technical change. But technological
change stemming from public and private sector research and development (R & D) is so rapid that managed adjustment is difficult and
can be very costly. William Lesser and David Lee (Chapter 8) explore
the economics of agricultural R & D. The major issues examined
concern the appropriate level of public funding and the division of R &
D between public and private sources. The authors note that many
studies have estimated high social returns to public sector agricultural
R & D in many countries. At first sight, it appears that such R & D is
underfunded but Lesser and Lee find that returns are typically
overstated. Nevertheless, they conclude that the social return to
agricultural research is high suggesting that additional funding would
enhance public welfare. Lesser and Lee then examine the trend towards
the private funding of agricultural research stimulated in part by the
potential of biotechnology to raise substantially the productivity of
agriculture. The heavy involvement of private sector funding in this
research raises several issues for policy makers including appropriate
legal protection for innovations and the regulation of new biotechnology products.

David Colman in Chapter 9, on 'Environmental Economics and
Agricultural Policy', notes that in North America and Western Europe
measures to control environmental externalities are now an ingredient
of domestic agricultural policy. This is a fairly new feature of the
relevant policy agendas and, in part, a reaction to the growing
influence of the environmental lobby (see also Josling, Chapter 3).
Traditionally, farmers have acted as stewards of the countryside; a
prevalent maxim among past generations of agriculturalists has been
'to live as if you are going to die tomorrow but to farm as if you are
going to live for ever'. Sustainable agriculture was part of the farming
creed but modern intensive farming is viewed by many non-agricul-
turalists as exploiting the land and using it in ways which generate
external costs in such forms as polluted water supplies, reduced food

quality and safety, and a degraded countryside and environment. Colman reviews the relevant economic principles that provide a framework within which such concerns, and those of sustainable agriculture, can be addressed by policy. Emphasis is placed upon alternative policy mechanisms to control the way farmers use their land and other resources. Using the UK as a source of examples, Colman then surveys regulatory instruments to control agricultural externalities; these range from subsidies for beneficial management to outright public ownership of land and from taxes to the issuing of tradeable pollution permits.

An implicit assumption in the traditional agricultural policy agenda has been that farming is the backbone of rural areas and that viable rural economies depend upon agricultural income levels. It has also been thought desirable that *agricultural* population levels be maintained in rural areas in order to both sustain the rural economy and conserve the environment. Disadvantaged regions – Less Favoured Areas (LFAs) – in an agricultural sense have been targeted for special support under agricultural policy in Western Europe. Kenneth Thomson in Chapter 10 addresses analytical and policy issues arising in connection with 'Less Favoured Areas and Rural Decline'. He notes there are definitional and classification problems that have to be resolved before rural development policy can be appropriately targeted. He discusses the various policy goals such as income redistribution, amenity preservation and the expansion of occupational choice (diversification of the rural economy) within the context of the declining linkages between agricultural prosperity and the state of the rural economy in many regions. In many rural areas with a disadvantaged economic base, part-time farming associated with pluriactive (multiple job-holding) farm households represents a core component of the local economy. These households are largely untouched by the prevalent price supporting commodity programmes while rural development strategies are not solely or even primarily advanced via agricultural policy *per se*. Perhaps not surprisingly, Thomson finds that 'there is no clear set of government policies addressed to the problems of rural economic decline'.

These chapters have been commissioned in order to inform students as to 'current issues' in the field of agricultural policy and related areas of analysis. Each one offers insights which students in agricultural economics will find useful as guideposts to existing knowledge or as pointers to future research. However, not all current issues in agricultural policy have been addressed, the most notable omission relating to agricultural development policies and problems in less developed countries (other than China). That is because these issues have been covered in the companion volume, *Current Issues in Development Economics*, edited by V. N. Balasubramanyam and Sanjaya Lall.

2 The Political Economy of Industrial Countries' Agricultural Policies

L. ALAN WINTERS[1]

2.1 INTRODUCTION

Agricultural policies in nearly all industrial countries' raise prices, redistribute income regressively and towards a small section of society, and impose economic costs both at home and abroad. In this chapter I consider why such an outcome is allowed to come about: why governments sanction it and electorates let them get away with it.

My basic thesis is that agricultural policy arises from the tension between a public opinion that abhors rapid change and values the supposed virtues of bucolic life, and an economic evolution that constantly disrupts traditional agricultural methods. As in all branches of economics, technical analysis alone, cannot answer the normative questions surrounding agricultural policy,[2] and so this tension has to be resolved politically; this opens avenues for discretionary market intervention, which, in turn, spawns political lobbying and bureaucratic manœuvring.

The final outcome thus depends on the interactions of the farm lobbies, the bureaucrats and the politicians as they struggle to resolve (in their own favour) the problems generated by the economic environment. Although there are a number of regularities observable in the outcome of such interactions, over anything but the longest of runs these interactions do not define a stable equilibrium in agricultural policy. Rather, the parties engage in an endless and uncertain game (in the technical sense), each 'winning' some rounds and 'losing' others, but all anticipating the next round, and all buffeted by the same exogenous shocks. The resulting compromises are hard to predict, and

11

given the longevity of most interventions, agricultural policy comes to resemble not a single elegant and effective structure, but rather an untidy accretion of differing, and sometimes conflicting, instruments.

This chapter aims to give a broad feel for the way in which this process shapes agricultural policy. The analysis starts with a sketch and a dismissal of a Panglossian view in which agricultural policy is optimal, but in which, given their limited horizons, economists cannot recognise it as such. From here, it moves on to consider less than perfectly competent governments and the goals they espouse. These goals I identify with the 'social will'. The next section deals with the importance of economic factors in shaping economic policy. The interaction of economic forces and social objectives leaves the major actors considerable discretion, so I then consider each of these – the politicians, the bureaucrats and the farm lobbies. In the last section, I consider two competing ways of pulling the story together: one stresses equilibrium and regularity – the 'political market-place theories' – while the other stresses the sequential and random nature of the most policy-making, examining processes as well as pressures.

2.2   OBJECTIVES AND JUSTIFICATIONS

The simplest approach to industrial countries' agricultural policy might be called 'social rationality'.[3] This argues that while protectionism may seem costly in terms of a community's economic welfare, this is only because the traditional notion of economic benefit is too restrictive: countries do not maximise national income because their citizens also have additional, and conflicting, objectives concerning income distribution, price and income stability, and national security. Once we recognise these, the arguments runs, we will see that industrial country governments are doing just the right thing after all. Few economists support such a view entirely, but for some – for example, Heidhues (1979) – it represents a principal mode of thought. It is also implicit in the traditional view – rejected by political economy analysts – that economic policy analysis based on welfare maximisation *does*, as opposed to merely should, determine policy decisions.

'Social rationality' discounts any notion of conflicting interests within government. By assuming that government action perfectly reflects well-defined social goals, it takes the politics out of political economy. It also assumes considerable sophistication on the part of governments, presuming them to be able to solve in practice the problems which, even in theory, keep academic economists awake at night.[4] Finally, it admits empirical testing only if all the additional objectives can be clearly specified independently of the policy decisions intended to achieve them. Since this is virtually impossible 'social rationality' can rapidly descend into mere apology for existing policy.

A natural – and fruitful – extension of 'social rationality' is to 'limited social rationality', which holds that governments try to achieve other targets but do not always succeed. This theory reduces the chances of formally deducing targets from observed behaviour, but in return wins a much wider range of application and relevance. Provided the additional targets can be identified independently of governments' policy stances, one can ask whether they have been achieved and if not, why not. This immediately opens the door to issues such as power and influence in policy-making, the role of institutions, and the importance of information and uncertainty. It also, incidentally, restores the legitimacy of economic policy advice, and allows industrial countries' agricultural policies to be challenged on the grounds of competence.

Table 2.1 lists the objectives of agricultural policy noted in certain official publications. Different countries weight them differently, but overall most policy-makers and citizens would find the list unexceptionable. It could not be termed innocuous, however, for it contains within it the seeds of all the conflicts that beset agricultural policy. For example, fair remuneration might conflict with reasonable prices, as might efficiency with adjustment relief, or stability of supply with conservation. Thus trade-offs become inevitable, and political factors come into play.

Even if the points in Table 2.1 do actually represent community preferences, their day-to-day execution rests with governments. Thus they represent not so much a perpetual maximand as a broad framework for government action, a boundary of 'reasonableness' beyond which governments cannot stray. Moreover, agriculture is not the only area of policy: thus agricultural aims have to be balanced against other objectives, not least the national budget constraint.

Before turning to the political arena, however, I shall briefly examine some of the issues raised by this list of social objectives. This is important because in many policy debates the proponents of agricultural support fall back on this list and assert that, since the bulk of the objectives are non-economic, they are not amenable to economic analysis and hence are the province of the economist no more than of any other analyst. This view is wrong: it is true that economists have no more right than anyone else to determine societies' goals and

TABLE 2.1 The declared objectives of agricultural policy in selected OECD countries

	EEC	Japan	Canada	Australia	New Zealand	Austria	USA	Switzerland	Finland	Iceland	Norway	Sweden
1. Satisfactory and equitable standard of living for farmers	X	X	X			X	X	X			X	X
2. Income stabilisation			X	O	X		X		X			
3. Stabilise domestic agricultural prices	X	O	X	X	X	X	X	X				
4. Ease adjustment to exogenous shocks	I	O	X	X	I		I					
5. Maintain healthy rural communities	O	X	O		I	X	X	X	X			
6. Regional development	O	O	O			X					X	X
7. Preservation and encouragement of family farming	X		X	I	O	O						
8. Environmental protection	O	O	I	I		X	O	X	X		X	X
9. Safe, secure, stable and sufficient food supplies	X	X	X			X	X	X	X	X	X	X
10. Fair prices for consumers	X	O	X				X		X			X
11. Agricultural efficiency and competitiveness	X	X	X	X	X	X	X	X		X	X	X

X denotes that the objective is explicitly referred to in the objectives section of the relevant national report.

O denotes that the objective is mentioned elsewhere in the text of the relevant national report.

I denotes that the objective has been imputed from the enactment of legislation directly *impinging* upon it, as reported in the relevant national report.

No entry indicates that no direct reference is made to the objective.

Source: Winters (1989).

constraints, but the objectives are none the less economic, both because they are amenable to money measurement (the criterion of 'economic' adapted by the famous Cambridge economist Pigou) and they involve trade-offs of the sort with which economics is concerned. For this reason I termed them SNOs (So-called Non-economic Objectives) in Winters (1989), where I argued that virtually none of them is efficiently pursued by current policy.

Observe first that the list in Table 2.1 envisages some maximal rate of adjustment for farmers, as for other folk. This is not absolute, but translates practically into the view that farmers should not have to face severe adjustment costs if the rest of us do not. This view embodies a widely held notion of 'fairness', and is particularly prominent if farmers (i) apparently face material declines in their welfare and (ii) if, in some sense, this is not their fault, for example, if it is due to changes in government policy, exogenous shocks (e.g. weather or disease), or external factors (e.g. from abroad). In these cases – especially if prompted by vigorous protests by the farmers themselves – industrial societies appear to be willing to countenance significant governmental farm support.

The abhorrence of adjustment implicit in the last paragraph is the phenomenon isolated by Corden (1974) in his 'conservative social welfare function' (CSWF). This holds that governments seek to prevent, and certainly never to initiate, events that significantly cut the welfare of any particular group of society. As well as meeting the community's sense of 'fairness', the CSWF is also attractive to policy-makers in that it probably promotes social harmony and political quiescence. Research on protectionism in general shows how much easier it is to win public and official support to prevent a fall in income than to create a gain – for instance, Lavergne (1983). In part this stems from a misplaced desire for concreteness in political debates: one can identify the farmer who is forced into bankruptcy by technical progress in pig farming, but not the two workers who would have jobs in the service sector if farming were allowed to contract. Jones and Krueger (1990) analyse this argument, while Fernandez and Rodrik (1988) show how uncertainty about whether they will be among the beneficiaries can lead risk-averse voters to reject a policy change even when they know that it will generate benefits in aggregate.

The CSWF lays great emphasis on the status quo, implicity assuming that it represents a feasible alternative to the policy under considera-tion. This helps to explain why major policy change is possible only at times of deep crisis, when, because the status quo is infeasible, everyone accepts that 'something must be done'.

Second, consider the security of supplies. Food, and hence agriculture, satisfies man's most basic need and arouses his most basic emotions. With the folk memories of food shortages during the Second World War still strong, it is difficult to overstate the strength of feeling on this issue in Europe and Japan. Heidhues (1979) argues that normal economic policy debate presupposes that 'more basic issues' such as survival are not at stake, and he quotes official reactions to the oil crisis (in 1973–4) and the fear of grain shortages (in 1972–5) as illustrating the primacy of security over economic efficiency.

The correct ranking of survival and efficiency is obvious, but using this to justify industrial countries' current agricultural policies is either foolish or disingenuous. Industrial countries need never fear debilitating food shortages arising from purely economic phenomena. It is inconceivable that they would be unable to purchase sufficient food on world markets after even the worst of world crops. Hence the 'economic security' argument hinges around cost, and it is clear that paying scarcity prices even as often as once every five years would be cheaper than paying relatively high prices every year to keep local output up.

More emotive is 'strategic security' – the ability to feed the population in times of severe political crisis. But it would have to be a very severe crisis indeed to make food unobtainable from any source – after all, the USSR coped easily enough with the USA's grain embargo in 1980. But in an extreme crisis the inputs necessary for the present high levels of output in Europe and Japan would not be available. Shortages of oil, fertilisers and pesticides would devastate current output levels, especially given the overexploitation of the land that current policies encourage. If security really mattered, industrial countries would surely tackle it via strategic stockpiles rather than output policies, especially given the perspective that nuclear weapons give to the likelihood of fighting a long war. Thus 'security' is an excuse – albeit a hugely effective one – for supporting industrial country agriculture. Winters (1990) explores this issue in detail.

Third, note the importance of uncertainty and instability in the list of objectives. The desire to know about one's fate – that is, to avoid uncertainty – and the desire to stabilise consumption flows over time figure large in private economic actions and are frequently invoked as justifications for economic policy interventions. For the latter purpose, however, one needs to identify the market failure that prevents people who desire certainty and stability from achieving it efficiently by private means. (Efficiently does not mean free.) For example, private insurance is available for many risks, and World Bank (1986) shows that increased public storage aimed at enhancing price stability is largely offset by a decrease in private storage. Moreover, if private insurance is not available because of market failures such as adverse selection or moral hazard, one must realise that these will also affect public insurance and policy substitutes for it, often with disastrous results, Dixit (1990). Thus while the argument that society should support groups whose industries suffer negative shocks has a strong intuitive appeal, not least because we would all like to think we would be so supported, it is difficult to show that doing so is efficient in terms of increasing welfare.[5]

A fourth interesting feature of the list of objectives is the promotion of rural lifestyles and the family farm. The virtues of the small farmer tilling his land and fighting the elements figure large in both European and American cultures. For example:

Those who labour in the earth are the chosen people of God . . . Corruption of morals in the mass cultivators is a phenomenon of which no age nor nation has furnished an example. (Thomas Jefferson, *Notes on Virginia*, 1781)

or on a humbler level:

In saving agriculture . . . we are saving a way of life in which the features are kindliness, freedom and, above all, wisdom. These are the qualities of the countryman and countrywoman. (R. A. Butler, speech in 1948, see Wilson, 1977).

Thus again policy-makers invoke an authority higher than mere economic efficiency to justify their agricultural policies. And again, given the propensity of policy to benefit large rather than family farms, one detects incompetence or disingenuousness. Yet again, however, the trick appears to work, for these emotions are deeply held and widely spread.

The list of objectives for agriculture is very laudable, and if any other sector of the economy were subject to such a perfectly targeted policy it would probably have similar objectives. However, no other sector does rival agriculture in this respect; agriculture is special in the degree of attention it receives and the question arises of why? There is no satisfactory answer to this, but I suspect that it resides in the above combination of a mistaken public perception of the worth of marginal units of agriculture and a cultural affinity towards farming, probably based on its historical importance. Public opinion surveys tend to find significant degrees of support for agricultural policy, although Variyam, Jordan and Epperson (1990) show that support drops away when questions are rephrased to make explicit the costs of agricultural policy to the individual.

2.3 ECONOMIC INFLUENCES

Social preferences represent one part of the environment for agricultural policy; the other part is defined by long-term economic conditions. The problems to which policy seeks to provide answers are economic: for example, the instability of agricultural supply, the secular improvements in technology and declines in prices, and the inelasticity of demand for agricultural products. Economics also basically defines the 'technology' available to policy-makers: the link between their inputs (policy) and their output (economic variables). For example, policies that increase prices will raise output and cut demand; subsidies to one factor of production will alter factor input mixes; rents will be captured by scarce immobile factors (land); rewards to mobile factors of production will be determined outside agriculture; restrictions on supplies of one good will stimulate purchases of close substitutes. Thus while I shall argue below that political factors are important determinants of the shape of agricultural intervention, the agenda of problems and possibilities is determined by economic conditions.

Such 'economic technology' helps to explain some of the differences in protection between commodities. Variable levy schemes tend to be worthwhile administratively only for major traded commodities and for homogeneous products. Production controls are more attractive when commodities are inelastic in supply – a feature often associated with high land intensity. Government purchase and control is easier when products must be processed – for example, milk and sugar – than where they need not – for instance, fruit.

These two directions in which economic conditions influence protection are illustrated in papers by Honma and Hayami (1986) and Gardner (1987). The former seek to explain nominal protection coefficients in agriculture for a sample of industrial countries over the period 1955–80. They find that declining terms of trade for agricultural goods explain a fair amount of the propensity to protect farmers. This is essentially economics defining the set of problems. Gardner, on the other hand, considers 'economic technology'. Examining eighteen commodities in the USA over the period 1910–78, he finds the degree of protection offered to a commodity directly related to the 'redistributional' efficiency with which income can be transferred to agricultural producers via that commodity. 'Redistributional efficiency' is the ratio of the change in producer surplus to (minus) the change in consumer surplus arising from one further unit of protection.[6]

A critical feature of the economic environment is its uncertainty. As well as leading to demands for protection, this also complicates policy-making. No one can predict the future shocks that agricultural policy will have to cope with, and hence it is difficult to design long-term policy. Neither are economists always adept at predicting the quantitative effects of policy, hence it can also be difficult to choose the correct level of interventions and difficult to decide, *ex post*, whether or not policy has been effective. Uncertainty means that policy-making is risky and that expectations are very important. One needs expectations not only about the consequences of the policy under immediate consideration, but also about a range of future issues. Much of politics proceeds by precedent, so, given the sequential nature of policy-making, one's attitudes to issues in year t must square with the attitudes that one expects to take to other issues in year $(t + 1)$. On the other hand, the passage of real time can ease some of the problems of decision-making, for it permits a 'wait and see' position and can resolve conflicts as data and information become available. This fact can help to explain the conservatism of agricultural policy, especially in dismantling redundant policy, for that can always be done next year, when the policy's redundancy will be even more obvious.

2.4 THE MAIN ACTORS

The social will may be as defined by Table 2.1 above, but it is implemented in practice through the agency of politicians and bureaucrats. Since the public cannot monitor their every move, and since they rely on administrators for much of their information, the latter have a great deal of discretion in designing policy. Indeed, I would argue that within some more or less vaguely defined boundary they have almost complete discretion. Thus a key factor in agricultural policy is the way in which administrators interpret economic shocks and social objectives in the light of their goals. I now consider how these goals are shaped and how they interact with the economic and political environment sketched above.

2.4.1 Politicians

I start with an unrealistic but informative model of direct democracy. Suppose, following Mayer (1984), that a referendum were held on whether to have a tariff on wheat imports. Imagine that all factors of production were sector specific, and that all farmers would each benefit from the tariff by a net present value of £g over its expected duration, while all consumers would each lose by £1. Since the number of consumers will outweigh the number of farmers, we would expect the tariff to be rejected. Now, however, assume that it cost each voter £c to vote – say, in lost time. If, not implausibly, $g > c > 1$, the vote would now support protection, for anti-votes would not be cast. This is so even though total producer gains may fall well short of total consumer losses.

Even this simple example illustrates some important points. First, while possibly not very relevant to voting, it is readily applicable to any process of making one's views known. Who would protest in the rain or even write to their MP over costs of say, 25p per year? Hence any British policy imposing say £10 million of social cost might get a free run through Parliament. Second, since the consumer costs of protection increase more than proportionately with the height of the tariff, at some tariff level the cost to each consumer will outweigh c, and at this level the tariff would be rejected. This suggests that great power resides with the 'gate-keeper' or agenda-setter, who decides what should be voted upon: a tariff of t may be passed in preference to a zero tariff while a higher one would be rejected. Third, the simple voting model overlooks one vital issue – free-riding. In the original model why would any producer incur costs of £c to vote? After all, he might figure that consumers will not vote and that since other producers will gain they will have a sufficient incentive to vote from the measure; hence cannot he save his £c without affecting the outcome? The difficulty is obvious, and can only be resolved by appealing to external pressures to vote or make one's opinions known – to which we turn below.

Once we recognise that voting on protection is indirect, via politicians, and that it is often tied in with other issues, the situation becomes much more complex. Voting in legislatures – Parliament or Congress – is often subject to log-rolling – voting coalitions whereby A and B agree to vote for each other's pet schemes. In the UK, party discipline is a means of log-rolling because it creates coalitions to vote for a multipolicy package. In the USA log-rolling is more *ad hoc* and hence more explicit, and is aided by the use of Omnibus Bills into which nearly anything can be written. Shepsle and Weingast (1981) show how the political incentive system encourages such practices among Congressmen anxious to get re-elected.

Log-rolling is clearly likely to create links between subjects, often inherently unrelated ones. This is important: it increases the leverage of pressure groups' financial contributions to, or publicly articulated support for, a politician, because the politician can use support on one issue to pursue other issues in which he is interested. Agricultural organisations seem well able to exploit multi-issue links: they generally have high public profiles and a lot of public sympathy, so that their endorsements matter. They also make campaign contributions – especially in the USA – not merely to legislators from rural constituencies but to key players throughout politics.

Log-rolling can also introduce random shocks, for political systems function by means of complex trade-offs, by which having received favours on one issue politicians feel obliged to offer concessions on another. The public choice school of theorists – see Mueller (1989) for a survey – holds that politicians make these trade-offs with the sole objective of re-election. This view may provide a useful approximation for analytical purposes, but it is probably exaggerated: concern for the disadvantaged, perception of the public interest and even principle may also play a role.

2.4.2 Bureaucrats

Politicians are not the only group which can dispense protection to petitioners – bureaucrats can also do so. Indeed, in Europe bureaucrats are typically in post longer than politicians and are frequently better informed and more powerful. Building on Niskanen's (1971) general theory of bureaucracy, Messerlin (1983) considers the implication of these facts for protection. He notes that senior bureaucrats become closely identified with the sectors they manage – their skills are rather specific, their prestige and status depend on how their sectors perform, and they often develop close relationships with managers in those sectors. He also observes that bureaux compete with each other for influence and that they resist external interference from politicians and particularly other bureaucrats in 'general' ministries such as Finance or Foreign Affairs. Finally, he notes that whereas politicians can frequently extract some of the political rents that their actions generate for their political institutions – for example, by diverting them to their own re-election campaigns – bureaucrats almost never can. Rather their rewards are related to the sizes of their budgets or their numbers of staff.

One implication of these observations is that bureaucrats offer more protection than politicians. Subject to constraints of political feasibility, politicians might offer a sector the tariff that maximises political rents, because implicitly they have a share of these rents. A bureaucrat, on the other hand, reaps no direct personal rewards from rents, but is interested instead in the size of the unit or the budget he administers; hence bureaucrats will tend to offer the tariff which maximises the extent of political activity or perhaps the tariff revenue collected. These will almost invariably be higher then the political rent-maximising tariff.[7] Bureaucrats will also favour more complex means of protection: these both generate jobs and reduce external interference and monitoring because no one else could understand how the system works. It is difficult to test such conjectures, but the case of agricultural protection suggests their plausibility. Agricultural bureaucracies grew very large during the Second World War, and have since maintained immensely restrictive and complex protection relying on quality and quantity controls. Attempts at reform have certainly been frustrated by civil servants in Japan and probably elsewhere as well.

Bureaucratic protection can also escalate because of limited competence – the fact that one bureau controls only a subset of available policy instruments. For example, protection is relative – protection for one sector means disprotection for the rest. Hence the Ministries of Agriculture and Industry might compete with each other to stimulate their own sectors by protection, escalating tariffs beyond the levels they would choose if they cooperated. New Zealand in the 1970s and the early 1980s provides an example of this sort of problem where agriculture required support to offset high industrial protection. Similarly, the Ministry of Agriculture might accept that reducing agricultural protection would be Pareto improving if simultaneously the Treasury increased income transfers to farmers. But because it cannot control the latter issue, the ministry dare not recommend the former. This is one of the reasons why ministries of Agriculture have only slowly come around to the idea of direct income support for farmers: as well as being dangerously transparent, they are too close to being a Treasury responsibility rather than an agricultural one.

It is only at higher levels of government that combinations of policies can be guaranteed, which is one reason higher levels are typically more liberal in their approach to foreign trade than are lower levels. Another is that the top levels of government are responsible for both the benefits and the cost of protection. Hence to stimulate trade liberalisation it is usually more effective to deal with the Ministries of Finance and Foreign Affairs, to which the domestic and foreign costs of protection matter, than the sectoral Ministries such as Agriculture, Industry or Energy.

2.4.3 Interest groups

Many interest groups press for protection, but those for agriculture are widely believed to be among the best organised and most influential in Western economies. In Britain, for instance, over 80 per cent of farmers belong to the National Farmers' Union (NFU). The NFU has a large professional staff at regional and national levels and has a privileged position in British policy discussions. When agricultural policy was a purely national concern – as opposed to the present situation under the EC's Common Agricultural Policy – the Ministry of Agriculture, Fisheries and Food was obliged by law to consult the industry before fixing product prices. Thus the NFU was granted access to the highest bureaucratic levels, a practice that continues today. In return, and as a means of re-enforcing its influence, the NFU provides a great deal of information and analysis not otherwise available to the ministry and even helps administer some policies. It and its related Scottish and Irish unions are the only farm representatives recognised by the ministry at top levels, and are readily taken as the competent bodies on farming issues. As one ministry official put it, 'if the farmers' unions have strong views on any subject, it is the duty of the Department to report it to other Ministers' (Wilson, 1977, p. 45).

In return for its close involvement in the bureaucracy, the NFU is somewhat muted in its political activities; but after policies have been announced in public, it expresses its views openly and has, at times, actively stimulated opposition to government policy. An interesting feature of the NFU is that, despite its wide membership, its officers and council are almost all drawn from the larger and richer farmers – specifically, from the grain barons rather than from the hill farmers. This fact may shed light on the view that the latter have fared relatively poorly from agricultural policy, although, on the other hand, the NFU and other European farm organisations go to great lengths in order to maintain the unity of the farm lobby.

The pressure groups in the United States operate much more explicitly within the political sphere, and broad farming groups do not have the same degree of influence as in Europe – possibly because of the greater contrasts between different types of farmers in the larger country. Rather, the running is mostly made by groups representing specific parts of agriculture, for example, the National Milk Producers Federation. Even within industry associations, however, conflicting interests arise from the different styles of farming across the United States, and astute opponents of sectional interests can sometimes exploit these differences. The farming lobbies operate partly by providing information and drafting legislation, but also by making explicit political contributions, by coordinating pressure on congressmen (organising delegations to Washington), and by political advertising and publicity. Their numbers, as well as their obvious importance in US politics are illustrated by Guither's (1980) book *The Food Lobbyists*. This is basically a directory of organisations and their activities, one which, says Representative Paul Findlay in the foreword, 'I will keep near my desk . . . [to] provide a ready index of the teams and players with which we *must* deal in the legislative game' (emphasis added).

The relationships between the different farm lobbies show a delicate balance between conflict and coalition. For example, Petit (1985) shows that in 1983/4, having decided what it could reasonably expect to achieve in the face of huge pressure to reduce the milk surpluses, the US dairy lobby explicitly sought an alliance with the tobacco lobby to effect it. The attraction of tobacco was that it urgently 'needed' additional support itself in that year, and had long been controlled by production quotas – the method of control that dairy interests now sought to introduce. On the other hand, having kept uneasily in the background for a while, the meat producers eventually opposed the dairy industry on the grounds that sacrificing meat interests to other farmers twice in two years was too much.[8]

Many public decisions may be seen as the outcome of lobbying and counter-lobbying by interested parties (Chappell, 1982; Becker, 1983; Esty and Caves, 1983), so it is important to ask what determines the effectiveness of a lobby. The first issue is free-riding. The results of lobbying are usually public goods within a sector – that is, one agent's benefiting from them does not preclude another's, for example, a price rise for the whole industry. Hence each potential member of a lobby would prefer other members to bear the costs of lobbying while he does not. Free-riding is much easier to prevent in small groups where culprits may be easily identified. It also appears to be easier to convert organisations that exist for non-lobbying purpose into lobbies than to start from scratch, and that lobbies which provide some private services have less difficulty in exacting members' dues to cover their public activities. US farm organisations, with their concessionary insurance, advice and inputs, are quoted as the classical example of this. Lobbies are also likely to be more effective the more unified are their members and the greater the threat they face.

It must also be recognised that farm lobbies are not without their allies. If the 'agro-industries' can earn rent on their sales to or purchases from farmers, they too have a strong interest in maintaining agricultural output. Since, for example, the large grain companies in the USA and the chemicals giants on both sides of the Atlantic appear to have substantial market power, it is not surprising to find them supporting agriculture in the lobbies. In the mid-1980s, for instance, ICI ran a series of full page newspaper adverts solely devoted to singing the praises of UK agriculture.

The previous paragraphs suggest several reasons why farm lobbies are more effective than consumer lobbies. Indeed the latter hardly figure at all in the debate about agricultural policy. A more effective counter to protectionist producer lobbies comes from other industries – user industries (e.g. food processors), or export industries whose markets are threatened by retaliation (see Destler and Odell, 1989). An example of the strength of exporters is the way in which China was able to obtain larger textile quotas in the USA in 1983 by threatening to stop buying US grain: the grain lobby suddenly discovered it opposed import quotas rather strongly!

Finger (1981) and Finger, Hall and Nelson (1982) introduced an important insight on the way in which bureaucracies and interest groups interact in the presence of 'administrated protection' – protection where the law defines a general case for protection which is then granted in specific cases by a legal or administered process. Examples include anti-dumping duties and emergency protection against import surges. The legal processes are technically complex and expensive and hence favour well-organised over general interests. This make administered protection attractive to an industry ·seeking support, but it is also attractive to politicians and bureaucrats. Although the net welfare losses from protection are substantial, they are usually small relative to the gross transfer involved. For example, Tyers and Anderson (1988) suggest that in 1980–2 agricultural policy cost EC consumers $55 billion, and benefited producers by $47 billion, giving net costs (after allowing for net tax costs of $1 billion) of $9 billion. Hence protection's most obvious feature is taxing Peter to pay Paul. Western political systems are poorly equipped to make such redistributive decisions, and administered protection is a way of insulating the authorities from them – that is, of taking the political sting out of redistribution. Finger (1981) argues that while the commissions and boards of experts are ostensibly designed to collect and process information, their real purpose is to slow down, obfuscate and confuse the situation. In that way, if protection emerges as the conclusion, the public will not blame the politicians but accept that if the law says that protection is necessary, it must be.

2.5 PULLING IT ALL TOGETHER

Agricultural policy arises from the interactions between the various actors in the game within the economic environment. We can discount the median-voter/direct democracy models as plausible descriptions of the real world and so I concentrate here on two characterisations of the making of agricultural policy: the political market place and the 'policy-as-a-process' school.[9]

2.5.1　The political market place

The political market place approach draws parallels between political and economic markets. Interest groups come to market with demands for support (protection) and prepared to pay for them in terms of campaign contributions, general political support, acquiescence to other policies, jobs for ex-politicians, etc. Politicians and bureaucrats, on the other hand, arrive with supplies of protection which they are prepared to dispense in return for suitable political rewards. The latter include not only the direct benefits just listed but also the provision of the means to insulate themselves from the adverse political consequence of the policies they are persuaded to pursue. Obviously the demand and supply prices depend on the costs and the benefits of the policies in question, and it is possible to persuade oneself that this market process leads to social optimality in the sense that only policies whose benefits exceed their costs will be undertaken. I do not wish to explore this contentious matter, but to show how the political market place helps to explain an important regularity.

Anderson (1989), Tyers and Anderson (1992), and more generally Anderson and Hayami (1986) use the political market place to explain why industrial countries tend to support agriculture while developing countries tend to tax it.[10] Consider poor countries first. The demand for agricultural support is weak: the sector involves very many producers, often poorly educated and with poor communications; farmers spend a high percentage of their income on food – their own (subsistence) or other local producers' – and hence suffer nearly as much from higher food prices as they gain; and material inputs are few, so there is little industrial support for agriculture. Moreover, the demand for industrial protection and cheap food from the small and articulate urban elite helps to offset any demands that agriculture might generate. On the supply side agricultural protection is costly: there are few alternative sources of tax revenue; national objectives frequently include industrialisation; and agricultural support would entail taxing the urban minority to support the rural majority, and hence would not go very far. Overall, therefore, the supply and demand curves for protection intersect at low or negative levels of support.

When countries industrialise, the situation is entirely reversed. The demand for agricultural support is high: the farm sector is small, easily organised, suffering a progressive loss of competitiveness; material inputs are large, so agriculture has industrial allies; and farmers typically earn a higher percentage increase in their net returns for each percentage increase in the price of their output;[11] and the elasticity of supply is higher, allowing a stronger response to any increase in price. The supply of protection is also higher: agriculture is valued culturally; agricultural bureaucracies exist with an interest in the sector; food takes a small share of consumers' income, and hence consumer resistance to price rises is lower; and agricultural support transfers resources from the majority to the minority, and hence offers big returns to beneficiaries at relatively low cost per loser.[12] Only when the budgetary cost (as opposed to the consumer cost) becomes too great do industrial country governments start to resist requests for support, probably mainly because the Treasury becomes involved as well as the Ministry of Agriculture. Hence for most industrial countries the supply and demand for protection intersect at higher levels of support.

The political market place approach has considerable appeal. It relates agricultural (and other) support to fundamental determinants in a coherent way and is able to account for a significant amount of the differences in agricultural policies observed around the world. However, while it offers insight into equilibrium outcomes, it does not really account for the dynamic aspects of political economy or the role of institutions and processes. Hence at least in the short run – and in political economy this can be long-lived – it provides only half the story.

2.5.2   Policy as a process

Petit (1985), Rabinowicz, Haraldsson, and Bolin (1986) and Moyer and Josling (1990) take up the factors missing from the political market place. Petit emphasises the sequential nature of, and uncertainty surrounding, the formation of agricultural policy, and the inertia they induce. In both the USA and France 'it took nothing less than the severe economic crisis of the 1930s and the arrival of a new government or administration' to establish the basis of current agricultural intervention. In both cases intervention had been widely discussed previously, but had failed to materialise, essentially because of political disagreements. But as agricultural prices slumped in the early 1930s it became widely recognised that 'something must be done'. The critical legislation, dated 1933 in the USA and 1936 in France, was followed quickly by the reversal of the decline in prices.[13] Fortuitous or induced, the evident 'success' of the new policies so legitimised intervention that it has never really been challenged since. Interestingly, while farm organisations had stimulated much of the preceding debate, they played little role in the policy innovations in the USA and actually opposed the legislation in France! Thus, in the extreme circumstances leading to major change, pressure groups would appear to have been secondary to economic pressures and political imperatives.

The story is different for the evolution of policy. No crisis or conjunction of political and economic events has seriously threatened agricultural intervention since 1935. Thus subsequent history has produced a series of incremental changes in which it is easy to detect the hand of farm interest groups and farmers' political power. Even so, we must remember that economic factors have still been of prior importance in defining the problems to be solved and the 'technology' of policy, and also that farmers have to compromise with other political pressures.

The farm lobbies – tacitly supported by the bureaucrats – have proved most adept at exploiting the conservative social welfare function to preserve existing instruments of agricultural intervention.

Thus there is a much greater tendency towards 'doing something' than towards 'undoing something', and agricultural policy has accumulated into progressively more complex piles. For example, the EC's milk surplus was tackled in 1984 by introducing quotas rather than by reducing support prices; similarly, in the face of excess demand for food in 1973, the USA restricted exports of soybean, but did not dismantle the production control machinery established over the 1960s, even though it was currently inoperative.

The lobbies are not omnipotent, however, and political compromise may be detected in several aspects of agricultural policy. First, coalitions are easier to construct for some policies than for others. For example, when US non-agricultural sectors objected in the early 1970s to excessive direct farm income support, farmers and urban Congressmen could none the less agree to stimulate food demand by extending the food stamp programme. Subject to two constraints – see below – it is politically easier to boost demand than to constrain supply, witness the USA's and the EC's food aid programmes and Japan's subsidised sales of rice as feedstuff. Second, agriculture sometimes gets linked with basically unrelated issues in top-level horse-trading. For example, in the early 1980s the British government demanded of the EC both lower agricultural prices (smaller increases) and a refund of Britain's 'excess' budgetary contributions. Invariably it sacrificed the former for the latter in the course of negotiations.

These two factors highlight one of Petit's most important insights: namely, that one cannot account for agricultural protectionism without examining the process from which it springs. This is partly because the rules of decision-taking influence the decisions taken, by affecting, for instance, the coalitions that can be formed or the set of issues that can be brought into one grand deal. It also means, however, that agricultural policy is somewhat unpredictable, for at any time it may become tied up with some non-agricultural event. For instance, President Reagan is reported to have signed the 1983 Dairy Bill, to which he was doctrinally opposed, because the re-election campaigns of several Republican Senators in dairy or tobacco states desperately needed fillips. The myopic nature of such political compromise, coupled with the short memories that Petit says policy-makers and lobbyists exhibit, results in policy proceeding in a series of irregular steps, often added to but rarely eroded. By ignoring the regular flux of coalition formation and the randomness of political shocks, the political market place theories of agricultural support miss an important dimension of the issue.

The principal constraint and the most common source of 'outside' political pressure on agricultural policy-makers is the public budget. The budget makes explicit some of the costs and redistribution involved in agricultural intervention, so both politicians and bureaucrats tend to prefer policies with low direct budgetary costs. Unfortunately for them, however, farmers' responses to intervention often cause policies that were once cheap to make huge budget demands in later years. For example, the EC's variable import levy system actually raised public revenue at first because the EC was a net importer of the goods concerned; but the high and stable internal prices and rapid technical change (possibly induced by the high prices) so increased output that export restitutions (subsidies) became necessary to maintain local prices above world levels. At that point, however, internal prices began to grow significantly less rapidly. By 1984 the budgetary burden had become so great that it threatened to bankrupt the Community – just the sort of crisis that could conceivably have led to dramatic policy innovations. In the event, the responses were piecemeal, increasing revenue somewhat and trimming outgoings by introducing dairy quotas. The acquiescence of the farm organisations in the latter probably reflects their realisation that they could have lost control of the situation if it had developed into a full-blown crisis. Similar pressures and compromise were evident in the USA over the same period.

A second source of constraint is the GATT or, on a broader view, international relations in general. Agricultural policy is aimed almost exclusively at domestic objectives, and the political coalitions important to its development mostly involve only domestic interests. Trade interventions arise as side-conditions, necessary to the effective implementation of domestic objectives. Occasionally, the foreign implications of policy become significant enough to influence the outcome. In some cases this takes the form of trade-offs within the agricultural sector, as for example in the establishment of the International Wheat Agreements or the GATT agreement on the minimum price of butter exports. In other cases, more general foreign trade or foreign policy issues are involved. Thus for many years the EC honoured the GATT tariff-bindings on tapioca agreed by Germany in the 1950s, despite their conflict with domestic goals. Similarly, the USA tolerated the EC's interventionist Common Agricultural Policy as a necessary price for the European integration she desired for general foreign policy reasons. The relative dominance of domestic over international pressures is well illustrated by the EC's unwillingness to compromise its Common Agricultural Policy during the Uruguay Round (see Chapter 4).

2.6 CONCLUSION

At the most fundamental level agricultural policy is determined by the interaction of a social welfare function that abhors change and entertains some notion of fairness with an economic system that constantly induces changes in both tastes and technology. On this broad canvas the details are painted by the policy-makers – the politicians and the bureaucrats – and the various interest groups of the economy. The latter seek to maximise their returns, but are constrained both by the extent of public sympathy and by the other objectives of the policy-makers. Public sympathy is greatest for policy to support the current income distribution, permitting intervention when the status quo is threatened but not encouraging its reversal when the crisis has passed. Policy-makers tend to favour complex and obscure methods of intervention whose costs are hidden but whose benefits are plain. Only the most extreme crises produce the confluence of interests necessary for dramatic policy innovations. The whole business of making policy takes place against a background of uncertainty – both about what the actual situation is and how policy will affect it – and in an environment of shifting alliances and priorities. The actual process by which bureaucrats and politicians reach decisions can be important to the final outcome, for it determines what issues can be traded off against agricultural interests and how effective coalitions can be formed. This generates at least some randomness in the formation of agricultural policy. Given the much lower priority accorded to dismantling policy than to imposing it, these random shocks tend to be very long-lived, leaving agricultural policy in industrial countries a costly tangle of potentially inconsistent instruments.

3 Agricultural Policy Reform in the USA and the EC

TIM JOSLING

3.1 INTRODUCTION

Agricultural policy reform is just the stuff of scholarly debate. One can argue at length over the definition of reform, the evidence needed to show that reform has taken place, the interpretation of that evidence and the significance of the findings. Such a debate would, in popular parlance, be labelled 'academic', implying a lack of relevance to practical affairs. But the underlying issues are ones of considerable importance. The basic question in the reform of farm policies need not be reduced to whether or not some particular policy has been 'reformed'. The issue is whether agricultural policies can be made to adapt to changing needs. This underlying question is relevant to issues in economic policy far removed from agriculture. It has to do with the process of policy change in an industrial democracy, the extent to which such changes in policy respond to changes in the economy and the way in which domestic economic policy is related to trade policy and to the international environment. Agricultural policy reform (hereafter, APR) is an interesting example of such policy change in action.

Agricultural policies in developed countries are, primarily, 'middle-class entitlement programmes'. Whatever their origins, their main effect is to support the income stream of a group of small businesses, often family owned, which provide the livelihood for from 2 to 5 per cent of the work-force. The programmes are financed by a combination of tax payments and market price support (implicit food taxes). The recipients are not predominantly poor nor are benefits related to poverty. Few would now claim that the markets for agricultural raw materials could not function tolerably in the absence of government programmes. Many now doubt that environmental and consumer health objectives are favoured by the present programmes. But they continue because society accepts the current distribution of property rights that entitle farm business to receive government assistance tied to the production and sale of their output.[1] To remove these entitlements is a political task few governments relish, even when they become costly and inconvenient. APR is the response of governments to the pressures on farm policies. It is the process of adjusting existing programmes to meet the new realities. The pace of reform differs in different countries. In some it appears glacial, and in these cases it is easy to argue that reform is absent. In other cases it is more cyclical, with waves of reform and backsliding in between. In such cases, one needs to see whether each successive reform push takes the policy towards a longer-run goal. In a few countries, APR can be dramatic, with the speed of change surprising those who (justifiably) base their predictions on the continuation of the status quo.

This chapter is about the process of APR in the USA and in the EC in the past decade. The discussion will be focused on three questions.

1. Have agricultural policies changed significantly in the 1980s as a result of pressures for reform?
2. Have these policies 'improved' in the sense of achieving their objectives with less cost and less conflict?
3. Are these policies headed in the 'right' direction, even if reform seems to be a slow process, or is there a likelihood of a reversion to the old ways of doing things?

To answer these questions it is necessary to describe the pressures under which agricultural policy has been working in the 1980s; to examine the policy changes and their significance; to give some empirical evidence on policy efficiency; to look at some possible future paths of US and EC policy; and to consider how the policies, reformed or not, are likely to stand up to future pressures.

3.2 THE PRESSURES ON FARM POLICY IN THE 1980s

Agricultural policy reform is a response to pressure. Left alone, policies tend to go on unchanged. Reform occurs when the benefits to change begin to outweigh the benefits to retaining the status quo. Three different sets of pressures can be distinguished which have combined to shift the balance of benefits in the 1980s. One pressure, dear to the hearts of most economists, is that coming from the rise to dominance of the paradigm of liberalisation and deregulation in economic matters. This sea-change in political thinking swept the world in the 1980s, reaching a climax in the apparent conversion of most of the world's centrally planned economies to the virtues of the mixed economy, with an entrepreneurial private sector running under governmental supervision. In many parts of the world, agricultural policies have changed significantly as a part of the rethinking of the role of governments, the rights of private ownership and the need for business incentives. Many countries which previously taxed their 'unproductive' farm sectors to free resources for the 'modern' industrial activities have reversed their policies to allow farmers to enjoy the rewards of their productivity.[2]

Developed country farm policies have not proved such an easy target for economic policy reform. Agricultural policies in the USA and the EC do not involve significant government control over the production activity. Though governments are sometimes involved in the post-farm handling of produce, parastatal agencies usually have heavy farmer representation. Most government intervention in markets is either done at the border or through domestic programmes of purchase, storage or set-aside of a quasi-voluntary nature. As a result there has been relatively little pressure from within agriculture itself to deregulate the sector and little scope for privatisation. Arguments to liberalise trade were, of course, made in the 1980s by consumer groups and by commodity traders, but these have never in themselves been enough to swing the course of farm policy.

In addition to the internal pressures from sectors seeking relaxation of government controls, the liberalisation/deregulation movement has been characterised by a growing disillusionment with the efficacy of government intervention in markets. The view that the 'old' approach to the problems of sectoral income and employment may not be viable began to permeate agricultural policy discussion in the 1980s. Countries felt able to pledge themselves to a 'more market-oriented' set of farm policies and began to look for programme alternatives that were more targeted and less distortive to the allocation of resources[3]. These views were bolstered by academic studies that pointed out the high cost of income transfers relative to the benefits achieved. If countries wished to continue to subsidise farm incomes, the least they could do was to make the transfers in a reasonably efficient way.

Unfortunately, such advice was not welcome in farming circles, where it seemed to be promising a permanent welfare status for farmers. With little inside pressure to 'get government out' of agriculture, and economic liberals pushing notions that ran counter to the mainstream of farm opinion, the liberalisation/deregulation process alone would have had little impact on farm policies.

Not unconnected with the liberalisation of domestic economic policies has been the growing dependence of the agricultural sector on developments in the non-farm economy and an increased vulnerability to macroeconomic shocks. Rural and urban capital markets are now indistinguishable in most parts of the EC and the USA; and agricultural labour markets are integrated with those in the non-agricultural sector, through the spread of education to rural areas and the growth of part-time farming. This implies that a policy of high agricultural prices benefits those with specific assets (land, or production entitlements) and influences the level of production, but has little effect on returns to labour, borrowed capital and other mobile factors. It also means that shocks from interest rate movements have a considerable impact on asset values in the farm sector and that urban employment and wage levels dictate farm labour incomes. This declining effectiveness of the old policy instruments, such as commodity price supports, and the search for new instruments to protect against macroeconomic disturbance feeds the appetite for policy reform. Though the realisation of the change in the market position of agriculture has come more slowly in Europe than in the USA, it is now adding to the frustration widely felt over the inability of even an expensive Common Agricultural Policy (CAP) to maintain farm incomes at a time of general economic weakness and high interest rates.

A third pressure on agriculture and on agricultural policy has come from the growing interdependence of the US and EC economies both among themselves and with other countries. This has arisen from rapidly expanding international trade, the growth of offshore capital markets, significant migratory flows of labour, and the growth of global corporations. Agricultural trade has grown less fast than has trade in other areas, but fast enough to make agriculture in the USA and the EC (and also Japan) much more dependent upon conditions on world markets. In the USA, a high proportion of crop output is exported, and world market weakness triggers problems for domestic policy. In the EC, low world prices often cause a budget crisis for farm spending. Weak market prices result from weak demand in foreign markets (a function of global economic activity and of the indebtedness of developing countries); from exchange rate movements; and from the policy interventions of other countries. Recognition of these influences has led to an awareness that interest rates and exchange rates can often be as important as domestic output prices in determining programme viability. The importance of these macroeconomic and trade factors in policy has generally increased over time with the growing interdependence. Macroeconomic influences were particularly strong in the early 1980s, but more recently attention has turned to the impact of farm policies on trade and on the trade system, and led eventually to the notion of agricultural trade reform to go along with APR.[4]

The combination of these three factors has materially changed attitudes towards farm policies and the operation of the policies themselves. Once thought to be a desirable way to achieve parity of income between a poor, undercapitalised, somewhat traditional sector of the economy and the industrial mainstream, price support policies are now credited with little else than the maintenance of high land prices and the production of embarrassing surpluses. The focus has changed from the policy changes needed to assist the agricultural sector to the changes needed to keep the policies. APR is less about finding new and better ways of helping agriculture than about rescuing agricultural policies from obsolescence.

3.3   FARM POLICY CHANGES IN THE 1980S

Farm policies are complex legislative packages, constantly under review and revision. However, it is possible to identify significant changes in the instruments used or in the level at which they are applied which can act as markers in the continuum of policy adjustments. The story of APR requires these markers as evidence: they are the outward manifestation of the reform process. In the case of the EC and the USA such policy changes are preceded by considerable debate and are often undertaken over considerable opposition. An examination of these changes therefore acts as a chronicle of the political troubles of the policies themselves. This section deals with the major policy shifts in the period of the 1980s in both the USA and the EC.[5]

3.3.1   US policy changes

US farm programmes started in the 1930s at a time when depressed rural incomes were held to be feeding the depression. The emphasis was (as it still is) on the maintenance of farm income and the stabilisation of domestic prices. The instruments at the disposal of the policy-makers included the non-recourse loan, whereby farmers could take out a loan at a fixed price using the commodity as collateral and could default on the loan with no penalty. This made the 'loan rate' an effective floor price for the market: the government through the Commodity Credit Corporation (CCC) would be left with the commodity at times of weak prices. In order to control supply, farmers were given acreage allotments, which specified the area that farms could devote to each crop covered by the programme. Marketing orders were established for some products which tied market allocations to the acreage quotas. The basic farm legislation was renewed in 1949, with much the same range of instruments, despite a vigorous debate on the use of direct payments in place of these programmes.

The first serious challenge to the viability of these policies came in the early 1950s, when the first post-war surpluses of grain appeared on US and world markets. The reaction was to introduce two new instruments, a programme of subsidised exports tied to development programmes (PL480 or Food for Peace) and a Soil Bank, into which farmers could place whole farms and receive conservation payments from the government. By 1962 the pressure of surpluses required further measures. One approach was to allow mandatory production controls when agreed by a majority of growers of the commodity in question. After an unsuccessful referendum of wheat growers in 1963 this option was abandoned. In its place was put a series of payments to those farmers who choose to participate in set-aside programmes, together with a lowering of the floor price (loan rate) to increase sales. The conditional payments were continued in the 1970s, evolving by the 1977 Act into 'deficiency payments' between a target price and the higher of the loan rate or market price. In addition, a subsidised storage programme was added in 1978, the Farmer-Owned Reserve, which aimed to stabilise prices by encouraging farmers to hold grain off the market in times of low prices. A federal crop insurance programme was also initiated, to act as a safety net for farmers adversely affected by the weather.

Many of these farm programmes are still in operation today, despite a turbulent period in farm policies over the 1980s. The decade came in with firm world market prices and record agricultural exports from the USA. Inflation was high and rising interest rates hit hard on capital intensive sectors such as agriculture. All pressures were for an easing of the financial problems of farmers and an encouragement to ride the export boom. But the newly elected President Reagan was concerned with decreasing government spending and deregulating industry: a draft 1981 Farm Bill from the administration aimed to keep budget costs low (below $2 billion) and to eliminate major parts of the farm programme, including the deficiency payment system for grains and the acreage allotment programmes for peanuts and tobacco. Farm-state legislators had little trouble defeating this attack on the programmes. Instead, Congress passed a bill which raised target prices and loan rates and established a scale of minimum price levels for the period 1982–5, rising by 6 per cent each year to offset anticipated inflation. These price increases came on top of those designed to offset the negative impact on agriculture of the 1980 US embargo of grain sales to the Soviet Union. Only the dairy programme was weakened, with support prices linked to market conditions rather than the historical concept of 'parity' prices.

The chickens soon came home to roost. Exports collapsed in the face of weak foreign demand and a strengthening dollar. Inflation dropped, leaving the price supports looking even more generous. Support costs rose dramatically, until in 1983 the EC could point out with smug satisfaction that US farm programmes cost more than did the CAP. The slump in farm markets together with high interest rates caused land prices in the USA to fall sharply, and bankruptcies to become common. The high interest rates attracted capital from abroad and drove up the value of the dollar, making exports even less competitive. Agriculture was in the worst depression since the 1930s.

Two stop-gap measures emerged over this troubled period. A new twist to the cereals programme gave farmers commodities from storage in exchange for acreage reductions. This Payment-in-Kind programme (1983) was seen as a convenient way of reducing stocks held by the CCC and encouraging supply control – all without any apparent cash outlay. Farmers were in essence paid twice for the same crop (once on delivery to the CCC and then again when they sold their PIK allotment) in exchange for not producing more. For dairy farmers, another approach was tried. A 1984 programme assessed a levy on milk producers, but this did not seem to have the desired effect and was followed by a dairy diversion scheme, which paid farmers to reduce milk production by between 5 and 30 per cent.

By the time the debate was joined for the 1985 Farm Bill, the scent of reform was in the air. President Reagan had just been re-elected in a landslide and continued his quest to contain bureaucracy with renewed vigour. The bill sent to Congress by the administration suggested phasing out the main price supports over a number of years, but this proposal received no support from Congress and was never seriously debated. In its place came a flood of farm bills that swamped Congress and confused the participants.

Three competing ideas emerged from the 1985 Farm Bill debate.[6] The first was to reintroduce mandatory supply control (the Harkin Bill), with quotas tailored to the size of the domestic market and with higher prices for that limited production. This proposal became identified with the cause of small farmers and with a broader neo-protectionist trade policy, and soon lost support. At the other extreme, two senators introduced a bill to replace price supports with generous transitional payments on the way to a market-oriented agriculture (the Boschwitz–Boren Bill), but that too represented too radical a departure from current practices. Most of the debate focused on the third alternative, price restraints applied to broadly unaltered policy instruments. This third approach was adopted in the 1985 Farm Bill. Public concern about the economic plight of farmers made it difficult for Congress to cut too deeply into support levels, but modest reductions in target prices were scheduled over the life of the bill, with loan rates adjusting to past market price levels. Conservation programmes received more attention, and a dairy herd buy-out programme was introduced which aimed to cut back the dairy herd by 1 million cows. A small step in the direction of decoupled payments was introduced in the cereals programme, with the freezing of base yields and acreage used in the calculation of deficiency payments. The incentive to farmers to expand in order to be eligible for more payments in the future was (at least in part) removed.

The 1985 Farm Bill also marked the start of an assault on export markets, driven by the notion that the fall in market shares was due to aggressive export subsidies by other countries (coupled with a high dollar). The bill extended the export enhancement programme (EEP) introduced earlier in 1985 to boost exports by giving away CCC stocks to firms winning export contracts, thus reducing their costs. In addition, funds were allocated to a targeted export assistance (TEA) programme, and an expanded programme of export credit guarantees. A modification of the loan rate for rice and cotton (the marketing loan) allowed farmers to pay back their CCC loans at the world price if lower than the loan rate. This gave farmers an additional subsidy equal to the difference between the world price and the loan rate and indirectly encouraged exports of these commodities.

Events since 1986 have been somewhat kinder to the farm programmes. A weaker dollar, a drought in 1988, some recovery in overseas markets, and a generally buoyant economy have led to lower programme costs and some recovery in farm incomes. The 1990 Farm Bill introduced few new programmes and steered clear of radical change. Cereal farmers will lose eligibility for deficiency payments on 15 per cent of their base acreage (the so-called triple-base acreage), in addition to that in the regular acreage retirement programme (ARP). The savings in support costs of this and other measures allowed the administration to cut the budget allocation to agriculture substantially, in line with the Budget Reconciliation agreement forged with Congress at the end of 1990. The 1990 Farm Bill continues a target price freeze, and extends the conservation reserve programme (CRP) to about 45 million acres. Dairy farmers will be assessed a 1 per cent fee to help with programme costs, with the promise of a new dairy programme to be discussed and implemented later in 1991.

The story of US policy in the 1980s is hardly one of radical reform, despite some strong rhetoric. But the threat of such reform has changed the direction of policy and the context in which it is decided. Budget stringency has proved the major force restraining farm programmes, with the external situation increasingly determining programme costs. Conservation programmes have prospered, widely regarded as having both positive environmental impacts and supply restraining effects. Export programmes have blossomed in an attempt to counter those of other countries. Meanwhile, the domestic price support policies have been made more restrictive, with lower payment limits per farm, and made less distortive of domestic production decisions. Though the programmes may look similar to those at the start of the decade, the seeds of change have been planted.

3.3.2   EC policy change in the 1980s

The EC's CAP has a much shorter history than that of US programmes.[7] The Treaty of Rome mandated only two sectoral policies, in agriculture and transport. Though generally supporting liberal internal markets, the treaty reflected the conventional wisdom of the mid-1950s, that agriculture needed a strong set of market regulations to control the internal price and avoid disruption from abroad. The opening up of the internal market to trade among EC members appeared to depend upon adequate protection from low world prices.

The main instruments of the cereals regime under the CAP were established in 1962. Imports would have to cross a threshold set in relation to internal 'target' prices, paying a levy equal to the difference between the world price and the threshold price. Exports (not so important at that time) would benefit by a variable subsidy, called a restitution, to step back down again to world prices. Intervention buying by national authorities (with Community funding) would put a floor in the market, at the intervention price. A common price level would be agreed annually, based on the recommendation of the European Commission. A transition period, until 1967, gave countries time to align prices with this common level. Germany had to decrease (and France to increase) prices to reach the new EC levels, a fact which coloured German attitudes to the CAP in early years.

The arrangements for other commodities followed shortly after the agreement on cereals. For livestock products, some variations on the cereals system were chosen. A milk target price was to be supported by import levies on milk products and by intervention buying of a few of these products (butter and skimmed milk powder). For beef, the guide price was to be supported by a variable levy on top of a fixed customs duty, with intervention buying for particular parts of the beef carcass.[8] Pig meat, poultry and egg producers were to be sheltered from the impact of the high internal prices for cereals by a mixture of duties and levies tied to those for cereals. For sugar, a 'temporary' system of quotas was introduced, which still exists. In the case of fruit and vegetables and many other products of smaller significance, a weaker form of protection was introduced, using fixed tariffs, optional support buying and deficiency payments.

This system has shown remarkable resilience over the years and the number of major changes to the commodity regimes has been limited. But the pressures on the policy have forced shifts both in the emphasis among instruments and in support levels. In addition, there have been a number of proposals from the European Commission for reform which have not found favour with the Council of Ministers. This process of policy change, with reforms proposed by the Commission and then diluted by the Council, is typical of the EC's method of policy change in contrast to that of the USA, where competing bills containing policy proposals vie for attention in the halls of Congress.

The problems with the CAP, and hence the first calls for reform, emerged as early as 1968 – right at the end of the transition period to common prices. Surpluses of milk, sugar and wheat (as well as some tree fruits) began to emerge. The first attempt at controlling surpluses was contained in the Mansholt Plan (Commission of the European Communities, 1968) which advocated that EC agriculture had considerable excess capacity; that structural adaptation should be stimulated to allow farmers to earn a living; and that price levels should be used to guide production (rather than support incomes on farms too small to be competitive). A weakened version of Mansholt's structural programme was finally passed in 1972, but the main thrust of the report was unheeded. The decision in 1970 to finance Community programmes from the EC's 'own resources', of import levies and customs duties, topped by a levy on countries up to 1 per cent of their value-added tax, meant that there were plenty of funds available to maintain the system of high prices. The high world prices in the mid-1970s obscured the problems with the policy and delayed the efforts to reform.

The Mansholt proposal included a call for a 'prudent' price policy, allowing inflation to erode the real value of price supports. Prices were indeed fixed until 1972, with inflation acting to administer a politically acceptable squeeze to farm incomes. A bout of high inflation in the early 1970s, coupled with fears of world-wide food shortages, led to an increase in prices of 9 per cent per year over the period 1973–7. 'Reform' was put on hold, with the Commission (in papers on 'Improvement' and 'Stocktaking' of the CAP (Commission of the European Comunities, 1973, 1975)) content to concentrate on policy management rather than directions or instruments. When it became clear in the late 1970s that the policy was getting too expensive, the first response was to implement a stricter price policy – to remove the incentives introduced by the generous policies of the preceding four years. Policy reforms were not yet under discussion: a Commission paper on the 'Future Development' of the CAP (Commission of the European Comunities, 1979) again focused more on managerial changes rather than changes in direction for the policy.

The first signs of a willingness to rethink the basic thrust of the CAP came in 1980 – at roughly the same time that the Reagan Administration was threatening the US policy with reform. The Council of Ministers had given the Commisssion a 'Mandate' in May 1980 to look at the budgetary problems of the Community. As agriculture consumed the lion's share of the budget, and was the main reason for the disproportionate burden borne by the UK, CAP reform was seen as an integral part of greater budgetary discipline. The agricultural component of the Mandate Report was contained in a Commission paper, the 'Guidelines for European Agriculture' (Commission of the European

Communities, 1981). The Commission used the opportunity to advocate a significant shift in policy, in particular by bringing support prices into line with those in the major competitors (e.g., the USA), and by limiting the open-ended nature of support to 'basic' quantities of production. This suggestion fell on deaf ears in the Council, and a rise in world prices denominated in EC currencies in 1980, in part due to the strong dollar, took the pressure off the CAP, actually reducing budget spending in 1981. About all that remained of this reform effort was the introduction in 1982 of somewhat ineffective 'guarantee thresholds' for grains, designed to trigger price cuts whenever output exceeded certain targets. Unfortunately, the price cut was to be taken from the proposed level of next year's price, which could therefore be chosen high enough to nullify any reduction. The notion of producer 'coresponsibility' for surpluses, the political spin put on the system of 'guarantee thresholds', did however provide the basis for later and less cosmetic cuts.

The effectiveness of guarantee thresholds was given a practical test in 1984, when the Commission reported that the threshold formula, if used, would imply a drop of 12 per cent in the milk price. The Council shrank away from such a major price change and opted instead for a system of quotas. This was the first major change in policy instruments since the CAP was established. But as an example of policy reform, the introduction of dairy quotas had one major shortcoming. Dairy quotas signalled a shift away from a competitive internal market towards control of supply by direct quantitative regulation. The notion of a liberal internal market for agricultural goods, supported only at the border, is inherent in the Rome Treaty: the Dutch had firmly rejected the notion of quotas on internal trade for farm products. Production quotas do not overtly contradict free trade, as they do not involve border measures, but the result on resource allocation is much the same. Output is determined administratively in a way that does not respond to price competition among regions. Only if the production quotas were to be made freely tradable (a condition so far rejected by the Commission) would output resemble that in a free internal market.

The next major effort at reform in the CAP came in 1986 when budget costs began to rise for cereals and for oilseeds. Under pressure to limit budget exposure the Commission developed further the notion of guarantee thresholds, extending them to other products, such as oilseeds, and making their operation more transparent. In the 'reform' package of February 1988, these ideas were put into operation. Coupled with the greater use of 'coresponsibility levies', the guarantee thresholds began to put an effective limit to the open-ended nature of price supports. If production exceeded the threshold level a cut in the current price, as well as in that for next year, would be triggered. Though this could always be countered by a generous price settlement, a parallel agreement on a budget ceiling for agricultural spending was put into place to guard against such generosity by the Council of Agricultural Ministers.

The fervent wish in Brussels was that the issue of CAP reform had been finally addressed. Controlled by the budget ceiling and the guarantee threshold system, the problems of agriculture would subside in visibility and allow the Community to do more interesting things – in particular to forge ahead with the completion of the internal market. Such an end to the agricultural policy problem was not to be: events intervened which put agricultural reform back on the agenda. This time the pressure came from outside the EC. The low world prices in 1986 had convinced many in the USA, Canada, Australia and other countries involved in the export markets for grains and livestock products that there should be a serious effort to curb the excesses of national policies. As an exporter of many products, the EC might have been willing to agree to this notion, but the thought of opening up the issue of reform again was not appealing. Instead the EC resisted the pressure from other countries to undertake further policy reform, first in the discussions leading up to the start of the Uruguay Round in 1986, then during the first part of the negotiations in 1987–8, and finally in the lead up to the 'final' meeting of the trade negotiators in December 1990. After being cast as the 'villain' in the 1990 (Brussels) meeting, the EC apparently decided that a modest programme of international reform was inevitable – and probably not inconsistent with the desired internal direction of policy.

The pressure on the EC to respond to the external pressure at the end of the Uruguay Round has yielded yet one more reform document from the Commission. This latest attempt at reform – the MacSharry Plan – is the most radical yet. The Commission proposed to move market prices, in particular for cereals, down towards world market levels, while compensating farmers for the loss in income. The compensation payments would be based on cereal acreage, calculated using regional average yields. For the larger farmers there would be a requirement that acreage be reduced in order to be eligible. Initially, it was proposed that such set-aside acreage would be only partially compensated. As a result, large farmers and those with high yields would tend to suffer under the policy change. This added a new twist to the national incentives for reform. The most ardent reformers in the Community have been those countries with good farm structures, who believe that they could compete at lower prices. The least enthusiastic are the countries that have a structure of small farms who fear that they would be badly placed in a more competitive environment. By tilting the compensation scheme heavily in favour of the small farmer, the Commission proposals managed to garner the grudging acceptance of those previously reluctant to agree to reform, but at the same time alienated the traditional proponents of reform. Subsequently, the 'MacSharry Plan' was modified so that all farmers, regardless of their scale of production, would receive compensation. Support for the plan was obtained from countries with medium- and large-sized farms and the plan received approval from the Council of Agriculture Ministers in June 1992.

3.4   HAVE FARM POLICIES IMPROVED OVER THE 1980s?

Have the agricultural policies in the USA and the EC improved over the decade of the 1980s? From the amount of debate that has surrounded the subject, and the amount of legislative time it has occupied, one might imagine that agricultural policies are more slim, trim and focused than at the start of the decade. From the shock given to the political system in both the USA and the EC by the rapid increase in budget costs in the middle of the decade, one would expect that at least the treasury exposure had been contained. But true reform is more than new proposals, legislative tinkering, or the switching of programme costs from the visible budget to less noticable sources. To be reformed, the policy must have got noticably better in achieving its objectives. But even that test may not be easy to administer: the objectives of policy are always difficult to quantify, and in a dynamic situation 'getting better' may mean 'getting worse less quickly'. But with these caveats, it is still interesting to see whether the quantitative evidence supports the notion that farm policies in the EC and the USA are performing better now than at the turn of the decade.

This quantitative evaluation is made possible by the improved availability of data on policies in a form which makes it possible to compare them over time and across countries. In particular there is now a consistent set of data on the magnitude of the transfer to producers inherent in the farm policies of the major industrial countries. Following the lead of the Food and Agricultural Organisation (FAO), which had attempted since the mid-1970s to monitor developed country farm policies, the Organisation for Economic Cooperation and Development (OECD) began in 1983 to calculate proxy indicators for the complex of national policy measures used in the agricultural sector. These indicators were based on the notion of a Producer Subsidy Equivalent (PSE) of a policy, defined as that subsidy which would substitute for the measure actually used and keep net receipts the same. An analogous measure on the consumer side, the Consumer Subsidy Equivalent (CSE), measured the subsidy to consumers – usually negative – inherent in the distorted market prices induced by the policies. The OECD has been calculating these indicators for most of its member countries for several years, providing a rich set of data on the quantitative aspects of farm policies. The calculations below take these PSE calculations for the EC and the USA over the period 1980–90 as a starting point to evaluate the efficiency of the policies in achieving their objectives.[9]

The PSEs capture the flow of transfers to the producers of a farm commodity through the manipulation of the prices of both inputs and outputs. Transfers that do not pass through the market are also included in the OECD figures, as are the provision of services that would otherwise have to be purchased in the market. The transfers from each policy can be added up to give an indication of the magnitude of the total transfer for each commodity. When expressed as a percentage of the actual farm receipts, the PSE shows the extent of those receipts accounted for by the transfer.

3.4.1 Level of producer transfers

The PSEs for the European Community for some major products, wheat, corn, milk, beef and sugar, are shown in Figure 3.1. Two conclusions stand out from calculations. First, the PSEs vary considerably over the period. This is often more a result of changes in world prices than of changes in policy: when world prices are high the preset policy prices generate less transfers. Thus EC sugar policy in 1980 generated few transfers at a time of firm world markets, but made up over 70 per cent of farm receipts for much of the decade. Similarly, cereal policies generated the greatest transfers in the period 1986–7 when fierce competition among subsidy programmes, coupled with weak demand, caused world prices to be weak. The second and most striking feature of the PSE values for the EC is their absolute size: beef, milk and sugar programmes regularly provided over one-half of

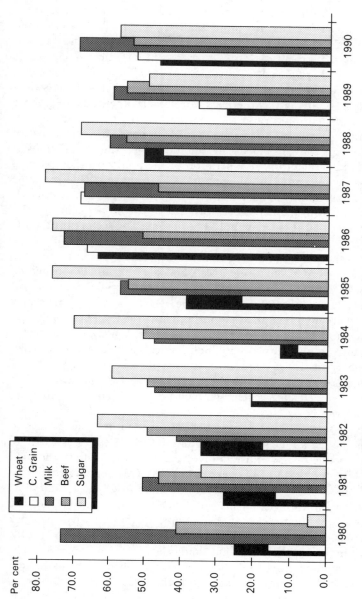

FIGURE 3.1 Producer subsidy equivalents: selected products, EC, 1980–90

Source: OECD PSE tables.

producer receipts of these products. Though no calculation of the social cost of producing these products has been made, it is quite possible that such costs are more than the level of non-subsidised revenue. Value added at private (i.e. subsidised) prices in the sector is probably in the range of 25 to 45 per cent of sales. Social costs doubtless exceed private costs for some purchased inputs, but the social cost of rural labour and some specialised equipment may be less than the private cost. If these two effects offset each other, any PSE more than 45 per cent should raise the question as to whether the market returns (at unsubsidised prices) are enough to cover the social cost of production. If the answer is in the negative, this constitutes a formidable indictment on the operation of the policy. In a developing country, we would proclaim such an industry to have a negative value added, and recommend its closure to improve national income. It would appear from the persistence of PSEs above 45 per cent in milk, beef and sugar that these may indeed be loss-making sectors for the EC economy.

The corresponding calculations for the USA are given in Figure 3.2, and show some broad similarities. Milk and sugar production benefited from high percentage transfers over much of the decade. Beef support is generally less in the USA than in the EC, but even in this sector where there are no direct price support schemes the level of support has hovered around 30 per cent of producer receipts. For the cereals sector the transfers are also surprisingly high, indicating that about one-half of revenue came from transfer payments in the 1986–7 period of depressed world prices. In both the USA and the EC, the levels of the PSEs have dropped since reaching a high-point in 1986–7, but they are still well above the levels of the early 1980s.

The percentage PSEs give an indication of the rate of assistance to the sector. To get an idea of the total amount of support it is useful to look at the value of the transfers involved. Figure 3.3 shows the total value of transfers in the EC over the period. This support rose from about 27 billion ECU in 1980 to about 56 billion ECU in 1986, falling back a little as world prices firmed towards the end of the decade. The figure shows the dominance of the support to the grass-fed livestock sector, dairy and beef, as compared with the arable crops. The profile of support in the USA is somewhat similar, as shown in Figure 3.4. The substantial support given to the livestock sector, even after taking into account the negative transfer through higher feed prices, is suprising. The support to the cereals sector varies with world prices, which were high at the begining of the decade, and with the shifts in domestic

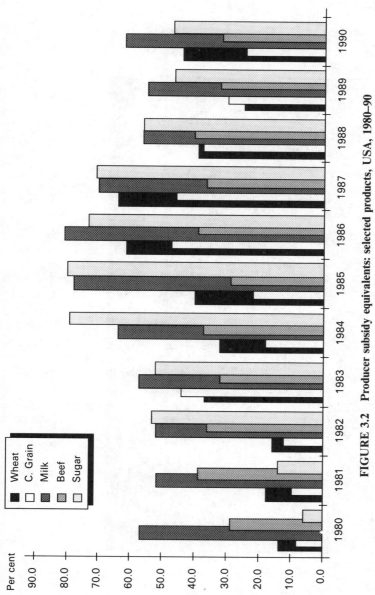

FIGURE 3.2 Producer subsidy equivalents: selected products, USA, 1980–90

Source: OECD PSE tables.

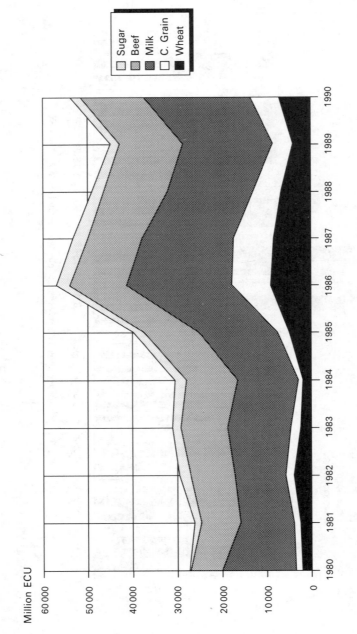

FIGURE 3.3 Total transfers to producers: selected commodities, EC, 1980–90

Source: OECD PSE tables.

51

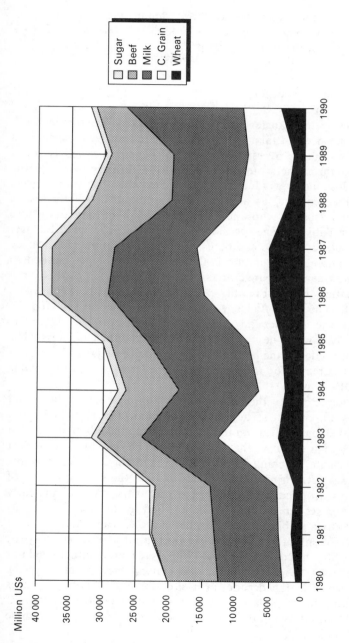

FIGURE 3.4 Total transfers to producers: selected commodities, USA, 1980–90

Source: OECD PSE tables.

policy, such as the expensive corn programme in 1983. The total transfers on these commodities reached a high of $40 billion in 1986–7 before falling with the firmer world prices.

3.4.2 Efficiency of transfers

The PSE records the transfer but not the cost of achieving that transfer. To do that we need to take a further step. The transfer effected by a subsidy to producers overstates the actual benefit received by farm families and the owners of factors specific to farming: some of the transfer is lost, as the inducement to overexpand the sector lowers output in the economy as a whole. This unrequited welfare loss is measured by a triangle whose height is the level of subsidy and whose base is the quantity change occasioned by the policy.[10] The PSE is just a notional subsidy and so can be used in the calculation of efficiency losses. The missing information is the elasticity of supply, needed to calculate the quantity change arising from the policy.[11] Armed with this information, one can readily calculate the size of the welfare loss triangle and hence the efficiency loss on the production side. To the extent that the policies also distort consumer prices, a similar calculation can be done for the consumption efficiency loss. The information needed is the level of CSE (as a percentage) and the price elasticity of demand for the products. These are also both available from the OECD work.

The economic cost of the policies is the sum of these producer and consumer welfare effects. The estimates are shown in Figures 3.5 and 3.6. The loss due to policies in the EC appears to have been about 3–4 billion ECU each year over the first part of the decade. In 1984 the cost began to escalate, reaching 9 billion ECU by 1986, at the time of low world prices. With firmer world prices in 1988 the economic cost of price support dropped back a little, but not to the levels of the early 1980s. High costs can presumably be justified for individual years, as the cost of price stability, though other more efficient policy instruments exist for smoothing out income fluctuations from year to year. More plausibly, the costs in the mid-1980s were neither anticipated nor acceptable: they were the unintended consequence of poor policy decisions earlier in the decade, in a situation where policy changes were not able to keep pace with events. More specifically, the EC entered the subsidy wars of 1986–7 unwillingly but with no credible policy alternative.

53

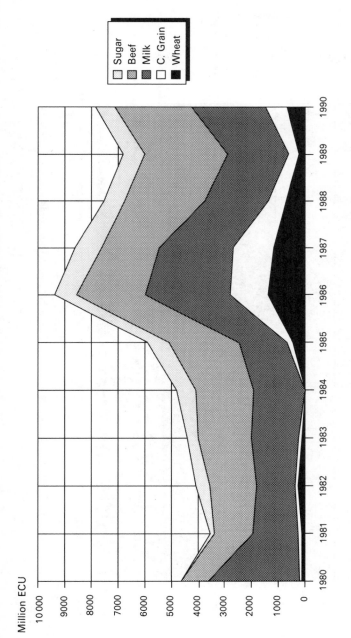

FIGURE 3.5 **Total economic loss due to policies: selected products, EC, 1980–90**

Source: OECD PSE tables.

54

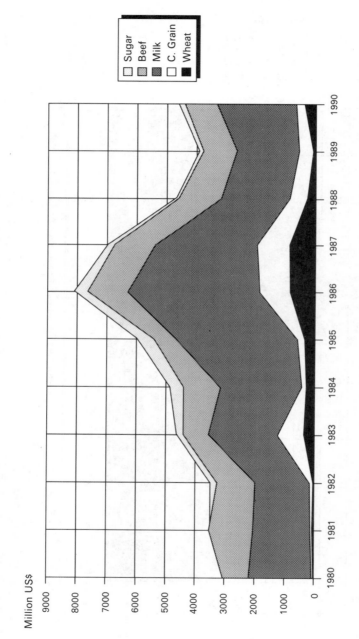

FIGURE 3.6 Total economic loss due to policies: selected products, USA, 1980–90

Source: OECD PSE tables.

The US position (Figure 3.6) shows a similar increase in economic costs over the decade, reaching $8 billion by 1986, much of it attributable to the dairy sector. Even with the greater flexibility of US policy (through the periodic Farm Bill debates) there is still an inertia which can account for an unacceptable run-up in efficiency losses. As was the case in the EC, some of the problem lies with world market developments, which are difficult to interpret and to react to in the policy arena. As was suggested earlier, a sudden price rise on world markets, for whatever reason, can easily undermine the case for policy reform. The EC misread the temporary strengthening of the dollar in 1983–5 as a tightening of commodity markets. When the dollar fell sharply in 1986 the internal policy prices were left high and dry. In the USA the unusual strength of export demand at the beginning of the decade misled people into thinking that a new era of expansion was at hand. The policy changes in the early 1980s took place against this backdrop. It was not until the time of the 1985 Act that the real costs of these programmes became clear, but by this time the plight of the farm sector, caught by falling land prices and rising real interest rates, prevented action.

The combination of rising transfers and rising costs poses the question as to whether the policies improved the efficiency of transferring income to the farm population. The most efficient transfers are those that do not distort production (or consumption) decisions. Such 'decoupled' policies have long been advocated by economists, but rejected by farmers as a form of welfare. There are ways of partially decoupling the programme transfers, in particular by tying full support payments to some form of supply restriction. The supply restriction in itself is not the object, except in the rare cases where monopoly rents can be extracted from a market: instead the aim is the containment of government liability. The effect is to reduce the amount by which output exceeds that in the non-subsidised situation, and thus reduce the efficiency loss from the transfer.

The efficiency in achieving the objective of a transfer to producers can be simply measured by the ratio of the unrequited costs to the transfer effected. The effective transfer is the efficiency cost (from both production and consumption distortions) divided by the gross transfer, as measured by the value-PSE, less the production efficiency loss (the welfare triangle on the production side). These calculations are given in Figures 3.7 and 3.8. In the case of the EC, the excess cost of transfer ranges from very small amounts (less than 5 per cent) for cereals in most years, to 20–35 per cent for sugar over much of the decade. The

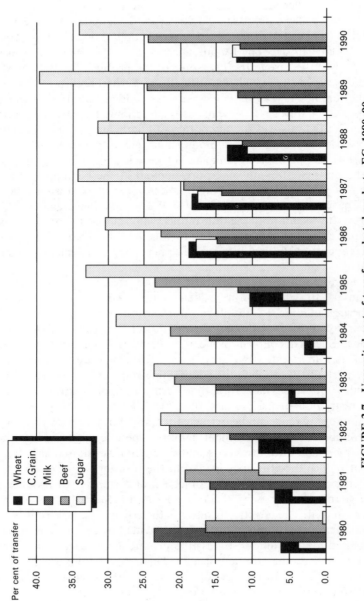

FIGURE 3.7 Unrequited cost of transfer: selected products, EC, 1980–90

Source: OECD PSE tables.

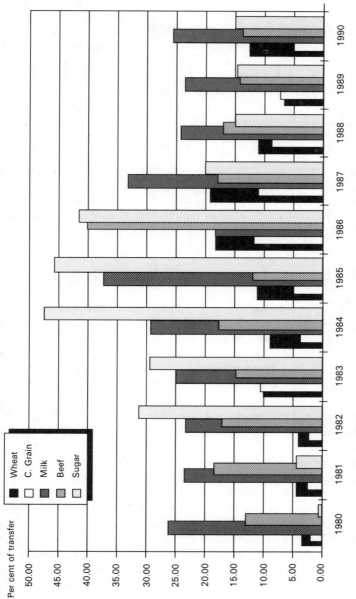

FIGURE 3.8 Unrequited cost of transfer: selected products, USA, 1980–90

Source: OECD PSE tables.

dairy and beef programmes tend to fall in between, with excess costs, relative to a 'pure' transfer, of 15–25 per cent. There appears to be little evidence of a significant improvement in the efficiency of transfer over the decade: the changes are once again a reflection of world price changes. This is to be expected, as efficiency losses increase by the square of the subsidy level whereas the transfers themselves vary in proportion to those subsidy levels. This picture is reinforced in the case of the USA (see Figure 3.8), where the most inefficient policies appear in the sugar and dairy programmes. In the absence of effective supply control on the domestic market, protection at the border has been the main policy instrument in these two markets. The inefficiency can be seen from the excess costs ranging from 15 to 45 per cent for sugar and from 25 to 40 per cent for dairy. By contrast, the other US programmes appear to be relatively efficient, though the cost of transfers to the beef sector has been about 15 per cent. US cereal policies would appear to have a modest percentage level of inefficiency, though as was discussed above the total economic loss can be quite substantial.

3.5   THE PROSPECTS FOR FUTURE REFORM

It is difficult to make the case from the analysis in the previous section that the policies in the EC and the USA have been substantially reformed over the last decade. The evidence points to escalating economic costs until 1987, to go along with the more visible budget costs. By 1988 the trend seemed to have been reversed, with costs declining and efficiency improving. The drought in the USA cut wheat production by about 30 per cent and sent cereal prices up by 50 per cent in 1988 and 1989; world prices for dairy products also firmed over that period. US farm support costs dropped almost as quickly as they had risen in 1986. In the EC, the budget cost of the CAP fell below the ceiling agreed in February 1988 in both 1989 and 1990, as export subsidies on cereals and dairy products declined. In April 1989, the EC and the USA, along with other GATT members, signed an agreement to freeze support prices for the 1989 and 1990 marketing years. Prospects for a constructive conclusion to the Uruguay Round, including a meaningful limitation on farm support levels and a move over time to reduce these levels, looked good. Though the reduction in support costs removed some of the political interest in the agricultural issue, the technical problem of phasing down support levels was made more tractable. In effect, the negotiators could argue that they had already begun the process of liberalisation of agricultural markets, since 1986, and needed merely to lock in the process for a further period.

Events have not been kind to this process of reform-by-accident. In the summer of 1990 the EC livestock market collapsed, under the weight of increased production, imports from Eastern Europe and a health scare which reduced consumption. In the ensuing debate on how to respond, one thing became clear: the time was not right to make major 'concessions' to the USA and the Cairns Group (a coalition of largely non-subsidising agricultural exporting countries) on farm support. The deadlock in 'final' Uruguay Round negotiations in December 1990 indicated that few EC members were willing to impose more hardship on their agricultural constituents. Though the talks resumed in 1991, and could still lead to an agreement during 1992, expectations are now for a much more modest agricultural package of trade reforms than once thought possible.

Where does this leave the process of agricultural policy reform in the USA and the EC? On the one hand is the clear evidence of both domestic and international discontent with the policies in their present form. There is ample documentation of the impact that excessive agricultural protection has on the non-farm economy and on trade relations. The political position of agriculture in both the USA and the EC depends largely upon the silent aquiescence of non-farm business in the passage of farm legislation. Whereas US agribusiness has been an advocate of reform, EC food and feed processing firms and machinery and input suppliers have tended to take the view that their interests are best served by a large and prosperous domestic agricultural sector.

Until EC reform is firmly backed by non-agricultural groups, its prospects are dim. The only effective domestic pressure for reform appears to be that of the budget. The 1991 spending on the CAP jumped by 30 per cent over the 1990 level, injecting a sense of crisis once again in the debate about the CAP. To the additional costs of export subsidies for cereals and relief for the livestock sector has been added the costs of German unification arising from the introduction of CAP prices in the former East Germany. This would seem to many to provide justification for a further increase in the budget ceiling, but it would again bring the issue of agricultural reform to the level of summit meetings. More likely in the short term is a series of measures to cut budget costs for the next year, leaving time for the current reform proposals to be debated.

As budgetary pressures for reform again become an issue in the EC, so international pressure through the Uruguay Round talks appears to be receding in importance. It now seems unlikely that a GATT agreement will force the main industrial countries to move faster towards reform than their own domestic policy constraints will allow. Over a chorus from the pundits of 'I told you so!', domestic politicians are taking back the initiative from trade negotiators. The trade tail tried to wag the domestic dog, and appeared for a time to be succeeding, but the dog seems now to have realised what was happening.

Two less traditional pressures for reform may turn out to be of more lasting significance. On the domestic front is the issue of the environmental impact of agriculture in the EC and the USA. Support for farm policies has in the past rested in part on the assumption that agriculture represents a sound and sustainable use of the environment. Farming was deemed to be the mainstay industry in the rural areas, and viable rural economies were thought to be dependent on agricultural incomes. It followed that price supports were necessary to sustain both the rural economy and the environment. The current perception in both the USA and the EC is somewhat different. The demand for clean air, pure water and an accessible countryside are often in direct conflict with large-scale, intensive, chemical-based farming systems. If high price supports were widely thought to stimulate such 'modern' farming, and hinder the small family holding, practising traditional farming methods and acting as a steward to the countryside, the reformers would gain as a powerful ally the large environmental lobby. This change in attitudes towards commercial farming is already apparent in the USA and is well under way in the EC. Similarly, as more and more rural families depend on non-farm incomes, the link between commodity prices and the state of the rural economy becomes more tenuous. This has led to pressures for a series of rural development programmes unconnected with commercial farming.

The other pressure for reform comes from the process of regional integration. In the case of the EC this manifests itself in the relations with EFTA and Eastern Europe. For the USA, the issue is of relations with Mexico and Canada, and of Latin America. Agriculture plays a sensitive role in the process of regional integration. The issue of farm policy coordination can arise in any regional trade agreement, as conditions of competition will depend on the internal agricultural policy regimes. The EC, anticipating a process of deeper integration, went straight for a common policy, though at the expense of a high level of protection against outsiders. The EFTA in 1960, by contrast, chose to exclude agriculture from its scope, thus avoiding the issue of policy harmonisation. When the EC and EFTA formed a free-trade area in manufactured goods, in the 1970s, they chose to exclude agriculture, and this has been the case with the talks for extending these agreements to areas such as services to create a 'European Economic Area'. Eventually, one suspects, agricultural trade will have to be included in these arrangements, though one can understand the reluctance of governments to open this 'can of worms'. This luxury of sweeping residual agricultural issues under the carpet will not work for Eastern Europe. The pressure will increase over time to allow these emerging democracies to sell agricultural produce into the markets of Western Europe. The CAP may well meet its match not in the GATT but in the arrangements for trade with Poland, Hungary and Czechoslovakia

The US regional trade agreements will also not be able to avoid agriculture. The Canadian free trade pact with the USA paved the way for coordination of policies by tying import controls to price support levels. An extension to Mexico of these arrangements could allow Mexican agricultural policy to be modified to take full advantage of the broader North American market. In the absence of a GATT agreement satisfactory to the USA, there may be an attempt to introduce on a regional scale some of the farm policy constraints discussed in the Uruguay Round.

Whether these new pressures for reform, from environmental concerns to the expansion of intra-regional trade, will succeed in toppling the USA and EC agricultural policies from their present position is not clear. Budget pressures, consumer discontent and trade frictions have not made a great impression on the policies over the 1980s. The key to the future of these farm policies may even lie outside the rich industrial countries themselves. Poor agricultural performance in the large land masses of the USSR, India and China could send prices up and rescue the price support policies in the 1990s as they did in the 1970s. On the other hand, a few years of weak export markets coupled with the relentless march of agricultural technology could quickly finish off the job tentatively started in the decade of the 1980s.

4 Agricultural Trade and the GATT

A. J. RAYNER, K. A. INGERSENT and R. C. HINE

4.1 INTRODUCTION

Agricultural trade has been a problem area in international commerce for several decades. Pervasive government intervention into the agricultural sector in many countries has distorted the location of world production and the extent and patterns of trade flows. Such intervention has restricted the gains from trade that accrue to world consumers arising from differences in the costs of production of farm commodities between countries. Furthermore, agricultural trade has not been effectively governed by the institutional framework for international trade relations that has been provided by the General Agreement on Tariffs and Trade, the GATT, since its inception in 1947. Rather, international trade rules have been adapted to conform with domestic agricultural programmes. Agriculture has been treated in a different way from other industries within the GATT and has not been subject to many of the disciplines which are intended to frame an orderly trading system[1.]

Agricultural protectionism has increased substantially over the past few decades. However, the costs and distortions associated with intervention fall when world markets are 'strong' and rise when they are 'weak'. During the 1970s, in the aftermath of the commodity price boom, agricultural trade was buoyant and public concern over agricultural support was muted. However, agricultural trade became a pressing economic and political issue in the 1980s. Growth in the global consumption of farm products slackened in the early 1980s under the influence of world recession and macroeconomic instabilities, whilst production kept increasing under the stimuli of technological advances and government support in the developed countries. Rates of protection for farm commodities rose rapidly to high levels. For OECD countries as a whole, agricultural protection expressed in terms of Producer Subsidy Equivalents (PSEs) 'soared from 28 per cent in 1980 to 47 per cent in 1986' (Sanderson, 1990, p. 2).[2] In terms of tariff equivalents, protection rose from 39 per cent to 89 per cent (ibid.). Protection was particularly high in Japan and the EC and rose sharply in the USA. Visible symptoms of policy failure included large costs to national budgets[3] and mounting stockpiles of commodity surpluses. Competitive subsidisation by exporters attempting to dump surpluses in restricted import markets depressed international prices and created trade tensions. Conflicts were generated between the major players – the EC, the USA and Japan – and caused considerable damage to smaller agricultural exporters such as Australia and New Zealand and to developing countries such as Argentina. Australia coordinated a group of fourteen, largely non-subsidising, exporters – the so-called Cairns Group[4] – to counter 'unfair' trading practices by the major players.

Escalating trade conflict in combination with mounting budgetary costs of agricultural support brought the issue of agricultural protectionism to the forefront of the international economic policy agenda. In the Uruguay Round of trade negotiations in the GATT, which commenced in September 1986, a high priority was given to reforming domestic farm policies which distort agricultural trade. The ministerial declaration which launched the negotiations aimed (i) to liberalise world farm trade, and (ii) to make it more orderly and predictable. Domestic agricultural policies were no longer regarded as sacrosanct since the negotiators called for 'the reduction of import barriers' and 'the phased reduction of all direct and indirect subsidies and other measures affecting directly or indirectly agricultural trade' and were committed to 'bring all measures affecting import access and export competition under strengthened and more operationally effective GATT rules and disciplines' (GATT, 1986).

The inclusion of agriculture as a major item on the agenda of the Uruguay Round of multilateral trade negotiations promised to redress the past neglect of agricultural trade in the GATT, and to remove the challenge posed by the prevalence and growth of agricultural protectionism to the credibility of the GATT framework for an orderly system of international commerce. Thus, much agricultural trade has not been conducted according to the rules and procedures of the GATT. Moreover, whilst successive rounds of multilateral negotiations in the GATT have fostered a process of trade liberalisation in industrial products, they have been unable to reduce agricultural trade barriers and distortions. The past failure of the GATT with regard to agriculture stems from two main factors: first, the proliferation of market distorting farm programmes enshrined in domestic legislation which employ non-tariff barriers (NTBs), domestic subsidies and export aids and, second, exemption of agriculture from certain rules of the GATT since its inception (Hathaway, 1987; Josling *et al.*, 1990). Four aspects of the differential treatment of farm products in world trade may be highlighted:[5]

1. NTBs are more difficult to reduce through negotiation than are tariffs so impeding the liberalisation of agricultural trade. Furthermore, Article XVI of the GATT has provided an escape clause for primary products as regards domestic and export subsidies: these are allowed provided that they do not enable a country to obtain 'a more than equitable share of world export trade'. This has enabled GATT members to argue that farm support programmes fall outside the scope of the GATT.
2. Article XI:2 of the GATT permits quantitative restriction of agricultural imports provided domestic production controls are also in place. Furthermore, the USA in 1955 obtained for itself the so-called Section 22 waiver allowing quantitative restraint on imports of farm products that interfere with the operation of its domestic farm programmes without parallel action to restrict domestic production. Strictly speaking, the 1955 waiver applies only to the USA and it has been a continuing source of resentment by other countries who have argued that the USA is not seriously interested in agricultural trade liberalisation.
3. The introduction of the protectionist Common Agricultural Policy (CAP) of the EC was not effectively challenged in the GATT, in part because of US political support for the formation of the EC. As a result, the bargaining power of the Community countries in the world trade arena was increased and they were in a stronger position to resist pressure for agricultural trade liberalisation.
4. The post-1947 success of the GATT in liberalising trade in industrial products by reducing mutually offsetting trade barriers, largely tariffs, reflected the interests of the industrial sector itself in expanding trade. However, the agricultural sector in many industrialised countries has felt threatened by trade reform.

Together with many developing countries they opposed efforts to liberalise trade in farm products and instead advocated the establishment of international commodity agreements to manage trade.

Although agriculture featured on the agenda of the seven rounds of trade negotiations in the GATT prior to the Uruguay Round, little was achieved in the way of liberalising trade in farm products. Governments were not willing to relinquish their sovereignty over domestic agricultural policy by agreeing to amend or abolish commodity programmes so as to reduce their trade distorting effects and limit the subsidies paid to farmers. Consequently, the conduct of agricultural trade is largely shaped by government policies. Section 4.3 of this chapter addresses these issues of agricultural policy and trade distortions. Specifically, it looks at the motivations for government intervention into agriculture in industrialised countries, assesses the costs and distortions of such intervention and considers if trade negotiations can assist the reform of agricultural policy. Section 4.4 highlights the main negotiating issues in the protracted discussions on agriculture in the Uruguay Round and section 4.5 discusses prospects for a reversal of the increasing protectionism and disarray in world agriculture. As a background to these issues, section 4.2 presents a brief summary of the main features of agricultural trade.

4.2 STRUCTURE AND PROBLEMS OF WORLD AGRICULTURAL TRADE

The developed countries dominate most aspects of world agricultural trade: as exporters and/or importers they were involved in 87 per cent of the $283 billion a year world food trade in 1988. Some 50 per cent ($141 billion) of this commerce takes place among developed countries, of which over half ($82 billion) is accounted for by intra-EC transactions under the Common Agricultural Policy. Livestock products and certain specialist crops like wine are traded largely between developed countries, while the tropical beverages (coffee, tea and cocoa), bananas and rubber are exported from the Third World mainly to developed countries. Wheat and coarse grains (maize, barley, oats, etc.) are increasingly traded in the reverse direction, that is from rich to poor countries, often on subsidised terms. The remaining major commodities – sugar, oilseeds, rice, citrus fruit, tobacco and cotton – originate in both rich and poor countries, who thus compete for markets predominantly (except for rice) in the developed world. In policy terms this commodity group is particularly sensitive in that support policies in the developed countries have a direct impact on the export prospects of Third World countries.

The main problems in world agricultural trade since the early 1950s have faced exporters rather than importers. Concern has focused on two issues: the downward trend in agriculture's share of world trade, and the instability of world commodity markets. Instability of prices reflects structural features (low short-run price elasticities of demand and supply), unpredictable shifts in supply due to weather and disease factors, and government intervention policies (see below). The decline in market share is a long-run phenomenon – before the First World War agriculture's share of world trade was over 50 per cent – and today it is less than 14 per cent. The decline reflects a slower growth in the volume of agricultural exports relative to that of manufactures, exacerbated at times by weakening agricultural export prices.[6]

The declining share of agricultural exports in world trade is due to a combination of factors – especially structural change, agricultural protectionism, shifts in comparative advantage, and the changing basis for international trade – only some of which are amenable to international negotiation. In the developed countries, which account for about two thirds of world food imports, low-income elasticities of demand for food and slow population growth generate only a weak expansion in the market for foodstuffs. Exporting countries complain too that protectionist governments reserve most of this expansion for local producers through subsidies and other aids. Similarly, greater efficiency in the use of agricultural raw materials dampens the growth of trade in these products, as also does the effort of developing countries to process more of their output of agricultural raw materials and to export them as finished products such as textiles and clothing. The relatively poor performance of agricultural exports in recent years also reflects the exceptionally dynamic growth in manufactures trade. This has taken largely an intra-industry form – that is, it involves a country's simultaneous import and export of similar products, motivated by the consumers' desire for a wide choice of product variety and the producers' need to achieve economies of scale in production. With factory re-organisation concentrating on fewer lines for export as well as domestic markets, a rapid two-way expansion of manufactures trade can take place without severe job losses and hence protectionist pressures. By contrast, in agriculture the scope for intra-industry trade growth is much less because of greater product homogeneity and the lesser importance of economies of scale.

During the 1970s, the downward trend in agriculture's share of world trade was halted by a combination of what now appear as exceptional circumstances. Food imports into developing countries more than doubled in volume during the decade, stimulated in part by the availability of credit from the Western countries. The leap in the price of oil permitted oil-exporting countries to quadruple their food purchases. The USSR turned to the world market to make up massive shortfalls in domestic grain production. Overall, there was a 54 per cent growth in the volume of agricultural trade which matched that of manufactures. However, the position changed dramatically during the 1980s: between 1980 and 1989, the volume of agricultural trade grew by only 26 per cent – one-third that of manufactures. At the same time, food export prices fell by 11 per cent whereas the unit value of manufactured exports rose by 20 per cent. Debt problems in the Third World, the decline in the oil price, and a recovery or at least stabilisation of production in the USSR, have all undermined the growth in agricultural imports. The only import markets to show substantial growth in the last ten years have been in Japan and the Asian NICs. Although heavily subsidised, Japanese food production was stable between 1980 and 1989, allowing imports to meet the whole of increased food consumption.

The 1980s experience has been particularly painful for the non-European food exporters because over a half of the modest growth in international food trade was internal to the EC, artificially stimulated by the Common Agricultural Policy. Excluding intra-EC transactions, the value of trade grew by only 15 per cent in 1980–7. Furthermore, while EC food imports shrank in real terms, the Community's subsidised exports expanded. Thus, although the USA remained the single largest exporter of food in 1989 with 14.5 per cent of the world total, its share had dropped quite sharply during the 1980s. Between them, the USA, Canada, Brazil, Australia, and Argentina – the leading non-European food exporters in 1980 – had very little growth in the nominal value of their food exports in the subsequent decade, and hence suffered a decline in real terms. These countries have consequently insisted on agriculture being at the centre of the Uruguay Round.

4.3 AGRICULTURAL POLICY AND TRADE DISTORTIONS

4.3.1 Motivation for agricultural intervention policies

An interventionist agricultural policy is the norm in OECD countries. Major objectives of policy include the maintenance of farm incomes, the stabilisation of prices and income, support of rural communities and ensuring the security and stability of food supplies.[7] There is a commonality amongst these objectives in that they are by nature defensive ; they seek to protect the agricultural sector specifically, and the food system at large, against both long-term adjustment and short-term shocks fashioned by forces internal and external to the country. There are two major, but interrelated, motives underlying defensive assistance to agriculture: first, to *redistribute* domestic wealth in favour of farm producers and, second, to *insulate* domestic food markets from trade shocks.

Redistributive policies or adjustment assistance programmes have been linked to the so-called 'farm income problem' or 'agricultural adjustment problem' in recognition that agriculture is a declining sector in an economy experiencing modern economic growth. In such an economy, there is a continuing decline in the *relative* importance of agriculture as measured by share of GDP and by share of the labour force.[8] This is called the agricultural transformation process. The roots of the process lie in rising agricultural productivity, on a par with productivity growth in other major sectors of the economy, and shifts in relative demand away from food products (Engel's Law).[9] As a result, there is continuous pressure for resources, especially labour, to move out of the rural sector and into the growth sectors of the economy. However, if there is imperfect immobility of resources, there is a possibility of a structural disequilibrium[10] known as the 'agricultural adjustment problem'. This 'problem' is typified by an income gap between urban and farm sectors although, depending on time and place, the income gap may be viewed as temporary or persistent/large or small. In the open economy, adjustment of agriculture may be exacerbated by growing imports of farm produce particularly if transport innovations or rapid technological change in competitor countries lead to large and rapid falls in real prices.

Whilst redistributive agricultural policies have by and large been introduced in times of 'crises' (see Winters, Chapter 2 above),[11] they have been sustained by the perception of an 'adjustment problem'. Under pressure from farm groups, the political agenda has responded to the fear, particularly in the agricultural importing or even agricultural self-sufficient economy, that the social and political fabric of rural society cannot withstand the burdens imposed by *laissez-faire* forces. With farmers regarding technology and input prices as given parameters, it is natural for them to demand intervention on farm product prices to effect income transfers. However, the pervasiveness of agricultural price support policies over time and across countries cannot be fully explained in terms of governments attempting to cope with a perceived adjustment problem. Rather, an alternative explanation can be given in terms of the failure of government to limit effectively the rent-seeking (or rent-preserving) activities of farmers, landowners and associated interest groups.[12] The result is a redistribution of income from society at large to the members of the farm lobby. Such activity tends to be more successful in agricultural importing countries where pressure groups can appeal to xenophobic feelings in society and where the costs of agricultural support fall partly on foreign producers (ibid.). However, if agriculture is shielded by policy against the forces of structural change and/or low cost foreign suppliers, then adjustment costs are shifted on to other sectors of the economy as well as on to countries specialising in farm exports.

Insulating policies shield the domestic market from fluctuations in international prices and reduce instability in internal producer prices. As a result, such policies can reduce the variability of agricultural gross income and provide benefits to risk averse farmers in the form of a reduction in income risk.[13] This argument can be demonstrated most simply by considering a country that is a small trader in a commodity on the international market. Without intervention, the domestic price is equal to the international price which is subject to random shocks from supply and demand forces and from exchange rate changes. Consequently, a policy which stabilises the producer price by severing the link between domestic and international prices reduces the instability of producer income.[14] However, the insulation of domestic commodity markets by a number of countries increases the instability of price on international markets and imposes a risk burden on exposed foreign producers.

Agricultural price support and domestic price stabilisation are major elements in *food security* programmes in agricultural importing countries. Such programmes typically equate food security with food self-sufficiency in staple items of the diet. Increased food self-sufficiency is achieved via administered price incentives and trade controls which reduce reliance on foreign suppliers. But the pursuit of self-sufficiency incurs domestic costs, creates tension in the international trading system and does not ensure food security unless the country is also largely self-sufficient in the inputs employed in modern agriculture, especially energy[15]

4.3.2 Instruments, distortions and costs

The pervasive government intervention into agricultural markets in OECD countries is effected, in the main, by instruments which distort producer prices, and commonly consumer prices, above international or border prices and reduce the instability of domestic farm commodity prices relative to world price fluctuations. Numerous mechanisms are employed which interfere with trade. These include variable tariffs and variable export subsidies, domestic subsidies such as deficiency payments, import quotas, voluntary export restraints, export promotion including targeted subsidies and non-emergency food aid and health and sanitary regulations.[16] In general, agricultural trade protection relies on non-tariff barriers. The domestic, trade and policy interdependence impacts stemming from the use of these instruments are sizeable and complex and are important considerations in the context of trade liberalisation negotiations. In what follows, we highlight a number of these impacts relying on counterfactual quantitative studies where available to indicate their implications relative to a 'free trade' benchmark.

Domestic costs[17]

Agricultural protectionism gives rise to consumer and/or taxpayer transfers and imposes domestic net economic costs. There are numerous studies of these impacts by international institutions with reference to a focus OECD country or to a group of such countries providing domestic cost estimates for a single year or for a run of years. Here we present the results from a widely referenced USDA study by Roningen and Dixit (1989a) which evaluates the domestic costs of protection in the USA, the EC and Japan.[18]

Table 4.1 indicates that farmers are supported at the expense of consumers and taxpayers of the same nation and that costs substantially exceed benefits. For the year in question, consumers and taxpayers combined typically lost around $1.5 for each $1.0 trans-

TABLE 4.1   Benefits and costs of agricultural support, 1986/7[1]

	Producer benefits	Consumer costs	Taxpayer costs	Net economic costs[2]	Transfer ratio[3]
		Billion dollars			*Per dollar*
USA	26.3	6.0	30.3	9.2	1.4
EC	33.3	32.6	15.6	14.9	1.5
Japan	22.6	27.7	5.7	8.6	1.5

[1] Estimates based on unilateral liberalisation by the country or region
[2] Net economic costs: Consumer costs + Taxpayer costs − Producer benefits with adjustment for transfer to other groups, e.g. quota holders.
[3] Transfer ratio: (Taxpayer + Consumer costs)/Producer benefits
Source: Roningen and Dixit (1989a), Table 8.

ferred to producers. However, it should be noted that the estimates are year-dependent since they depend, *inter alia*, upon the state of the world market and the exchange rate of the dollar against the ECU and the yen.

Distortion of trade flows and depression of world prices

Agricultural protectionism encourages domestic production and, commonly, discourages domestic utilisation of farm commodities thus decreasing imports/increasing exports. As a result, trade flows are distorted from the pattern and quantities that would occur under free trade and can even give rise to trade reversals. For example, it has been estimated that protection given to EC producers under the Common Agricultural Policy led to the Community being a net exporter rather than a net importer for many commodities in the early 1980s (IMF, 1988, p. 17). Furthermore, by encouraging domestic self-sufficiency, protection policies depress commodity prices in the residual international markets to the detriment of producers in unprotected countries. There are many studies which estimate the extent to which world commodity prices are lowered by protection or, conversely, would be raised by liberalisation.[19] As one example, Tyers and Anderson (1988) estimate that *liberalising* (eliminating) all OECD protection policies would raise real international food prices by an average of some 30 per cent by 1995 in comparison to the levels likely to occur if protection levels of the mid 1980s were continued with. The costs of protection fall quite heavily on non-subsidising agricultural exporters since, *ceteris paribus*, they sell a lower volume of exports at lower prices. Tyers and Anderson estimate that the food producers of the Cairns Group suffer a loss of some $15billion a year because of protection in the industrialised countries. On the other hand, consumers in the Eastern bloc and the LDC importers of temperate-zone products are the gainers from low prices on world markets. However, these gains are small in relation to the costs that lower prices impose on farmers in developing countries and to the costs of agricultural protectionism in the industrialised countries.[20]

Overall, protectionism in the industrialised countries combined with low food prices in the developing world (see World Bank, 1986) causes a regional misallocation of resources in global agriculture; a phenomenon that has been called 'world agriculture in disarray' (Johnson, 1973, 1991). The proliferation of NTBs is an additional reason why global agriculture is slow to adjust to changing conditions of production and trade.

Increased instability on international markets

Domestic market price insulation is measured by the proportion by which domestic price risk is smaller than that in corresponding international markets and is equal to unity minus the elasticity of price transmission from the world market to the domestic market for a specific commodity. Tyers (1990) presents evidence to show that domestic market insulation is substantial in most OECD countries and in several developing countries. However, the food exporting countries of the Americas and Australasia have low degrees of insulation. In general, the degree of market insulation is determined by the choice of policy instruments employed in domestic farm support programmes (ibid.). For example, the substantial insulation of EC farm product markets stems from the CAP system of variable import levies and variable export restitutions (subsidies). Estimates of the degree of insulation for certain OECD countries are presented in Table 4.2.

Domestic market insulation by one or more countries increases instability on international markets and imposes a risk burden on economic agents in those countries who remain exposed to turbulence in world markets. Thus, world markets are thinner or more residual in nature and have to make greater adjustments to quantity shocks so amplifying price instability.[21] Consequently, insulation by many

TABLE 4.2   Extent of food market insulation (per cent)[1]

	Short run	Long run
EC10	83	62
Japan	76	53
USA	30	22
Australasia	39	22
Argentina	39	30

[1] Insulation measures the proportion by which domestic food price risk is smaller than that in corresponding international markets, averaged across seven commodity groups including grains, livestock products and sugar.
Source: Tyers (1990).

countries substantially reduces the risk spreading capacity of world markets and increases the risks faced by all other countries. Tyers (1990, p. 222), using a model of world trade in the important temperate-zone commodities, shows that 'world food markets would be very much less volatile were agricultural trade policies to be liberalised, or changed so as to be non-insulating' by, for example, converting existing import barriers into ad-valorem tariffs only. Moreover, this reduction in volatility would 'make most domestic agents in most countries better off (by virtue of reduced price risk) than they are at present' (ibid., p. 227).

Two other consequences of undue world market instability should be noted (McCalla and Josling, 1985, chapter 10). First, governments have difficulty in discerning the current and future trend of international prices as a guide to price setting under their domestic farm programmes. Second, the development plans of developing countries can be disrupted by variability in their food export earnings and import bills.

Trade disputes and policy interdependence

Agricultural price support policies protect high cost production which displaces imports and, in some cases, disrupts export markets; a range of instruments is deployed to restrict imports and to aid otherwise uncompetitive exports. These price supports generate friction in international trade as import markets shrink and competition intensifies for the remaining export markets. A large number of US–EC and US–Japanese trade policy disputes concern trade in agricultural commodities (Josling, 1986). Political capital, with a high opportunity cost, becomes tied up in resolving these disputes. Moreover, trade friction over seemingly unimportant agricultural issues can erode cooperation on other, more pressing international problems.[22]

Although policy decisions on agricultural intervention are taken at a national level, trade links the policies of different countries. As a result, there is policy interdependence. One aspect of this interdependence concerns policy offsets: protectionism tends to lower international prices and so a fraction of farm price support in one country is used to offset the impact of support in other countries. For example, Roningen and Dixit (1989a, p. 27) suggest that in 1986/7 over 40 per cent of support to US farmers 'merely offset the losses created by policies of other industrialised countries', although the offset share of support was much lower in the EC and Japan. Likewise, policy costs in one country are affected by the extent and form of protectionism elsewhere. For example, subsidisation of grain exports by the EC and by the USA raises the budgetary costs of support to both countries; on the other hand, restrictions on land planted to grains in the USA tends to reduce support costs in the EC. Similarly, the variability of policy costs in any one country are affected by insulation practices and public stock-holding policies adopted in other countries. Furthermore, retaliation is a common occurrence in agricultural trade. A recent example is the use of targeted export subsidies for grain by the USA, a policy innovation introduced to counteract the employment of export subsidies by the EC.

4.3.3. Can trade negotiations assist policy reform?

By the mid-1980s, national agricultural policies were under scrutiny in most industrialised countries. Rising budgetary costs of farm support against a background of weak international commodity markets were a major reason for reviewing existing policies. Trade disputes and conflicts between the major players – the EC, the USA and Japan– and the considerable economic damage to smaller agricultural exporters generated by protectionism also provided pressures for change.[23] Finally, the domestic consumer and taxpayer burdens and the trade distortions stemming from existing policies were made transparent by authoritative studies conducted by respected institutions, such as the World Bank, OECD and the USDA. Under internal and external pressures, agricultural policy makers began to look for ways to reform farm support policies.

Against this background, the Uruguay Round of Trade Negotiations included the liberalisation of agricultural trade on its agenda. For the first time in the GATT, domestic farm policies were on the negotiating table. The case for using trade negotiations as a vehicle to reform domestic farm policy has been put succinctly by Hathaway (1987, p. 3):

At no time since World War II have so many countries been considering changes in their agricultural policies. It is in the interests of all countries that these changes take place with as little disruption as possible to their agricultural economies. Dislocations can be reduced if all major participants agree on directions and rules and the GATT is the only effective negotiating forum to include the various countries concerned.

However, shifting the focus of agricultural policy reform from uncoordinated domestic political agendas to the international bargaining table offers both promise and difficulties. We look at these two contrasting aspects in terms of, first, static measures of economic surpluses gained or lost from a reduction in protectionism, and second, the exposure of domestic agents to international price instability and, third, food security concerns.

Static welfare gains and losses from liberalisation

Various studies, such as those by Tyers and Anderson (1988) and Roningen and Dixit (1989a), illustrate the advantages to be gained from multilateral reform by the main agricultural trading nations as opposed to unilateral reform by a single major player. Specifically it is in the economic self-interest of the major players to pursue agricultural liberalisation and the losses imposed on domestic farm sectors are smaller if reform is coordinated internationally. Consider for example, some of the results of the Tyers and Anderson study as set out in Table 4.3.[24]

It is apparent from the table that it is in the economic self interest, as represented by net economic welfare, of both the USA and the EC to pursue unilateral liberalisation (gains of $3.3 billion and $21.4 billion respectively). Moreover, it is highly likely that it is in the interests of the USA to liberalise if the EC liberalises and *vice versa*. Thus, the USA gains $3.1 billion if all industrialised countries including the USA liberalise as opposed to $1.7 billion if only the EC liberalises; similarly the EC gains $17.6 billion if all industrialised countries including the

TABLE 4.3   Welfare effects of liberalisation (1985 $ billion per year)

1995 effects on net economic welfare

Liberalisation by:	USA	EC	All industrial market economies
USA	3.3	−1.9	1.1
EC	1.7	21.4	22.7
All industrial market economies	3.1	17.6	50.9

1995 effects on producer welfare

Liberalisation by:	USA	EC	All industrial market economies
USA	−21.5	5.0	−13.9
EC	7.6	−88.6	−70.9
All industrial market economies	3.1	−73.7	−122.9

Source: Tyers and Anderson (1988, p. 211).

EC reform their agricultural sectors but loses $1.9 billion if only the USA liberalises. Consequently, trade liberalisation is a dominant trade strategy for both countries and constitutes a Nash equilibrium in a game theoretic representation of US and EC trade strategies.[25] The table also illustrates the point that the loss in producer surplus in a liberalising country is smaller the larger the number of countries that liberalise. For example, EC producers lose $89 billion from unilateral abolition of protection but $74 billion if all industrialised countries liberalise. US producers lose $22 billion from a unilateral US liberalisation but gain $3 billion from multilateral liberalisation.[26] Thus an internationally coordinated reform promises substantial economic benefits whilst reducing the dislocation imposed on each domestic agricultural sector.

An additional presumed advantage of pursuing reform on the international stage is that the policy process is less susceptible to lobbying by domestic farm interests. The rationale for this is twofold: first, trade ministers as well as agricultural ministers are involved in the negotiating and ratification procedures; second, there is linkage between progress in agricultural negotiations and achievements in other negotiating areas in the GATT system.

However, there are risks attached to the strategy of pursuing domestic farm reform via international trade negotiations. As pointed out by McCalla and Josling (1985), experience suggests that trade talks polarise the participants into mercantilist exporters seeking to expand their markets and protectionist importers clinging to their self-sufficiency . . . countries meet on this battlefield to berate each others' policies'. Confrontation rather than cooperation may be the outcome. Moreover, the clear enunciation of gains and losses from liberalisation provided by authoritative studies during the negotiations may inform the likely losers and intensify opposition to reform. As a result, attention may be focused on the costs of reform to the farm sector rather than on the benefits to the public at large. Even an announced policy of compensation for the abolition of or reduction in price support may galvanise the losers into action. In this connection, farmers may oppose the substitution of direct income support (DIS) for price support for two reasons: first, a distrust of political pledges and, second, a repugnance for being dependent on 'charity'. Nevertheless, if offered the choice between DIS and no support, then they are likely to opt for the former.

Mutual assurance and international price instability

The use of insulating policy instruments by most countries increases world commodity price instability and the price risk faced by non-insulating countries. A single country would lose by a unilateral switch to non-insulating policy instruments since its domestic price instability would increase. However, if all countries refrained from insulating domestic markets, the volatility of international food prices would decrease considerably because of the risk spreading capacity of the world market (Tyers, 1990). It has been argued that the mutual assurance provided by a multilateral agreement under the auspices of the GATT might be a decisive factor in persuading governments to 'take the plunge' in reducing or abolishing market insulation policies (Runge *et al.*, 1987; Tyers 1990). Thus, if a critical mass of participants in trade negotiations agree to a rules revision outlawing insulating instruments then benefits are available to all. For example, variable import levies lie outside GATT disciplines at present; if they were replaced by fixed tariffs then market insulation would fall and international food price instability would be reduced.

Whilst the provision of international market stability requires collective action, it will not necessarily be achieved via trade negotiations seeking to liberalise trade. The attainment of a critical mass of participants willing to forgo insulating policies is hindered by the heterogeneity of nations' exposure to trade and by the temptation to free ride on the actions of others. Furthermore, reliance on international markets to spread risk requires governments to allow world price variations to influence domestic markets even during times of unusually large price movements. As pointed out by McCalla and Josling (1985, p. 227), ' It requires that governments are sufficiently convinced of the longer-term benefits of trade to resist the temptation to intervene for shorter-run objectives.' This may not be easy at times when extreme weather conditions have an undue effect on world production or when exchange rates linking the dollar price of commodities to national currencies are volatile.

Food security concerns

Trade negotiations could assist the reform of food security policies in food importing countries by providing assurance as to the dependability of supplies from exporters. Specifically, importer concerns over food security could be met by commitments from exporters to eschew the use of export embargoes and restraints, and to forgo policies that give their domestic consumers prior access to domestic supplies and that insulate internal markets from world market instability. In return, importers would be required to loosen restraints on import access. However, difficulties lie in persuading both importers and exporters to cede the primacy of domestic policy measures in favour of more open trade.

4.4 THE AGRICULTURAL NEGOTIATIONS IN THE URUGUAY ROUND

4.4.1 Background and initial negotiating positions on agricultural trade

The early 1980s witnessed a general malaise in the world trading system including a slowdown in trade, widening trade imbalances especially for the USA and Japan and a growing disregard of international trading rules as embodied in the GATT. Recognition of the dangers which might attend the breakdown of the GATT system led eventually to the initiation of the eighth round of multilateral trade negotiations under the auspices of the GATT in September 1986 at Punta del Este in Uruguay.

The USA was the principal instigator of the Uruguay Round, even though Japan made the first formal proposal for a new round of MTNs to be launched. The US administration, under President Reagan, saw strengthening of the GATT as a key weapon in its battle against domestic protectionist pressures. The Uruguay Round agenda therefore reflected largely US priorities. These included the liberalisation of trade in services and trade-related investment measures (TRIMs), the international enforcement of intellectual property rights (TRIPs), and the 'graduation' of Newly Industrialising Countries to a status obliging them to liberalise their import regimes. Above all, the USA sought to bring the protection of agriculture firmly within the ambit of the GATT and, having done so, to reduce it.

The Uruguay Round was launched against a background of rising agricultural protectionism. The monitoring of agricultural support and protection by international institutions such as FAO and the OECD has been carried out in recent years via the 'producer subsidy equivalent' measure or 'PSE' (OECD, 1991). The percentage PSE, defined as the ratio of the total PSE to the total gross value of production, is a convenient measuring rod of support and protection, although it has its drawbacks (see Peters, 1991). Empirical estimates of average percentage PSEs for the three broad aggregates of 'crops', 'livestock products' and 'all products', covering the years 1979 to 1986 are shown in Table 4.4 for six members of the OECD. These data confirm that, amongst these countries, protection during this period was highest in Japan, where agricultural exports are negligible, and lowest in Australia and New Zealand where agriculture is strongly export-oriened. Canada, the EC (10) and the USA, occupy intermediate positions between these extremes. But the most salient point confirmed by these data is that between 1979, the last year of the Tokyo Round, and 1986, the opening year of the Uruguay Round, levels of agricultural protection in all those countries were tending to rise, particularly during the second half of the period.

Negotiations began in February 1987 and were scheduled for completion in December 1990. By the end of 1988, six countries or groups of countries had tabled initial negotiating positions in GATT on the reform of farm trade. Prominent amongst these were papers by the USA, the EC, Japan and the Cairns Group (CG) of agricultural exporters. The USA sought the elimination of all forms of trade distorting farm supports, phased over a period of ten years; only

TABLE 4.4   Net percentage PSEs, 1979–86

	1979	1980	1981	1982	1983	1984	1985	1986
Australia								
Crops	3	5	8	15	8	9	13	19
L/S products	9	11	11	15	13	11	15	15
All products	7	9	10	15	11	10	14	16
Canada								
Crops	13	15	16	20	19	25	39	54
L/S products	36	34	36	36	37	40	39	45
All products	26	25	26	28	28	33	39	49
EC (10)								
Crops	45	25	30	42	26	24	44	66
L/S products	38	38	31	31	36	36	43	47
All products	40	35	31	34	33	33	43	52
Japan								
Crops	79	71	65	77	79	81	86	93
L/S products	52	49	51	46	50	48	47	53
All products	68	61	58	62	66	67	69	76
New Zealand								
Crops	2	4	10	13	8	9	10	15
L/S products	15	16	23	28	37	18	23	34
All products	15	16	23	27	36	18	23	33
United States								
Crops	8	9	12	14	34	21	26	45
L/S products	31	29	32	31	31	34	36	41
All products	21	20	23	23	33	28	32	43

Source: OECD, Up-dating of PSE/CSE Analysis: Country Notes, Paris, 1989.

'decoupled' payments such as direct income supports not linked to production or marketing and food aid might be permitted to continue.[27] The CG allied itself with the USA in pressing for major agricultural liberalisation and its position paper sought the elimination of all domestic farm subsidies and border measures with trade-distorting effects, but with a more flexible time-scale than the USA.

These proposals were condemned as unrealistic by the EC and Japan. The EC negotiating paper contemplated negotiations on concerted and reciprocal reductions in support but subject to various restrictions, whilst Japan expressed concern over 'non-economic' objectives such as food security and rural employment. The initial negotiating positions of the major players are summarised in Table 4.5. These revealed deep divisions between the major contestants, particularly the EC and the USA, about the nature, extent and pace of reform.

TABLE 4.5   **Main elements of initial negotiating positions, 1987–8**

United States

- Eliminate all trade-distorting subsidies over ten years
- Eliminate all import barriers, including use of sanitary or phytosanitary regulations to hinder trade over the same period
- Make commodity-specific policy changes in conformity with existing or revised GATT rules for achieving the agreed phasing out of government support
- Use an aggregate measure of support such as the PSE to establish initial levels of protection and monitor progress with their elimination

Cairns Group

- Freeze and then reduce all domestic subsides and border measures with trade distorting effects over ten years by an agreed amount as the first step towards their eventual elimination
- Use an AMS for monitoring progress

European Community

- As a *short-term* strategy, enter into international agreements on prices and market sharing for commodities in surplus (in the EC) such as sugar, cereals and dairy products
- For the *longer term*, negotiate concerted and reciprocal reductions in support, over an agreed period, to achieve more balanced support amongst commodities
- Use an AMS for monitoring progress with long-term support reduction, but allow credit for supply control and adjust for exchange rate variations.

Japan

- Eliminate export subsidies over an agreed period
- Negotiate tariff reductions using the traditional request-and-offer procedure
- Keep GATT waivers permitting retention of import quotas to buttress food security
- No need for an AMS to monitor progress with agreed reforms

4.4.2   Mid-term review and Geneva Accord[28]

A mid-term review of progress with the Uruguay Round negotiations was held in Montreal in December 1988. The objective of this meeting was to anticipate the types of agreement being sought in all fifteen negotiating areas, to identify major obstacles remaining to be overcome and to devise means for removing these. In the event this objective was successfully achieved in eleven areas, but not in the remaining four, including agriculture, a major sticking point. Although many disagreements on how to advance the negotiations on agriculture remained, the key stumbling block was US insistence on a prior commitment to the elimination of all forms of trade-distorting protection in the face of EC determination not to concede major liberalisation of the Common Agricultural Policy. Lack of progress on agriculture was regarded as the major obstacle to further progress overall: a decision was made to adjourn the talks until April 1989, with Mr Dunkel, the Secretary-General of GATT, being given the responsibility to resolve the impasse on farm trade.

In the breathing space provided by the Montreal adjournment the major protagonists were sufficiently daunted by the prospect of a breakdown of the whole round to cooperate with the Secretary-General in finding a mutually acceptable compromise. Both the EC and the USA appear to have decided independently against allowing their failure to agree on agriculture to jeopardise their own self-interest in reaching agreement in other areas unconnected with agriculture. Most crucially, the Geneva Accord, reached in April 1989, contained no reference to the *elimination* of trade-distorting support and protection. Rather, the objective was to be 'substantial progressive *reductions* in agricultural support and protection sustained over an agreed period of time'. Thus, by signing the Geneva Accord, the USA abandoned the 'zero option'. But the EC also made a significant concession. Whereas the Accord allowed credit only for reduced support and protection measures already carried into effect since the Punta del Este Declaration (i.e. since 1986), the EC had earlier claimed credit for measures taken since 1984. The Accord also stipulated a freeze on all forms of farm support from April 1989 to December 1990, 'within the scope of existing (domestic) legislation and GATT commitments'. This short-term package gave negotiators a further breathing space to reach agreement on the specifics of long-term measures of agricultural policy and trade reform over the next eighteen months to the conclusion of the Uruguay Round at the end of 1990. An important feature of the Geneva Accord was that proposals for long term reform were to be organised under the separate headings of internal support, import access and export competition: these proposals are summarised in Table 4.6.

The revision of negotiating positions following the Geneva Accord revealed some common ground between the USA/CG and the EC on the issue of replacing NTBs (including variable import levies (VILs)) with tariffs, although the EC's partial tariffication proposal was more cautious than the US bid to eliminate border protection within ten years. However, whereas the USA/CG were insisting that there must be separate and specific commitments to (i) reducing internal support, (ii) improving import access, and (iii) reducing export subsidies, the EC was unwilling to comply with this demand. The EC would go no further than advancing the 'formula approach' to reduced support and protection, spanning all three of these aspects, based upon an agreed Aggregate Measure of Support (AMS). Although the EC had couched its own reform proposals in terms of its own AMS, namely the Support Measurement Unit (SMU), there was little or no serious debate or negotiation at this stage on the form of the AMS, due to US hostility to the formula approach. The USA and the CG also proposed a three tier classification of internal support measures: those which were very trade distorting ('red') and would be phased out; those which were less distorting but would require 'GATT discipline' ('amber'); and those deemed not to distort trade ('green').

4.4.3 Position papers and collapse of negotiations in 1990; impasse in 1991

Little real progress was made with the Uruguay Round agricultural negotiations during the early months of 1990. But, in the middle of the year, Aart de Zeeuw, chairman of the negotiating group on agriculture (NG5), produced a draft Framework Agreement on Agricultural Reform. The de Zeeuw framework agreement essentially endorsed the formula approach advocated by the EC for reducing trade-distorting internal support but steered close to the US/CG position on border protection and export competition. The de Zeeuw initiative was unable to break the deadlock but it was agreed that all parties would table their 'final' negotiating positions by December 1990. The offers made at this stage by the principal contestants, under the previous headings of 'internal support', 'border protection' and 'export competition', are summarised in Table 4.7.

TABLE 4.6   Main elements of post-Geneva Accord long-term reform proposals (1989)

United States	Cairns Group	European Community	Japan
		Internal support	
• Adopt three-tiered approach to disciplining domestic support	• Adopt three-tiered classification of support measures and discipline policies accordingly (like the US Proposal)	• Negotiate a gradual reduction in overall support using the Support Measurement Unit (SMU) as the AMS	• Retain significant domestic support to achieve food security and the desired level of self-sufficiency
• Eliminate most trade-distorting ('red') policies over ten years	• Agree and adopt target reductions of support expressed in commodity-specific AMS terms, taking account of both support price levels and the quantites subsidised	• Rebalance support amongst commodities to permit the EC to increase protection of oilseeds and cereal substitutes	
• Permit least trade-distorting policies – decoupled from current production ('green') – to continue			
• Subject intermediate group policies – production related but not commodity-specific ('amber') – to monitor reduction and GATT discipline			
		Import access	
• Prohibit use of VILs, VERs, MIPs, and all other import barriers not explicitly permitted by the General Agreement	• Tariffy all existing NTBs such as import quotas and reduce the tariff	• Replace VILs and NTBs with a 'partial tariff' consisting of two elements:	• Retain border protection for reasons of food security
• Convert all 'permitted' NTBs (under Art. XI of the GA) to tariff quotas to be phased out over ten years	• Tariffy and reduce broader instruments of protection, such as VILs (cf. US proposal to ban their use)	(1) A 'fixed tariff' based on the difference between the internal or support price and an external reference price expressed in domestic currency at a fixed exchange rate	• Retain and clarify Art. XI: 2(c) of the General Agreement to that end
• After ten years the final bound tariff to be the sole permitted form of import protection		(2) A 'corrective factor to offset world price and exchange fluctuations ouside prescribed limits	

Export competition

- Eliminate export subsides over five years except for food aid

- Phase out export subsidies over/up to ten years

- Rely upon negotiated reduction of the fixed tariff element of border protection using the AMS formula approach, to bring down export assistance as well (but not eliminate it)
- Improve GATT rules on export subsidies by revising Art. XVI: 3 of the General Agreement

- Eliminate export subsidies over an unspecified period
- Buttress food security of importing countries with GATT rules pertaining to the use of export restrictions by governments of exporting countries

TABLE 4.7 Main elements of 'final post-framework agreement reform proposals (late 1990)

United States	Cairns Group (excluding Canada)	European Community	Canada
Export competition			
• Reduce export subsidies expressed in terms of both aggregate budgetary outlays and the total quantity of exports assisted by 90 per cent over ten years from 1991–2, but relative to a 1986–8 base: exempt *bona fide* food aid	• Reduce export subsidies by 90 per cent over ten years from 1991–2, relative to a 1986–8 base, including the reduction of per unit export assistance, as well as aggregate budgetary outlays and and quantities of exports subsidised • Exempt least developed countries (LLDCs) from all reform provisions	• Rely on proposed 30 per cent reduction in internal protection (expressed in terms of an AMS) to reduce export assistance as well via the implied reduction of the fixed component of the partial tariff • Strengthen Art. XVI of the General Agreement through negotiation of export market shares	• Eliminate export subsidies over ten years from 1991–2
Internal support			
• Reduce most trade-distorting ('red') support policies by 75 per cent over ten years from 1991–2, but relative to fixed external reference prices based on 1986–8 • All support reduction commitments to be commodity-specific, but concede use of AMS to monitor implementation	• Reduce 'red' support policies by 75 per cent over ten years from 1991–2 relative to fixed external reference prices based on 1986–8 (subject to review in 1995–6) (virtually identical with US position) • Offer concessions to LDCs – total depth of cuts in support reduced from 75 per cent to only 45 per cent; implementation period extended from ten to fifteen years (not offered by the US)	• Reduce support of main products, expressed in terms of an AMS, by 30 per cent over ten years from 1986 and relative to fixed external reference prices also based on 1986 • Allow AMS credit for support reductions already implemented between 1986 and 1990, leaving only 'residual' reductions to be honoured between 1991 and 1995	• Reduce 'red' support policies by (only) 50 per cent over ten years from 1991–2 relative to a 1986–8 base • Offer concessions to LDCs on terms identical to those offered by the 'majority' Cairns Group

Border protection

- Bind all tariffs and tariff equivalents (converted from VILs and NTBs) at their 1986–8 level and then reduce them by 75 per cent over ten years from 1991–2
- Tariff quotas corresponding to base period imports to be expanded by 75 per cent over ten years and eliminated thereafter
- Permit resort to tariff snap-back mechanism under specified conditions, but only during the ten year transition period
- End legality of import quotas under the GATT by abolishing Art. XI:2(c)

- Bind all tariffs and TEs at their 1986–8 levels before reducing them by 75 per cent over ten years from 1991–2 (identical with US proposal)
- Expand tariff quotas corresponding to base period imports by 75 per cent prior to their elimination (identical with US proposal)
- Permit resort to tariff snap-back mechanism under specified conditions (following US)
- End legality of import quotas by abolishing Art. XI:2(c) (following US)
- Grant concessions to LDCs involving smaller cuts in tariffs and TEs and an extended time frame

- Agree to define the 'fixed component' of the earlier proposed 'partial tariff' as the difference between the internal support price (ie the 'intervention' price) and the fixed external reference price increased by 10 per cent (to reflect Community preference)
  NB The Community did not complement this proposal with any specific offer to reduce the fixed component of the partial tariff beyond stating that a 30 per cent reduction in the AMS (see above under 'internal support') will provide a reduction of border protection
- Agree to application of 'corrective factor' to offset all exchange flucuations (relative to the 1986–8 base level) plus a proportion of world price fluctuations

- Bind all tariffs and TEs other than import quotas at their 1986–8 levels before reducing them by (only) 50 per cent over ten years from 1991–2 or to a maximum of 20 per cent, whichever is higher
- Increase product volume subject to lower tariff rate quota during transition period
- Clarify and strengthen Art. XI:2(c) to confirm legality of import quotas when used to buttress domestic supply control

The main adjustments in the agricultural negotiating positions of the major Uruguay Round contestants, as revealed by the quantitative offers tabled in October–November 1990, were:

- The concessions made by the USA/CG to the EC in substituting 75 per cent cuts in internal support and border protection over ten years from 1990 for their elimination, and in replacing the elimination of export subsidies in five years with their 90 per cent reduction over ten years.
- The specific offer by the EC to reduce internal support and protection by 30 per cent over ten years from 1986 expressed in terms of an AMS (i.e. the SMU).

However, the December 1990 ministerial meeting in Brussels that was to have brought the Round to a successful conclusion turned out to be a fiasco. Although progress had been made in many of the fifteen negotiating areas, nothing could be agreed in the agricultural negotiations.[29] Delegates from the agricultural exporting countries, including the USA, withdrew from all negotiations and the meeting adjourned in failure.

The crux of the disagreement on agriculture was that the USA and CG were unable to accept the EC's refusal to offer specific commitments to improving import access and reducing export assistance. The EC's trade competitors were apparently prepared to negotiate on the depth of cuts in support and protection, as well as the time-scale, but they were not prepared to compromise on the issue of making specific commitments in each of those three areas of contention. They were unwilling to settle for the EC's argument that a specific commitment to reducing internal support, expressed in terms of an AMS, was sufficient to ensure that border protection and export assistance would be cut commensurately. They suspected that, one way or another, the EC would manipulate its AMS calculations so as to avoid having to make commensurate reductions in those two areas, whenever this served the EC's interests. There was also the point that the USA and CG wanted deeper cuts in export assistance, and at a faster rate, than in the remaining two areas. Finally, the USA and CG remained adamantly opposed to permitting the EC to rebalance protection across commodities to enable tariffs to be levied for the first time on Community imports of oilseeds and cereal substitutes.

The negotiations were revived following an 'emergency' initiative by the GATT Secretary-General, Arthur Dunkel. In February 1991, all contracting parties agreed to renew agricultural negotiations on the basis of reaching 'specific binding commitments to reduce farm supports in each of the three areas: internal assistance, border protection and export assistance'. This agreement on the objectives of the agricultural negotiations led to the resumption of negotiations in June 1991 in all fifteen areas covered by the Uruguay Round. In addition, President Bush was able to persuade Congress in May 1991 to extend his 'fast track' negotiating authority, effectively extending the US deadline for concluding the Uruguay Round until June 1993.

The negotiations made little progress throughout most of 1991 with agriculture remaining the pivotal issue. However, at a USA–EC summit on 9 November 1991, President Bush lowered US demands as regards cuts in agricultural subsidies.[30] Despite this initiative, the USA and the EC could not resolve their differences and, on 20 December 1991, Dunkel again revived the talks by putting forward a draft 'final act' agreement (see below) which required further concessions from both the USA and the EC on agriculture and which the EC, in particular, was likely to find hard to accept .

In 1991, as from the start of the Round, a resolution of the deadlock in the agricultural negotiations appeared to be linked to a reform of the CAP such that EC farm policy moved away from trade distorting support. An EC Commission paper on CAP reform – the MacSharry Plan – produced in January 1991 and revised in July 1991, proposed lowering support prices much closer to world market levels whilst supplementing farmers' incomes by 'compensating payments' and by 'compensatory aid' to cereal producers for 'set-aside' of arable land.[31] However, consensus on CAP reform along the lines proposed by MacSharry could not be reached by the EC agricultural ministers during 1991. In addition, in early 1992 a number of member states were arguing that CAP reform must follow rather than precede a GATT deal.[32] Commissioner MacSharry responded by threatening to introduce price cuts without compensation in order to cajole ministers into acceptance of his reform plan. Breaking the historial sequence of events followed so far, it is germane to observe that the legal text of a somewhat modified version of the MacSharry Plan was finally adopted by the Council of Agriculture Ministers on 30 June 1992. There were two main changes from the revised draft version of the plan. First, the cereal support reduction (over three years) was changed from 35 per cent to 29 per cent. Second, all producers, regardless of scale of production, would qualify for compensation, subject to their agreement to set aside a designated proportion of their arable land. But whether the adoption of the MacSharry Plan can 'save' the Uruguay Round remains to be seen at the time of writing (July 1992).

4.4.4 The Dunkel draft agreement (December 1991) and prospects

The Dunkel draft agreement covered all areas of the negotiations and included a proposal to establish a Multilateral Trade Organisation (MTO) which would serve as an umbrella for the agreement and provide a foundation for the extension of a liberal trading system. Dunkel stated that, due to the urgency of concluding the Round after nearly five years of negotiation, time would not permit revision of his plan: it must be accepted in its entirety, or not at all. Easter 1992 was set as the provisional date for the conclusion of the Round. In areas other than agriculture, the provisions of Dunkel's 'final act' were based substantially on provisional agreements already reached in the relevant negotiating groups. But in agriculture, where no consensus had been reached upon how to resolve the outstanding issues of the *amounts* of the agreed reductions in support and protection, Dunkel had to devise his own 'draft agreement' for consideration by the negotiators.

The main body of the Dunkel text on agriculture deals with the three principal areas of contention: namely, improving market access, reducing domestic support and improving export competition. In addition, criteria are specified for identifying the 'green box' domestic support policies permitted to be exempted from support reduction commitments, including decoupled income payments. A common *implementation period* of 1993–9 applies to all the cuts in support and protection but the *base period* from which reforms are to be made over the implementation period differs between (i) domestic support reduction and improved market access (1986–8) and (ii) export subsidy reduction (1986–90). The key provisions are :

1. *Improved market access*: an average reduction of 36 per cent in custom duties, including those resulting from the tariffication of all NTBs (e.g. import quotas, variable levies and minimum import prices), subject to a minimum reduction of 15 per cent in each tariff line. Import duty reductions are supplemented by minimum access opportunities set at 3 per cent of the importer's base consumption in the first year of the implementation period rising to 5 per cent in the final year. In addition, special safeguard provisions intended to cushion the effects of unusually large import surges are specified.

2. *Domestic support reduction*: a uniform 20 per cent reduction, applying individually to all supported commodities with credit allowed already for actions taken since 1986. The AMS is defined as the difference between the internal price and the external reference price (expressed in domestic currency) times the quantity supported, i.e. $(P_s - P_r)Q_s$, with adjustment permitted for any producer levy. This definition does not give any credit for supply control as envisaged by the EC's SMU proposal. Exempt 'green box' policies are those that 'have no, or at most minimal, trade distortion effects'. Examples include publicly financed R & D, early retirement schemes for farmers and land retirement (subject to a minimum retirement period of three years).

3. *Criteria for decoupled payments*: direct payments to producers qualify for exemption from reduction commitments provided they are tied solely to *base period* criteria where payments are related to prices, volume of production and employment of factors of production. In addition, eligibility to receive payments must not be dependent upon the continuation of production after the base period.

4. *Export subsidy reduction*: budgetary outlays on export subsidies to be cut by 36 per cent (by commodity) and, simultaneously, the volume of subsidised exports to be cut by 24 per cent.

The prospects for a successful agreement based on the Dunkel draft probably hinge less on the quantitative reductions proposed in support and protection than on the resolution of a number of related issues. A particularly difficult problem is that the criteria for decoupled income support exclude both the current US deficiency payments and the 'compensatory payments' for the cut in producer price support which are a central feature of the MacSharry Plan for CAP reform. Unless the USA and the EC surrender their right to base direct payments on current rather than base period prices and/or production, the Cairns Group countries are likely to object that such payments are a concealed export subsidy. Moreover, the political feasibility of Dunkel–style decoupled payments, which even producers whose current production is zero would be entitled to receive, must be in some doubt. For both these reasons it is difficult to see Dunkel's criteria for discriminating between 'green' and 'amber' box domestic support policies gaining unanimous acceptance. Some relaxation of Dunkel's proposed rules of acceptability appears inevitable if an agreement is to be reached.

As far as improved import access is concerned, the Dunkel proposals make no provision either for the retention of import quotas or for raising protection, except for temporary safeguard clauses. Canada, and possibly Japan and the EC are likely to strive to retain quotas in some form. Moreover, the EC will not easily abandon its rebalancing proposal to limit imports of cereal substitutes. Finally, the EC has so far only accepted partial tariffication of variable import levies and full tariffication remains a sensitive issue.

On the issue of export competition, the EC is resisting the Dunkel proposal for a restriction on the volume of subsidised exports. It is potentially easier to control the CAP budget (of which export restitutions form a part) than the volume of production. But, by the same token, the USA and the Cairns Group competitors of the EC in export markets are likely to hold out for the retention of the volume restriction.

In short, despite over four years of painstaking and detailed discussions, as of July 1992, important obstacles remain to be surmounted if the agricultural negotiations are to come to fruition and bring farm trade within the GATT framework.

4.4.5 Issues

Some measure of consensus exists amongst the major participants in the Uruguay Round that the budget costs and international trade frictions associated with present farm support programmes must be reduced. But, the specific objectives of the principal contestants have not coincided and as a result the negotiations have been difficult and protracted. The USA and the CG have shared a common purpose in seeking reforms that would ensure that agricultural trade and export shares be shaped more in the future by underlying comparative advantage than has occurred in the past. They have attempted specifically to reduce the trade distorting effects of EC agricultural policy and to improve access to the markets of Japan and other developed countries. For the CG, an agreement that made farm trade subject to the GATT norms governing international commerce would be useful in order to end the damage imposed on their agricultural export sectors by the US–EC subsidy war. The EC and Japan have attempted to retain a substantial measure of national policy autonomy and have resisted pressures for liberalisation that would bring about a significant reallocation of resources in world agriculture. The EC has made commitments to only a modest scale and pace of reform such that it would preserve a degree of Community preference. Japan has been concerned primarily to maintain its restrictive import regimes ostensibly on the grounds of food security, but also because of protectionist pressures from an influential farm lobby.

The technicalities of the negotiations have been organised under the three headings of internal support, import access and export competition. The discussions on internal support have focused on the extent and pace of reductions as monitored by aggregate measures of support (AMS). Some consensus has emerged on a number of the main elements of an appropriate AMS, in particular with respect to the use of a fixed external reference price as a comparator to the domestic producer price.[33] Having a fixed reference price in nominal terms implies that future national rates of inflation will have an important influence on the impact of any agreement. The negotiations have also been concerned with strengthening the GATT rules by attempting to reach agreement on allowable (green) policy instruments for providing income support to farm producers. However, whilst there has been general agreement amongst participants that the AMS should only take into account policies which distort trade, drawing the dividing line between support measures to be reduced (amber) and those to be exempt (green) has been a difficult negotiating issue. The Dunkel proposals take a strict line on the definition of decoupled payments which would be allowed into the green box.

The choice between the alternatives of (i) relying upon AMS reduction commitments (as preferred by the EC) and (ii) strengthening of GATT rules, also applies to border protection and export assistance. On border protection, the measure of consensus already reached between the main contestants upon moving to the tariffication of NTBs is important. The EC's offer to convert its VIL to a partial tariff appears to represent a genuine willingness to bring border protection 'within the GATT', despite its provisos giving farmers a measure of protection against adverse exchange rate fluctuations. Another vital issue concerning border protection concerns the legality of agricultural import quotas. Is Article XI to continue to permit these, at least under specific conditions? Or are agricultural commmodities to be brought fully into line with other traded goods in this respect, by banning selective import quotas without exception?

There appears also to be a strong prima facie case for strengthening GATT rules and codes of behaviour covering export subsidies. Regardless of whether primary products continue to be treated exceptionally under Article XVI, GATT rules need to be more precise in defining an export subsidy. At present, Article XVI:1 merely requires GATT contracting parties to report 'any subsidy, including any form of income or price support, which operates directly or indirectly to increase exports . . . from, or reduce imports into, its territory'. This definition is far too vague and imprecise to permit effective surveillance and monitoring. Easier definitions to apply and observe could be either (i) any subsidy permitting exports to be sold below the domestic market price, or (ii) any subsidy permitting exports to be sold below the domestic supply price. If export subsidies continue to be permitted up to some limit, at least for an interim period, then agreement will be needed on limits, monitoring and enforcement. A broad choice exists between per unit and aggregate limitation and, if the latter, between restricting export volume alone, export value alone, or both. The USA is anxious to improve restrictions on subsidised EC exports but there is a danger that this could lead to market sharing to the detriment of other exporters.

The AMS reduction and GATT rules revision approaches to agricultural trade reform are not cut and dried alternatives. For example, if AMS reduction is followed, agreement must be reached on which (amber) policy instruments are covered by the AMS and which (green) ones are exempt. One argument in favour of the AMS reduction option might be lower costs of administration, monitoring and enforcement. In contrast, a thoroughgoing revision and/or extension of GATT rules and codes of behaviour, together with their enforcement, would throw a substantial burden of extra work on the GATT Secretariat. Indeed, some commentators have argued that a major revision and extension of the General Agreement to new areas would scarcely be feasible without the upgrading of the Secretariat to a fully fledged International Trade Organisation (ITO), as originally visualised by the architects of the Havana Charter which the USA failed to ratify in 1948. In fact, such an organisation, to be called a Multilateral Trade Organisation (MTO), is likely to be established if the Uruguay Round is successful.

4.5   OUTLOOK FOR REFORM AND LIBERALISATION[34]

A gradual reform of agricultural policies in the developed countries is already in train and will continue regardless of the outcome of the multilateral trade negotiations if only because of domestic budgetary pressures. The MacSharry Plan for EC agriculture is only one example of this trend. The reform process may be impeded but is unlikely to be halted by political pressures exerted by well-organised farm blocs. These unilateral reforms have a general tendency to reduce distortions imposed on international food markets and are complementary to the pressures to bring agriculture within the rules of the GATT.

In the Uruguay Round, agriculure has been brought to the forefront of multilateral trade negotiations for the first time and it is unlikely to revert to its exceptional position of being outside the disciplines of the GATT. Negotiations in the Uruguay Round have seen movement towards a compromise which falls short of complete liberalisation of agricultural trade. However, for an agreement to be concluded, an intermediate position between the EC and US negotiating stances will have to be found which is preferable to failure for each participant.

In conclusion, the Uruguay Round negotiations represent a historic opportunity to bring agricultural policy under international disciplines. A compromise agreement would be a major step forward in the ongoing process of domestic and international agricultural reform since the commitments entailed would lock governments into the reform path. Even a modest accord in the Uruguay Round is important for at least three reasons: first, it will discourage a resurgence of agricultural subsidisation and market insulation; second, it will reduce the disarray in world agriculture; and third, it will be an acknowledgement by the major developed countries that they have a responsibility to preserve and extend the open, rules-based multilateral trading system. The issue is not whether there will be agricultural reform but whether reform will be implemented unilaterally or orchestrated multilaterally.

5 Transformation of Agriculture in Central-Eastern Europe and the Soviet Union: Major Policy Issues and Perspectives[1]

CSABA CSÁKI

5.1 INTRODUCTION

Eastern Europe and the Soviet Union are at present undergoing fundamental economic and political transformation. Far-reaching changes going far beyond the reforms of earlier years characterise the agrarian economy of Eastern and Central Europe where the creation of a new agricultural structure based on private ownership, true cooperatives and the market economy has now begun. The Soviet Union also wishes to overcome its serious economic difficulties with comprehensive economic and political reforms, though here the changes have not yet affected the most important basic elements of the so-called socialist economic and political system. This process is still far from finished in any of the countries concerned. Most of the details have yet to be clarified, especially in the Soviet Union and there is a very high degree of uncertainty as regards future developments. However, there can be no doubt that all these changes will fundamentally reshape agriculture as a whole in the respective countries and will influence the behaviour and role of the region in the system of international agrarian relations. This study was written to survey the problems of Bulgaria, Hungary, the former GDR, Poland, Romania, Czechoslovakia, and the Soviet Union. Due to the preliminary stage of

96

transformation in the Soviet Union, the discussion of major issues of transformation is based mainly on the experience of the smaller Central-Eastern European countries.

5.2 THE AGRICULTURAL SITUATION IN CENTRAL-EASTERN EUROPE AND THE SOVIET UNION

5.2.1 The state of agricultural production

Eastern Europe and the Soviet Union account for around 20 per cent of the world's agricultural resources (see Table 5.1), and 8 per cent of the world's population. The region has around 12–16 per cent of world livestock. The highest density is of pigs and poultry, while cattle-raising is of lower intensity. More than 17 per cent of the world stock of pigs and 12 per cent of the stock of cattle are to be found here.

In these countries, agriculture is still a dominant branch of the national economy and the agrarian sector is more important than in the majority of developed countries. The share of agriculture in net national product is between 8 and 20 per cent with the lowest proportion in the GDR and Czechoslovakia and the highest proportion in Hungary and Romania. The proportion of the population engaged in agriculture is similar (9 per cent in the GDR, 10.6 per cent in Czechoslovakia, 13.9 per cent in Hungary, 14 per cent in Bulgaria, 14.2 per cent in the Soviet Union, and 22 per cent in each of Poland and Romania). The agriculturally active population is showing a tendency to decrease but at a rate which slowed down in the second half of the 1980s.

The natural conditions for agriculture are favourable in the region on the whole. All the smaller countries can be found in a temperate continental climatic zone. In the northern countries the climate is more humid, cooler, and the soil quality is poorer. But the conditions of agriculture are above average in Romania, Hungary and Bulgaria. The Soviet Union has a vast diversity of agro-ecological conditions and, on the whole, this country also has tremendous potential for agricultural production especially in comparison to the level of population. The proportion of agricultural area within the total territory is different in each country For example, this proportion is 70.5 per cent in Hungary, 53.3 per cent in Czechoslovakia and 13.3 per cent in the Soviet Union.

The agriculture of the respective countries developed quickly in the first years of the 1970s but then the process slowed down (see Table 5.2). At the beginning of this period, the annual growth of production

TABLE 5.1 Population and arable land resources of Eastern Europe and the USSR – 1988

	Population, total		Economically active population			Arable land	
	Million	*As % of the world*	*Total million*	*Agric. million*	*Agric. in total %*	*1000 Ha*	*As % of the world*
Bulgaria	8.99	0.18	4.5	0.6	13.3	3825	0.3
Czechoslovakia	15.62	0.31	8.2	0.8	9.8	5000	0.4
Germany DR	16.67	0.33	9.5	0.8	8.4	4694	0.3
Hungary	10.60	0.21	5.2	0.7	13.5	5048	0.4
Poland	37.86	0.74	19.3	4.3	22.3	14480	1.1
Romania	23.05	0.45	11.6	2.6	22.4	10080	0.7
EEUR/6	112.79	2.21	58.3	9.8	16.8	43127	3.1
USSR	283.68	5.55	143.6	20.4	14.2	228200	16.6
EEUR + USSR	396.47	7.76	201.9	30.2	15.0	271327	19.7
World	5112.00	100.00	2285.0	1083.0	47.4	1373200	100.00

Sources: FAO Production Yearbook 1988 (Rome: FAO, 1989); Hungarian Statistical Pocket Book, 1989 (Budapest: KSH, 1990).

TABLE 5.2 Growth of gross agricultural output since 1970 (annualised percentage change in volume)[1]

	1971–75	*1976–80*	*1981–85*	*1986–88*	*1989*	*1990*
Bulgaria	2.2	2.1	1.2	−0.3	0.3	−1.4
Czechoslovakia	3.8	2.7	3.4	3.8	0.0	1.3
German DR	2.2	1.4	1.6	2.2	−2.7	2.5
Hungary	3.9	3.9	2.4	0.2	−0.2	−0.9
Poland	3.2	0.6	−0.5	2.8	1.3	−9.0
Romania	4.7	4.7	2.0	9.9[2]	−4.9	2.4
USSR	2.5	1.7	1.1	2.9	1.3	−2.3

[1] Annualised changes between periods shown and previous five-year period.
[2] 1986–87.
Source: UN ECE common data base.

was about 3 per cent. By the middle of the 1980s, it had dropped to 1.5–2.5 per cent . However, as Table 5.2 indicates, agricultural performance has differed widely between the seven countries over the last two decades. Average annual output in monetary terms in constant prices rose most in Czechoslovakia, the GDR, Romania, and the USSR. In the remaining countries, the annual growth rate was somewhat lower. Net output growth was, however, much smaller and intercountry difference less marked. Nevertheless, agricultural growth of more than 2 per cent a year, which is characteristic of the whole region in the long run, is quite high, even in international terms.

As indicated by Table 5.2, there were quite striking changes in the annual rate of growth of agricultural production within each country, generally in line with movements in overall economic growth.

In all the countries under review, a major agro-political objective was to increase the degree of self-sufficiency and especially to increase grain production. The proportion of grain-crops inside the sown area settled at about 54–58 per cent. The development of grain production can be seen in Table 5.3. However, despite rising yields and concomitant increases in production, imports were still needed to meet increasing demand. Whilst the efforts made to increase grain production cannot be considered unsuccessful, the grain trade balance of the seven countries is still negative and only Hungary exports a considerable amount of grain, about 2 millions tons a year.

Crop yields are generally low and highly variable and only approach Western European levels in Hungary, the GDR and Czechoslovakia.

TABLE 5.3 Production of grains (millions tonnes)

	Bulgaria	Czechoslovakia	GDR	Hungary	Poland	Romania	Eastern Europe	USSR	Total
1976–80 (ave.)	7.8	10.0	9.0	12.6	14.5	14.4	78.3	205.0	283.3
1981–85 (ave.)	8.2	10.4	10.4	14.4	22.2	21.7	87.8	180.3	268.1
1986	8.5	10.8	11.7	14.3	25.1	24.1	94.5	210.1	304.6
1987	7.2	11.8	11.3	14.2	26.1	17.5	88.1	211.4	299.5
1988	7.8	11.9	9.8	15.0	22.7	14.5	86.7	145.0	281.7
1989	8.0	11.7	10.8	14.7	26.8	14.3	91.3	211.0	302.3

Source: Statistical Yearbook of the respective countries.

However, the region is relatively more backward in animal husbandry than in plant production. The standard of animal husbandry is lower than in Western Europe. This backwardness is reflected in the breeds kept, in the animal hygiene situation and especially in the unfavourable fodder utilisation rate. The large-scale agricultural units (cooperative and state farms) predominate in animal husbandry in the region. But, in general, the share of household plots and small farms (private production), is greater in animal husbandry than in crop production. This applies above all to Poland and Hungary where the private producers keep more than half of the stock of livestock.

The trend in meat production is closely related to the situation of animal husbandry. Table 5.4 shows the trend in meat production in the region. In 1989, the countries under review accounted for 18 per cent of world meat production. As with the trend in the stock of livestock, the growth rate of meat production in the past two decades has lagged behind that in the rest of the world, especially in the case of the countries of Central and Eastern Europe whose share of world output in the past two decades has declined by around 20 per cent. The growth of meat production in the Soviet Union has also been slightly below the world average.

Data in Table 5.5 provide information on the technical conditions of agricultural production. The total capacity of tractors has grown considerably in all the countries though the number has decreased in the GDR and in Hungary as a consequence of structural changes. In addition, there has been a shift to tractors of larger engine size.

TABLE 5.4   Meat total production (1000 MT)

	1975	1980	1985	1989	1989 as % of 1970	1989 as % of the world
Bulgaria	553	651	723	814	147.2	0.48
Czechoslovakia	1,304	1,426	1,486	1,635	125.4	0.97
GDR	1,721	1,783	1,914	1,987	115.5	1.18
Hungary	1,297	1,441	1,595	1,588	122.4	0.94
Poland	2,786	2,858	2,513	2,801	100.5	1.66
Romania	1,337	1,774	1,835	1,628	121.8	0.96
EEUR/6	8,998	9,933	10,066	10,453	116.2	6.19
USSR	15,060	14,981	17,131	19,970	132.6	11.83
World	119,853	141,081	151,209	168,860	140.9	100.0

Source: FAO Production Yearbooks, 1975–1989 (Rome: FAO).

TABLE 5.5 Tractors used in agricultural production (1000)

	1985	1986	1987	1988	1989	1990
Bulgaria	55	54	54	54	n.a.	n.a.
Czechoslovakia	137	139	140	141	n.a.	n.a.
East Germany	158	162	165	168	n.a.	n.a.
Hungary	55	54	54	53	52	50
Poland	924	989	1,044	1,101	1,153	n.a.
Romania	184	194	184	183	n.a.	n.a.
USSR	2,789	2,854	2,735	2,692	2,689	2,630
World	24,504	25,284	25,535	25,865	n.a.	n.a.

n.a.   not available.
Source: *Agriculture and Food Processing 1990* (Budapest: Ministry of Agriculture, 1991).

Fertiliser consumption grew until the second half of the 1980s. In 1988, average fertiliser use per hectare of agricultural area in active ingredients was 268 kg in Hungary and 310 kg in Czechoslovakia but only 127 kg in Romania and 117 kg in the USSR. The world average in that year was 99 kg/ha.

5.2.2 Food consumption

In the first half of the 1980s, the standard of living in most of the countries was still improving. But in the second half of the decade this increase came to a halt; furthermore, living standards have declined in almost every country in recent years .

In most of the countries, calorie consumption per capita reaches or surpasses the Western European standard, being around 3300–3500 calories a day. However, there are large differences in food consumption patterns between Eastern and Western Europe (see Table 5.6). Generally speaking, cereal consumption is higher and fruit consumption is lower in Eastern Europe. Soviet, Romanian and Polish meat consumption per capita is well below that of the EC countries although meat consumption in the GDR, Czechoslovakia and Hungary is not dissimilar. Finally, the range of vegetables available to Eastern European consumers is limited and cabbages and tomatoes are the main items purchased.

In earlier years, rationing played a considerable role in the trend in food consumption in the region. However, in Poland, Czechoslovakia

TABLE 5.6   Consumption of major food products, 1989 (kg/capita)

	Meat	Milk and dairy products	Sugar converted to white sugar	Cereals converted to flour	Vegetables	Eggs
Bulgaria	79.3	275	35.0	146	136	136
Hungary	78.2	134	34.0	408	88	315
GDR	100.2	n.a.	41.4	90	106	106
Poland	76.1	415	46.2	119	115	115
Romania	52.0	132.6[1]	20.3[1]	175[2]	113[1]	n.a.
Czechoslovakia	88.0	253	40.4	113	81	345
USSR	67	636	42.5	129	9.5	268

[1] Data of 1985.
[2] Data of 1980.
Source: CMEA Yearbook (Moscow, 1990).

and Hungary the market is now determined by the relations of supply and demand and there are no longer shortages. In the Soviet Union, Bulgaria and Romania there is still disequilibrium with excess demand at current consumer prices and the satisfaction of consumer demands depends fundamentally on the quantities available; queuing and the quantitative shortage of food remains a permanent phenomenon.

In 1990, the food market was fundamentally transformed in Poland, Hungary and Czechoslovakia. Governments ended consumer and producer subsidies for food as well as most agricultural export subsidies. Parallel with this, the real income of consumers declined and there were general economic difficulties. There were substantial rises in the price of food, especially meat (30–40 per cent), and domestic consumption fell considerably (in Hungary and Poland by around 20–25 per cent in the past year). The dismantling of export subsidies meant that sales abroad ceased to be profitable. As a result, unsold stocks accumulated, there was a reduction in the numbers of livestock and production fell. Poland and Hungary have witnessed a fall in the consumer price of meat for the first time in many years. It would appear that the obsolete and monopolistic food processing industry is responding slowly to these changes.

The situation in the food markets is evolving differently in Romania, Bulgaria and the Soviet Union. In Romania, production increased in 1990 as a result of the lifting of the restrictions of the Ceaucescu regime. There was also a substantial increase in meat production in the Soviet Union. Despite this, there were even more serious difficulties in supply in the big cities than in earlier years, although there was undoubtedly a decline in imports. The unfavourable situation can be explained principally by the disruption of the traditional internal delivery and supply relations and not by the trend in production. As a result of the relaxation of the earlier strict production and supply quotas and the strengthening of the aspirations of the different regions for autonomy, there was a substantial decline in the quantity of food delivered to the big cities at official prices. The attempts to set price ceilings, affecting the free markets, also had an unfavourable influence on supply to the big cities. However, at the same time, the level of supply in the rural producing areas improved tangibly.

5.2.3 Eastern Europe and the USSR in international agricultural trade

During the 1970s and 1980s import demand for agricultural products increased in most of the Eastern European countries and the USSR. Those developments represented not only unsatisfactory production performance, but also structural changes in domestic output in all the seven countries. The Soviet Union increased imports of meat and other livestock products – largely to ease social tensions. In the USSR, imports accounted for about 8 per cent of total meat consumption, while grain imports have risen from close to zero in the early 1970s to over 30 million tonnes per annum in recent years. On the export side, Eastern European countries to the West suffered substantial losses of market share – partly because of the effects of protectionism but also because of underdeveloped processing, lack of quality control and a shortage of packing and marketing capacities in the Central-Eastern European countries themselves.

In 1986–9, Eastern Europe and the USSR together were net importers of agricultural products amounting to about US$15 billion net imports annually. The deficit of the Soviet Union is about US$14 billion while the contribution of the six smaller countries is around US$1 billion. Three of the other six countries can be classified as importers – GDR, Czechoslovakia and Poland, and three as exporters – Hungary, Romania and Bulgaria. The export-surplus of Hungary is especially prominent; in 1989, more than one-third of the total European CMEA agro-export came from Hungary.

The region as a whole is a net importer of cereals (averaging around 36 million tonnes during 1986–9), oilseeds (nearly 2 million tonnes), oilseed meals (6 million tonnes), and sugar (5 million tonnes). Soviet imports alone accounted for about 15 per cent of world trade in cereals in 1986–9. Eastern Europe was a net exporter of meat (743 thousand tonnes) while the USSR was a net importer (636 thousand tonnes) during the same year. The region as a whole imports substantial amounts of coffee, cocoa and tropical fruits.

The share of agricultural products in total trade varies between the countries. In Hungary, farm products account for about 25 per cent of exports; corresponding figures for Bulgaria and Czechoslovakia are 18 per cent and 6–7 per cent respectively. On the import side, the USSR comes first and Romania is in the last place. Romania's import rate of this product group is less than 10 per cent. The foreign exchange outlay on agricultural trade and the export receipts are very important for the balance of payment of all the countries. This statement is particularly valid for the countries with relatively large amounts of debt, where the hard currency balance of agricultural trade in both positive and negative directions can be of significant importance when the financial problems of a particular year are to be solved.

Agricultural trade links are mostly with the OECD countries. The USA, Canada, and Australia are the major grain and oilseed suppliers. Western Europe is the most significant export market for the quality food products of the Eastern European countries though the share of the six smaller countries in total Western European import is extremely low, 2.5–2.7 per cent. In past years, there was a negative agricultural trade balance with Western Europe. Food exports directed to the non-European OECD countries are not significant; although Romania's, Hungary's, and Poland's sales in the North American markets (primarily meat products and highly processed foodstuffs) are worth mentioning.

Particular attention must be paid to the agrarian trade within the former European CMEA region. Traditionally, the smaller European countries, above all Hungary and Bulgaria, and to a lesser extent Romania and Poland, exported food products to the Soviet Union according to long-run agreements. The main sugar supplier of the Soviet Union is Cuba. The Soviet partner paid in energy and raw materials for the foodstuffs. In the 1980s, about half of the Hungarian agrarian exports and more than two-thirds of the Bulgarian food products found their market in the Soviet Union. This network of relations has now been disrupted radically. In the Soviet Union, the energy transportation facilities are becoming more limited and the Soviet balance of payments is unfavourable. By the end of the 1980s, Soviet imports from Eastern Europe had declined significantly. However, the Soviet Union seems to be able to get food on credit mainly from the well-developed countries, and recently food imports from the OECD countries have grown rapidly.

Food trade with the developing countries does not rank with trade with the OECD countries. Exports to the LDCs are rather modest in both value and volume, however, imports from developing countries have increased rapidly in the 1980s. The imports consist of tropical agricultural products, above all coffee, cacao and raw materials of agricultural origin.

5.3   EARLY ATTEMPTS AT AGRARIAN REFORM

In the 1950s and 1960s, the so called socialist reorganisation of agriculture was carried out in all the six smaller countries. Practically speaking, it was equivalent to the collectivisation, according to the Soviet model, of an agriculture consisting mainly of smallholders. The state farms and agricultural cooperatives came to be dominant in all the countries, except Poland, by the middle of the 1960s. The organisation of large-scale socialist farms, as they are called, was accompanied by the introduction of central planning which established targets for agricultural production. A considerable recession accompanied the reorganisation in all the countries except Hungary. After a relatively short period of time, it was obvious that the central administrative direction retarded the growth of agricultural production. Some other signs of the unsatisfactory functioning of the system also appeared. For this reason, the first attempt to reform of the socialist agricultural systems was introduced in the second half of the 1960s.

Two alternative reform paths were promulgated. One group of reformists pressed for improvements in central planning techniques whilst the other group sought decentralisation and the introduction of economic incentives. However, the introduction of market mechanisms was viewed as a risky experiment, being outside the experience and ideology of the policy makers. Consequently, although limited decentralisation reforms were introduced, traditional methods of central planning prevailed except in Hungary. In Hungary, the so-called 'indirect–direct system' was introduced; this provided the basis for a rapid development of agriculture.

Apart from the Hungarian experiment, the limited attempts to bring in new agricultural management systems did not appear to have had any positive effects on farm production by the early 1970s. Moreover, the decentralisation process was retarded by political forces opposed to existing private plot production. But in the second half of the 1970s a new situation arose in the region. Changes in the world's economy, the oil crisis, and the neglected reaction to all this increased the tension over economic problems. It was becoming more obvious that agriculture organised and directed by earlier methods was not able to keep up with the demands of consumers. That is the reason why the desire for change came into prominence again at the end of the 1970s when the second wave of reforms began.

Reformers sought to modernise the economy and make it more flexible in response to changing economic conditions via the introduction of the 'direction system', discussed but barely implemented in the first reform period. Although the command character of economic management was weakened, the reforms were stilted by numerous restrictions on the marketing of produce, the dominance of state purchasing, the lack of correspondence between government set prices and underlying supply–demand relations and the continued use of plan instructions. Moreover, political change was not on the agenda; as a result, fundamental economic reform of the traditional socialist system could not be introduced at the highest political levels.

The third period of agricultural reforms in Eastern Europe started in 1985–6 and lasted until the end of 1989. The general economic crisis of the region and its poor growth record under communist rule can be considered as the antecedents of this wave of reforms. In addition, in some of the countries a serious debt crisis was also relevant.

The failure of previous reforms and the sharpening political tensions hastened the demand for radical changes combining economic with political reforms. In this period, the central objectives of agricultural reforms were as follows:

- to improve efficiency and quality against the simple quantitative increase of production;
- to move towards a price policy which reflected the real costs of production;

- to increase the role of financial incentives;
- to enhance the freedom of decision-making of firms;
- to widen the possibilities of private agricultural production.

The third wave of reforms was not introduced equally into the countries of the region, since the political changes of the second half of the 1980s did not occur at the same pace in the various countries. In the GDR and Romania, the decision-making freedom of companies was restricted and decentralisation hardly figured on the political agenda. Agricultural reform intentions were expressed more clearly in the Soviet Union but very little change occurred. In Bulgaria and Poland, and in Czechoslovakia to a lesser degree, the independence of companies, economic incentives, the use of the price mechanism, the role of financial instruments and the support of private production were all considerably increased and reinforced. In Hungary, where these arrangements had already been put into practice earlier, the decentralisation of the food industry and foreign trade was carried out in part and the idea of transforming the weakest cooperatives into a loose cooperation of private producers also arose. But, in the smaller countries, these changes coincided with the final days of the planned economy and did not produce perceptible results. The attempts at agricultural reform were interwoven with the planned changes of great significance forced by the difficult economic circumstances and political tensions, and the economic machinery of the party-state had no time to carry them out.

In the second half of 1989, the political wave sweeping Eastern Europe created a new era in the development of the agrarian sector. Practically speaking, the sequence of attempts to refine the socialist agricultural systems was over. Efforts which aimed at the formation of a completely new agrarian structure were high priority for ambitious reformers. However, radical change can so far be observed only in the GDR, Hungary, Poland and Czechoslovakia where, together with the introduction of a real multiparty system, the power of the communist party also came to an end.

Progress in a similar direction is going on in Romania and Bulgaria. Although the positions of the new post-communist parties are more stable, the political perspectives for the future are still uncertain, and for the same reasons it is very difficult to predict the expected developments in agriculture. The character of change in the Soviet Union is similar to that of the Eastern European countries. The events of August 1991 have created the political conditions for a real change in agriculture; however, there is a long way to go in the USSR before a detailed agenda for the transformation of agriculture emerges.

5.4 MAJOR ISSUES IN THE TRANSITION[2]

The legacy of the decades of socialism is largely similar in all the countries. The agricultural sector of Eastern Europe and the Soviet Union on the eve of the transition is characterised by (Brooks 1991):

- large, inefficient farms with high costs of production;
- high levels of food consumption relative to market economies of comparable prosperity;
- subsidised food prices;
- excess demand for food at those prices;
- pervasive monopoly in food processing and distribution.
- macroeconomic imbalance, including budget deficits, inflation and foreign debt.

The main direction of the transformation of agriculture reflects these initial conditions and, just like the general economic political changes, can be stated relatively simply. In every country, the objective is to develop an agricultural structure based on individual incentives and private ownership. The principal characteristics of the new system and the critical points of the future can only be outlined. But it is clear that the most important tasks in developing a market-oriented and competitive agricultural structure are the following:

(a) legislate for a market in landed property;
(b) alter the farming structure so that the present large-scale farms are replaced by small- and middle-sized agricultural private ventures and a system of cooperatives of various types together with state or communal farms;
(c) change government attitudes so that they are supportive of the emerging private ventures, and to bring about the transformation of the cooperative sector;
(d) promote a real agricultural market which guarantees the conditions of fair competition by its rules, physical conditions and institutions;
(e) introduce an agricultural policy which serves the efficiency of agricultural production by means applied in the market-oriented,

well-developed countries and maintains income parity for agricultural producers;
(f) alter the role of government, including the redrafting of the macroeconomic relations of agricultural economy;
(g) pay attention to the environmental impact of agriculture in policy-making.

These actions are elements of a package that preferably should be implemented in a coordinated way relatively quickly. Experiences of the transformation of agriculture under way in other former socialist countries indicate that consistent reform packages, if implemented quickly, lead to faster and more visible positive results than partial, stop-and-go actions. Furthermore, political transformation, the introduction of a democratic multiparty political structure, is an essential precondition of a successful move toward a market economy in any former socialist country.

5.4.1 Reprivatisation of landed property

The legal status and redistribution of land property rights affects farmers' incentives to manage land and invest in its productivity. Consequently, one of the biggest dilemmas of the present period of time in Eastern Europe and the Soviet Union concerns the appropriate restructuring of land property rights. It is obvious that the creation of marketable landed property and the rehabilitation of land as a valuable resource in agricultural production is unavoidable.The correspondence of the farming structure with the market economy conditions is also necessary. Several possibilities can be considered.

However, it is first worth surveying the landed property relations in Eastern Europe. With the exception of the Soviet Union, land was not completely nationalised after the war; cooperative landed property and various forms of private landed property existed too. Over the course of time, the proprietary rights were merely formal as land could not be traded, and with the abolition of the land market, land lost its character as a valuable resource.[3] Of course, it is not accidental that one of the most debated political and economic questions concerns landed property together with political change. Today, all over Eastern Europe, there is a multitude of opinions concerning reprivatisation of which the following are among the most important:

- to keep the present forms of property and to make use of the land through leasing;
- to give the land as property to all those people who want to be employed in agricultural production;
- on the basis of proprietary rights before collectivisation, to give land to all those who want to work in agriculture, together with financial compensation of the earlier proprietors who did not take an active part in agricultural production;
- to treat the land ownership issue as an integrated element of an overall compensation and privatisation package;
- to set up the landed property relations existing before collectivisation without any restrictions.

The land ownership issue was the focal point of heated political debates throughout Eastern Europe in 1991. Parliaments passed legislation related to land in Romania and Bulgaria in February, in April in Hungary and in May in Czechoslovakia. Each of these laws recognises private land ownership and the rights of land owners just prior to collectivisation and sets up a procedure for reinstating property rights, but the actual treatment of problems is different.

In *Romania* and *Bulgaria*, households can claim a limited amount of land based on a variety of evidence to support their claims. In Romania, the restitution of former land ownership was started relatively quickly and has taken place without any intention of creating farms of optimal size, or envisaging how farming will take place after the land is distributed. The Bulgarian approach attempts the construction of appropriate holdings through administrative assignment. Alhough this method by its nature is slow, political tension has delayed almost any implementation so far.

In *Hungary*, the initial attempt to return agricultural land to former owners in 1990 was blocked by the Constitutional Court, with the ruling that land ownership must be treated similarly to that of other assets. In 1991, land owners and dispossessed owners of other property were granted vouchers redeemable for agricultural land and other assets providing essentially monetary compensation for prior land and other asset owners. Landowners who continued to hold title to land managed by cooperatives are granted the return of their managment rights unconditionally. In *Czechoslovakia*, the law mandates return of agricultural land to previous owners who will cultivate it. Very little interest in claiming land has been reported so far.

In *Poland*, where most of the land has always been in private ownership and use, the future of state farmland – about 20 per cent – has not been discussed yet. Land ownership represents a more complicated issue in the *Soviet Union*, where land was nationalised in 1917 and collectivised later on. Solutions similar to the above mentioned land laws of Bulgaria, Czechoslovakia, Romania or Hungary are feasible only in the Baltic area where previous owners can be identified. In the rest of the USSR, it is difficult to imagine any kind of restitution of former land ownership. The settlement of land ownership and tenure issue represents probably the most crucial condition for a real transformation in agriculture.

5.4.2   Change in the farming structure

The agrarian structure was formed by the collectivisation process of the post-war period. The objectives of collectivisation were similar in the various countries, but there were large differences in the methods of execution and in the structural development. In the GDR, Czechoslovakia, Bulgaria and Romania, the socialist reorganisation of agriculture was carried out in line with the Soviet model. In these countries, the typical form of agricultural enterprise was the state or cooperative large-scale farm of several thousand hectares. In Bulgaria, agro-industrial complexes came into being as a special formation, fusing the state and cooperative farms. In the middle of the 1980s in Bulgaria, 150 gigantic complexes were working and spanning the majority of the agricultural territories. One of the particular characteristics of East Germany was the separation of plant cultivation and animal husbandry farms. Collectivisation was unique in Hungary where the independence of the cooperatives has always been relatively large. Poland preserved the predominance of private farms but the government impeded the natural progress of this agricultural structure based on private ownership for a long time.

The classical private farms survived the reorganisation of agriculture in only a small number of countries. The private sector was marginalised and, above all, household farming and part-time agricultural production was largely eliminated. Political judgement of this activity was also frequently changing. Hungary was the only place where the farm household and complementary agriculture was continuously tolerated and often supported by the system. The production structure of private agriculture was also rather specialised. The private growers dealt primarily with animal husbandry and garden plots/horticultural production whilst grain production and the cultivation of the tillage areas were almost exclusively concentrated on the big farms. The share of private production was at its lowest, about 10 per cent, in the GDR while apart from Poland this share was the highest in Hungary where one-third of production came from the private sector in recent years. In Czechoslovakia, the contribution of private production to total agricultural production was 10–12 per cent, and in Bulgaria it was about 25 per cent.

The question arises, what will be the future of cooperatives and state farms in the transformation of the East European agricultural economy? It is obvious that these farms in their present form are not suitable for the requirements of the market economy. They are too gigantic and are not geared to profit-making in their organisation so that transformation, including privatisation, is unavoidable.

At the time of writing, the future of cooperative farms is the most debated issue. In the early stages of the transition, the complete disappearance of these farms was expected. It is now quite clear that a remarkably high proportion of cooperative members do not want to pursue completely independent farming, at least in the short term. They desire well-defined and freely transferable ownership rights and also wish to pursue their rights of decision-making and individual ambitions, combined with the protective network of cooperation. Therefore, it is probable that only a small proportion of cooperatives will be fully dismantled. New forms of cooperatives focused more on service processing and marketing will emerge on the basis of the present structure. This looser form of cooperation will probably open the way for the move toward individual farming in a later stage.

Private production is gaining strength and will grow everywhere, and the number of private farms will also increase. However, the conditions for fully independent private farming beyond the level of production for self-consumption and local markets do not exist in most regions; this is the main reason why a sizeable proportion of cooperative members are reluctant to pursue completely independent farming, which they see constrained by numerous factors. Most of them have not accumulated sufficient savings to start independent farming operations in all respects, nor do they have the collateral that would be required to obtain credit on reasonable terms. In rural areas in all the countries, only savings banks that perform no other function are operating. The agricultural banks, in larger settlements, only settle payments for planned activities of large-scale cooperative and state farms. There are no branch banks or staff able to process credit applications or handle private farmers' credit needs. Also, there is an almost total lack of input and output commerce outside the rigid state monopoly system. There is no network of rural shops selling inputs and instruments for farming and no system for farm-level purchase or wholesaling of agricultural products. Auction centres, farmers' markets and means of transportation are also lacking. Technical service, machinery and tools for private farming are not widely available, and, above all, cooperative members and state farm employees have only a limited knowledge of running business operations, financing, accounting, taxation and risk-taking.

Due to these difficulties, cooperation will be essential for private farmers in finance, marketing, and using machinery and other (e.g. irrigation) services. New private service cooperatives might be based on the core of the existing farms. However, farmers should be free to choose what forms of cooperation they prefer and the new cooperation has to be based on private ownership and competition. There is no experience and only limited information available concerning private cooperatives. Therefore, the foundation of the new cooperatives should be supported by governments. International assistance might also be appropriate in this area (based on Danish and Dutch experiences) in the form of training and direct technical assistance. Promotional programmes (advice, technical assistance, etc.) should also be organised to help those farmers who choose fully independent private farming.

As far as the state farms are concerned, the privatisation processes which have been started in other parts of the economy should be taken into account. A small number of state farms which are of a joint-stock character will be set up with an important role in the supply of seed-grain and breeding stock, and in the provision of extension services. Some of them can be expected to function as diversified agribusiness companies. They may also play a major part in introducing foreign capital into agricultural production. However, it is probable that most of the state farm lands will be transferred into private ownership.

5.4.3   A real market for agricultural products

Direct government control of agricultural commodity and input marketing has distorted resource use and created serious food shortages and social tensions. All the Eastern bloc countries have already taken the first steps to dismantle the command economy and introduce a market system in agriculture. As the experiences of Poland,

Hungary, and Czechoslovakia indicate, the next and crucial step is a reform of agricultural price policy. The main element of the reform still needed, especially in the USSR, is free market agricultural producer pricing, with intervention price policies used only for basic grains and animal products (not delivery targets) to eliminate excessive random and cyclical price fluctuations. Free market consumer pricing of agricultural commodities should also be expanded beyond horticulture and livestock products emanating from private plots and animals. In the least developed part of the region, a limited amount of low-priced basic food items may need to be provided at the existing government ration shops during a short transition period, with food aid and imports used to secure availability of the rationed products. But food subsidies should be completely eliminated within a few years. Freeing of market prices for agricultural inputs and services should parallel a reorganisation of the input supply and service sector.

The state monopoly of foreign trade is another serious obstacle. Foreign trade has to become a right and potential activity of each business entity in agriculture. Together with the disappearance of the state monopoly of foreign trade, a new foreign marketing structure including competitive trading houses and direct sales by producers should take shape relatively soon. Centralised decision-making with licensing should be replaced by a coordinated system of tariffs, customs and taxes. Steps toward the liberalisation of foreign currency regulations are also crucial for the development of viable agricultural trade.

The new agro-economic structure presumes that free markets for the food economy can be developed and activated. The total market system must supply the input, domestic food and international agricultural and livestock product markets. The tasks required for the creation of such a system have organisational, institutional, legal, and regulation aspects. A fundamental requirement is to make the processes of agricultural production through to retail sale and the supply of the means of production into a unified system combined with free economic relations.

The supply of basic inputs and machinery services has critical importance for the emerging private sector. At the time of writing, neither the required structure of distribution nor the critical input goods to be supplied exist in most East European countries. The shortage of fertiliser, other farm chemicals and machinery in operational condition often resulted in low yields in previous years. Tractors and other machinery suitable for small-scale farming are also not available in the majority of the countries concerned.

As development of a private-based commercial system is the most suitable way for supplying inputs and machinery services, a network of farm supply shops should be created relatively soon. For the short term, especially in the USSR and southern part of Eastern Europe, the new types of cooperative can be the major institutions of supply, if they are established soon. In the long run, private firms, including some foreign ones, are likely to be involved. However, the development of a nationwide commercial network of supply will take several years in all the countries under consideration. Therefore, imported tractors and other farm machinery should be offered both to the service enterprises and to private cooperatives and farmers. Credit availability to cover inputs and services should also be organised.

The government's role is to assist the emergence of wholesale marketing and encourage retailing and processing firms to develop their own purchasing activities. It should encourage competing buyers by subdividing state-owned trade and processing monopolies. Government assistance and promotion has critical importance now because the emerging private but primitive farmers' markets provide very limited opportunities for marketing, and the old system is further paralysed by the shortage of products. Therefore, it is vital to create the actual facilities for farmers' markets and a wholesaling network tuned for private farming as soon as possible.

Whilst, at the time of writing, the need to create a marketing structure for farm products represents the major problem, at a later stage, the new infrastructure should include improved facilities such as auction halls, city markets, regional cooperative packing and grading facilities, and transportation equipment. Market information services for farmers should also be made available, such as radio and television programmes and farm newspapers. The more developed domestic agricultural markets will require a commodity exchange. (The first commodity exchanges are already operating in Hungary as well as in the USSR.) More efficient and coordinated international marketing for agriculture should be supported by commercial-based export marketing organisations.

5.4.4 New role of government and a new macroeconomic framework for agriculture

The transition to a market economy requires a fundamental change in the role of government in agriculture and in the economy in general. Direct government intervention in the agricultural economy, such as establishing mandatory targets for production and/or delivery of goods and central distribution of investments and inputs has ended. The appropriate government role in the agricultural sector will be to establish the general rules and facilitate the conditions for the smooth and prosperous operation of markets and independent business organisations. This role is no less important than the previous one; however, it requires a different philosophy, means, and institutions.

The abolition of central planning calls for the development of a new macroeconomic framework for agriculture enabling the implementation of agricultural policies of the government by economic means used in other market economies. All the East European countries aim to develop an internationally competitive agriculture with sustained growth. They also seek to establish private ownership and market control. This will require a macroeconomic framework for agriculture that includes an appropriate price policy and system of taxation supportive of production and improved well-being of the farming population. In addition, parallel with the liberalisation of producer prices, an agricultural tax system should be introduced to avoid sudden rural income inequalities, maintain urban–rural income equity, and increase government revenues.

In a move towards a new macroeconomic framework for agriculture, all the Eastern bloc countries except the USSR took substantial steps towards liberalising consumer and producer food prices and eliminating subsidies during 1990–1. The liberalisation has been almost 100 per cent in the more developed northern countries (Poland, Hungary, Czechoslovakia), while in Romania and Bulgaria it has been less complete. The full results of these moves cannot be analysed in detail here. However, one can safely conclude that food price liberalisation in Central-Eastern Europe has been a success. Food prices increased everywhere by 30–40 per cent but have lately started to decline in response to excess supply. Consumers' adjustment has been remarkable, while change on the producer side seems to be much slower. The food price liberalisation was carried out with virtually no safety net; citizens were granted partial monetary compensation but targeted programmes of direct food relief were not attempted anywhere. The promising experiences of Central Europe should give encouragement to the forthcoming price liberalisation in the USSR.

The dismantling of the bureaucratic structure of central planning is a very important task on all levels. What is needed more than changing the names of the various ministries is the radical modification and merger of some of them. Units related to central command and direct interventions should be fully dismantled, while those remaining should be managed and new units organised to meet the needs of a free market system. Market regulation, (not management) and trade policy functions should be taken over by the Ministry of Agriculture and other government agencies. As transition proceeds the whole structure can be further simplified, with fewer institutional units and employees. Changes are needed in the structure of the administration at the levels of regional units, as well. Of course, the overall structure should be redeveloped within the framework of the general reform of local administration and self-government. In some of the countries such as the USSR, a huge bureaucracy relating to the implementation of the central control still exists at regional level. There is no need for its continued existence in its current form – a relatively small administration would be adequate to enforce agricultural regulations, promote development and provide extension and market information services.

The current change, however, will substantially reduce the number of those employed in administration. The ongoing change at cooperatives and state farms will also free a large number of skilled agricultural technicians who at present are working in various farm managerial positions. Most of these experts will be needed in the extension and training services. However, the future careers of this group of experts should be assisted by providing retraining opportunities and financial assistance to enter private business.

The mainly private ownership-based agriculture requires extended service channels to disseminate new technologies and information to farmers, with the establishment and financing of an extension network being the responsibility of the government. The existing research and service stations and universities provide good starting points. However, the national extension service network should be designed carefully.

5.4.5   New legal framework required

The establishment of a market economy requires the development of a new legal framework, essential both for the transition to and for the operation of the new system. As far as agriculture is concerned, several legal instruments are needed as almost immediate pre-conditions of a smooth transition. A land law that defines specific ownership and land use rights – establishing private, communal and public land ownership – is essential. It should describe the process of distributing ownership titles, the way of handling former owners' claims and principles of land ownership policy, for example, limits on holding size, foreign ownership and land ownership transferability. A law on the transformation of agricultural cooperatives is also necessary and should specify the process to be followed in transferring land and other assets of cooperatives to private ownership. It should be a basic principle that new cooperatives be based only on private property and voluntary membership. Law on the transformation of state farms, the necessary privatisation and management changes, should be similar to that for other state-owned enterprises.

The legal framework should also have components that can be completed in a later stage of transition. These ought to include a law that establishes the basic principles of private cooperatives for agriculture and other sectors, together with an agricultural marketing law creating a regime that describes the rules of such markets – setting the principles of fair competition, anti-cartel policy and quality control. Also at a later stage, general regulations for agriculture, forestry and hunting and fishing have to be established according to the new ownership structure and economic management philosophy. And it will be essential to harmonise legislation related to agricultural trade with that of the EC.

5.4.6 More attention to the environment

The countryside of Eastern Europe as well as the USSR has experienced environmental damage due to inadequate agricultural practices, reflected especially in the serious degradation of soil resources in hilly areas. There are also striking signs of industrial pollution of agricultural land and water resources. Throughout the world, the development of modern agriculure has resulted in an energy-intensive technology strongly dependent on industrial inputs and disruptive of the natural ecological processes. This gives rise to harmful environmental effects which rich countries have attempted to counterbalance with a whole system of interventions and supports, but poor countries are obliged to suffer. The developed countries are now beginning to discard as obsolete those technologies thought to be revolutionary in developing countries. It would be the task of environmental policy during the transitional period to restore damages done by and to agriculture that are still reparable, and promote the development and spread of environmentally friendly technologies for agricultural production, including appropriate land use and tillage practices and integrated pest management. The most dangerous industrial mismanagement, oil pollution of water and soil, should be stopped immediately.

The increased assertion of environmental protection requirements means, above all, that protection of environment and sustainable land use must have a high priority in setting new agricultural policies. Greater scope must be given to materials and energy-sparing technologies, and protection of the soil and the safeguarding of its quality must become fundamental criteria for agricultural production. The proportion of waste-free or recycling technologies should be increased, technologies preserving the original property of the basic material should be given greater emphasis, and the use of chemicals rationalised.

5.4.7 Rearrangements of intersectoral linkages

A basic requirement for the adaptation of East European and Soviet agriculture to the developed market-economy model is that the process of agricultural production and marketing, and the production and supply of capital goods, must form a uniform intertwined system. Both the strategies of agricultural domestic marketing and exports, and the structure and mechanism by which they are conducted, require that producers are supported by an agricultural marketing policy coordinated at the national level. The experience of developed countries which export agricultural products shows that there is a need for a market policy differentiated for the individual markets, with the whole process of production and marketing mobilised appropriately. Processing is a bottleneck that is a particularly serious handicap for food exports. It cannot be overemphasised that, with demanding international markets, improved food processing is an indispensable condition for international competitiveness and the improvement of export efficiency. Naturally, better processing is becoming increasingly important for domestic consumers too. The actual development of food processing should take place as a private sector activity, but the government could promote this by providing incentives for both domestic and foreign investors.

The future of agriculture in the region cannot be separated from other areas of the economy, with the success of restructuring in the agricultural sphere dependent to a considerable extent on the evolution of conditions outside the sector. The creation of a market economy and a system of private ownership in itself will make the conditions for improved performance of the agriculture sector far more favourable. However, the pace at which industry and basic infrastructure change and the extent to which the domestic industrial and service background to agricultural production expands and develops are of decisive significance. Without appropriate input and output marketing/processing/transport facilities and services, agriculture sector growth will be seriously constrained.

The desired state of East European and Soviet agriculture cannot be reached without relaxing the pressure which the lack of alternative rural (and urban) employment opportunities has on agriculture. Increased non-agricultural activity in rural areas will have a very significant and positive effect on demand for agriculture products. The development of rural industries is of interest not only to the whole country but to agriculture as well. Therefore, the establishment of promotional programmes for rural industries such as handicrafts, labour-intensive industrial activities, food processing and tourism seem to be necessary.

5.5 FUTURE PERSPECTIVES AND ANTICIPATED MARKET BEHAVIOUR

It is not easy in the new situation created by the changes in agricultural policy either to predict the market behaviour of the countries of Eastern Europe or to forecast their probable exports and imports of agricultural products. In analysing the future possibilities and influences on the agricultural markets of the region, an attempt must be made to answer three questions.

1. What will be the trend in food production and, in particular, in grain and meat production?
2. Can an increase in food consumption be expected and what will be the trends in the domestic markets?
3. How will the international environment evolve? How far will the trade policy conditions for the agricultural exports of the countries concerned improve and how will their relations with each other change?

As far as agricultural production is concerned, the characteristic of the recent past has generally been a decline in the growth rate of output, in some countries amounting to stagnation, especially in the livestock sector. The explanation for this can be sought in the following factors:

- the high degree of obsolescence of the technical basis of agricultural production and food processing;
- the low yields and the outdated conditions of animal farming;

- the acute lack of capital;
- the inflexible operating structure;
- the unfavourable effects of the first steps taken in the direction of a market economy;
- the political tension and uncertainty caused by the changes under way (such as land law).

Despite these negative factors, the change in political and economic regimes has already created in part the conditions for advancement. The opening up of the economy to market forces and privatisation is paving the way for easing the shortage of capital, the appearance of foreign capital, the import of efficient technologies and the radical transformation of the entrepreneurial structure. The question is how rapidly these influences will predominate in the countries concerned and thus result in the stabilisation of agricultural production. In those Eastern bloc countries where the shortage of food, especially meat, remains the decisive factor, the unsatisfied demand at existing prices could be an important incentive for increasing production. However, the liberalisation of prices and the dismantling of subsidies has begun here too, and it is probable that an equilibrium of demand and supply will be reached at a lower level of consumption than at present .

In view of the above, three alternative medium-term development courses for agricultural production in the region seem possible:

either (1) under the influence of the fall in demand resulting from the general economic crisis and the tensions and uncertainties produced by the political changes, the growth of agricultural production will halt and production will decline for a number of years to come. Recovery or possible increases in output will not occur until the second half of the 1990s.

or (2) The reform measures and the liberalisation of prices will make their influence felt on agricultural production relatively quickly. There will be no decline in production, indeed the growth rate of food production may accelerate over the short term and an appreciable upswing may begin in the near future.

or (3) The region's agriculture will remain in a state of stagnation. Production as a whole will increase slightly or will stagnate with big fluctuations, remaining below the world growth rate right up to the end of the decade.

It is my conviction that there will be a considerable degree of differentiation in the development of agriculture in the countries of the region. In fact, the chances exist for all three scenarios in each of the countries. Very probably none of the three scenarios outlined will characterise the whole of the region. In my opinion:

- The countries with the most developed agriculture (Hungary, Czechoslovakia, and I would also list Poland here) will be characterised by the first trend outlined.
- The greatest probability of the second course is in Romania and Bulgaria and could be the case in the Soviet Union too, if the trend in conditions is optimal. However, the probability of the latter is quite small.
- It is probable that the Soviet Union will be characterised by the third trend, assuming that the reform process will be slowed down by internal disintegration and that the political and economic tensions will become prolonged.

In recent years, food consumption in the countries of the region has reached a relatively high level. By the mid-1980s, together with the end of the rise in living standards, the growth of food consumption practically came to a halt, while the structural transformation of food consumption slowed down and, in some cases, took an unfavourable turn.

It is likely that no real improvement can be expected in the income situation and standard of living of the population as a whole in the countries concerned within the next few years. However, there will almost certainly be an increase in the differentiation of incomes and social tensions can also be expected to grow stronger. The following conclusions can therefore be drawn:

- A substantial quantitative growth of consumption or expansion of demand cannot be expected for the basic kinds of food products.
- Demand can be expected to shift in the direction of lower-quality goods and the cheaper kinds of food.
- As a result of the differentiation in incomes, there will be an increase in the demand for the more highly processed, top quality food products.

The international agricultural trade system of the region is undergoing a fundamental transformation. The system of relations which concentrated the food sales of the East European countries within the

CMEA, or the so-called socialist bloc, on the Soviet Union has disintegrated.

The deep economic crisis of the Soviet Union is also having a very serious impact on the food exports to that country from Eastern Europe. In 1990, there was a considerable decline in the agricultural exports from the countries of Eastern Europe to the Soviet Union and it is probable that not even the 1990 levels can be maintained in 1991. Despite this, it is improbable that this system of relations will entirely disappear. The comprehensive energy supply system running from the Soviet Union to Eastern Europe and the forecast oil glut on world markets, together with the agricultural market conditions, especially meat surpluses, of the East European countries, will forge these relations once again though probably on differing bases from those of earlier years. However, it is unlikely that the agricultural trade conducted by the countries of Eastern Europe with the Soviet Union will reach earlier levels within the foreseeable future.

There are also hitches in the agricultural trade conducted among the countries of Eastern Europe. In this area, the lack of liquidity raises rigid barriers. However, the developments of the recent past indicate that within the framework of the emerging market economy these relations will be revived relatively quickly and become substantial.

Simultaneously with the disintegration of the traditional CMEA relations, the conditions for agricultural trade conducted with the developed world have become more favourable. In the case of the agricultural exporting countries of Central-Eastern Europe, the earlier, largely politically motivated, discriminative measures have given way to well-intentioned preferences. There can be no doubt though, that the European Community in particular, and most of the other countries concerned are protectionist as regards the conditions of agricultural trade. Despite this, t. e conditions for access to export markets for meat and other products of the Central Eastern European countries are already clearly more favourable than at any time in the past two decades. Association with the European Community offers further possibilities for some countries (Czechoslovakia, Hungary, Poland).

The Soviet Union is replacing agricultural imports from Central-Eastern Europe with more purchases from OECD countries. Almost without exception, these are agricultural products (mainly grain and meat) supported by credit and at favourable prices, although generally of lower quality. It would appear that, guided in part by political motivations, the developed countries are prepared to continue extending credit to the Soviet Union for the purchase of meat products. In view of the economic situation of the Soviet Union and the growing internal political tensions, how long this practice can be continued is an open question.

The opening up of food production to market forces in Eastern Europe and, to a lesser extent, in the Soviet Union can also be expected to find expression in the appearance of foreign capital. At present, processing and sales represent the bottleneck in agricultural production in the countries of Central-Eastern Europe. It is in precisely these areas that the entry of foreign capital and the appearance of the multinational food corporations can be expected. As a result, an improvement will occur in the quality and range of East European processed agricultural products, leading to greater competition in export markets where conditions are, moreover, already becoming more favourable. At the same time, the appearance of foreign capital in Soviet agricultural production in the near future is not likely.

The creation of a market economy and the spread of fully market-compatible solutions will not be achieved overnight in food production and sales. The payment problems of the countries concerned will probably remain serious. Consequently, trade policy, especially of the Soviet Union, will continue to place great emphasis on bilateral relations and on the requirements of trade equilibrium with the different partners. Even over the medium term, a substantial part of the agricultural trade will be conducted not on the basis of free foreign exchange but as part of complicated, in cases multilateral, barter-type agreements. The proportion of such deals will remain high in the case of relations continuing or newly established with the Soviet Union.

On the basis of the above, the following general conclusions can be drawn regarding the expected behaviour of the region in the international market:

(1) The Central-Eastern European region has a substantial comparative advantage and existing production capacity in agricultural production. The conditions for greater exports than at present are already in place on the production side. However, the economic difficulties of these countries and the lack of funds available for export subsidies obviously restrict export ambitions. At the same time, international payment obligations constitute an incentive for an increase of exports to the developed countries and the limitation of imports. Since the expansion of agricultural exports is easier to achieve over the shorter term than the increase in sales of manufactured goods, it can be expected that the countries

concerned will make greater efforts to increase agricultural exports, and especially meat, to the markets of all developed countries.

(2)   Expansion of exports can be expected despite the stagnation or possible decline of production. The stagnation of domestic consumption and the shrinking Soviet market will create the necessary commodity surplus for this. Over the short term, the reduction of breeding livestock will further increase the quantity of meat available for export. The expansion of East European exports can be expected to be accompanied by an upgrading of quality, so that they are better adapted to the market, and more effective marketing. This could lead to an appreciable increase in market share for certain products. There can be no doubt that Central-Eastern Europe could become a tougher, more aggressive actor in the markets for some food products, notably pork, poultry, fruit and vegetables.

(3)   Although it has the potential for self-sufficiency in food products, the Soviet Union will remain a net agricultural importer over the medium term. However, the Soviet economic difficulties will almost certainly prevent the expansion of the level of food imports established in earlier years, and it is probable that in the coming years imports will remain below the exceptionally high levels of the second half of the 1980s. As a consequence of the structural transformation already outlined, there could be a further expansion in 1991 of food imports from the developed countries to the Soviet Union. In the final analysis, over the medium term the volume of Soviet purchases will be determined by the readiness of the dealing countries to extend credit and by the terms of such credit.

6 The Quest for Sustained Growth in Chinese Agriculture[1]

TERRY SICULAR

6.1 INTRODUCTION

During the past decade, the Chinese government has undertaken substantial reforms in agricultural policy. These reforms have reduced administrative interventions in the rural economy, increased reliance on economic 'levers', decentralised economic decision-making, and expanded the role of markets. Mandatory planning of production and procurement has been reduced, and direct government investment in agriculture has declined. Increasingly, the government has relied on pricing and incentives to guide agricultural production, marketing and investment.

These measures have been undeniably successful in promoting agricultural growth. Between 1978 and 1989 the gross value of agricultural output (in constant prices) nearly doubled, agricultural productivity and farm incomes rose, and the quality and quantity of food available to consumers improved vastly. Success was most apparent, however, prior to 1985. Since 1984 agricultural performance has weakened: annual growth in the gross value of agricultural output has fallen from average rates of 8 or 9 per cent to average rates of 3 to 4 per cent. The slowdown was most abrupt for crop production, output of which dropped in absolute terms in 1985 and stagnated thereafter (see Table 6.1).

China's agricultural policy in the 1990s will almost certainly aim at sustaining growth in agricultural, and especially crop, production. Effective policies, however, require a clear understanding of the reasons for the slowdown in the late 1980s. Several explanations have

TABLE 6.1   Growth in gross value of agricultural output (per cent growth over previous year, constant prices)[1]

Year	Growth in value of agricultural output	Of which: crops
1979	17.6	7.2
1980	1.4	−0.6
1981	6.5	5.9
1982	11.3	10.3
1983	7.7	7.9
1984	12.3	9.9
1985	3.5	−2.0
1986	3.4	0.9
1987	5.8	5.3
1988	3.2	−0.5
1989	3.1	1.8

[1] Includes crops, forestry, animal husbandry, aquaculture, and sidelines; does not include rural industry
Source: State Statistical Bureau (1990b) p. 53.

been proposed. Some observers argue that growth could not be sustained at the rates attained in the early 1980s because agricultural growth had to decelerate as the one-time gains from decollectivisation were played out. Some have attributed the slowdown to the declining amount and uneconomic distribution of land. Small family farms with numerous, fragmented plots could not capture economies of scale, and China's limited and shrinking arable land area constrained further growth. Others have blamed the slowdown on reduced investment in farming. Certain of these factors undoubtedly weakened agriculture's performance in the late 1980s; however, none of them explains why growth slowed so abruptly in 1985.

This chapter presents a different explanation for the slowdown: certain policies enacted in 1983–5 caused the abrupt change in agriculture's performance. Beginning in 1983 but especially in 1984–5 the Chinese government implemented a set of measures that individually and as a group affected agriculture negatively. These measures included policies directly aimed at agriculture; for example, reductions in the prices and incentives farmers received for deliveries of crops to the state. Equally important, and too often overlooked, were changes in industrial, commercial and financial policies that had repercussions for agriculture. One such policy change was the 1983 decision to sanction the development of private rural enterprise. In 1984, the government enacted policies that promoted the development of private and collective rural industries and permitted rural residents to leave the land to set up private businesses. Together with certain other non-agricultural measures discussed below, these actions caused a flood of resources to flow out of agriculture.

In the wake of such agricultural and non-agricultural policies, agricultural growth declined abruptly and, in the absence of comprehensive countermeasures, remained weak in the years that followed. Inflation hindered agriculture's recovery. Only with the retrenchment in 1989–90, when the environment for non-agricultural activities worsened, did agriculture begin to recover.

The discussion below examines economic policies that contributed significantly to the initial acceleration and consequent slowdown in agricultural growth during the 1980s. Section 6.2 discusses decollectivisation and production planning. Then section 6.3 examines procurement and pricing of farm products, and section 6.4 analyses policies affecting agricultural investment. Section 6.5 discusses non-agricultural policies that contributed to agricultural trends. Foreign trade of agricultural products and relevant policies are examined in section 6.6. Finally, section 6.7 concludes that sustained growth in Chinese agriculture is possible, and raises some lessons for policy in the 1990s.

6.2 DECOLLECTIVISATION AND PRODUCTION PLANNING[2]

Decollectivisation and reforms in production planning are closely related in that both have affected who makes economic decisions in agriculture. Decollectivisation has shifted the basic decision-making unit from the collective farm to the household. Reforms in production planning have changed the degree and nature of administrative control over the basic decision-making unit. These reforms have been given credit for the burst of agricultural growth in the early 1980s; some claim that they also underlie the agricultural slowdown in the late 1980s.

Decollectivisation has been treated extensively elsewhere, and so is discussed only briefly here.[3] During the early 1980s, the household contracting system, under which land was contracted to individual households who could then make their own input decisions and dispose as they wished of their output after meeting their tax and quota sales obligations to the state, became widespread (see Table 6.2). By linking rewards directly to effort, the contracting system enhanced incentives and promoted efficient production based on economic considerations.

Reforms in production planning accompanied decollectivisation. Prior to 1980, collective farms faced mandatory targets governing sown areas, yields, levels of input applications, planting techniques, and so on. Of these targets, those governing sown area were most important, in part because they were relatively easy to monitor and enforce. During the early and mid-1970s, sown area targets governed the planting of all major and many minor crops, and they covered a substantial proportion of cultivated area.

During the reform decade the government moved away from mandatory production planning. The number of production planning targets in agriculture was reduced substantially in the early 1980s. Production planning began to pay greater attention to local soil and weather conditions, economic considerations, and the desires of producers. As surpluses of grain and other crops emerged in 1983 and 1984, mandatory planning of production no longer seemed necessary, and in 1985 the government announced that mandatory production planning in agriculture was no longer permitted. Thereafter planning targets were to serve only for guidance or reference. Local implementation of the production planning reforms varied, but the overall effect was to reduce the degree of intervention in agricultural economic decisions. These reforms contributed to agriculture's rapid growth in the early 1980s by permitting the diversification of agricultural production, greater regional specialisation, and a decline in the previously overintensive cultivation of grain.

The slowdown in the late 1980s has raised questions about decollectivisation and the relaxation of controls over farming. Chinese publications have given increasing attention to the potential drawbacks of the household contracting system. One drawback is that decollectivisation may have reduced agricultural investment. Rights to land under the contracting system have remained vague. Because farmers do not have a secure and permanent claim to the land, they are reluctant to make long-term investments. Decollectivisation, by weakening collective organisation, has apparently also contributed to a decline in water conservancy and irrigation investments.

Another alleged drawback to the household contracting system is that small, fragmented farms are less productive than large, consolidated farms. This view underlies recent proposals to promote farm reconsolidation as a solution to the current agricultural malaise.

Although household labour could undoubtedly be saved if each household's plots were consolidated, it is questionable whether combining small farms into large farms would bring about additional gains. Studies of other countries, and some preliminary evidence from China, have shown that land in small farms is not significantly less productive than that in large farms.[4]

Although the government has not reversed decollectivisation or rehabilitated mandatory production planning, it has encouraged increased collective leadership by local governments and the formation of cooperative organisations. In many places, household land contracts now specify the land area that households are required to plant in grain.[5] In some localities, village cadres directly manage certain aspects of agricultural production. For example, a county in Shandong has promoted a programme called the 'five unifieds', that is, unified ploughing, sowing, irrigation, harvesting and threshing by villages.[6] Implementation of the 'five unifieds' requires considerable planning and coordination of agricultural production at the village level.

Measuring the extent of collective management of farm production is difficult. Western field researchers have observed the continued importance of village-level management in some localities.[7] A recent survey carried out by the Ministry of Agriculture's Policy Research Centre (Table 6.2) provides more systematic evidence. Although the surveyed villages report that by 1987 over 95 per cent of their land was contracted out to households, the role of collective organisations was apparently still quite large. As late as 1987, 40 per cent of the land in these villages was ploughed, 45 per cent of irrigated area irrigated, and roughly one-third of fertiliser, insecticide, and diesel oil inputs supplied in a unified fashion by villages (or groups). The proportion of villages planning crop layout and rotations also remained high: in 1987, 63 per cent of the villages set plans for crop layout and rotations, and 58 per cent set plans for farmland basic construction.[8] The importance of collectives in farm management is highest in the eastern regions, where over three-quarters of the land is under unified ploughing and 80 per cent of villages set plans for crop layout and rotations. The statistics suggest that the role of collectives in farm management has declined less than previously thought.

Involvement of local leaders in the management of farm production is qualitatively different from central planning through vertical channels. Local leaders are more likely to be aware of local conditions and the desires of the farmers. Their interests and aims may conflict not

TABLE 6.2   Survey statistics on collective (unified) production and planning activities

	1978	1984	1987 All	East	Central	West
I. Per cent of cultivated area						
A Under unified management	99.4	5.0	2.4	—	—	—
B Contracted to households	0.2	93.2	95.7	—	—	—
C Other	0.4	1.8	1.9	—	—	—
II. Per cent of land under unified ploughing	—	49	40	76	34	20
III. Per cent of irrigated land under unified irrigation	—	47	45	85	36	16
IV. Per cent of inputs subject to unified supply						
A Chemical fertilisers	—	56	32	50	30	21
B Pesticides	—	54	28	51	26	23
C Diesel oil	—	48	33	65	29	20
V. Per cent of villages (groups) setting plans for						
A Crop layout and rotations	73	64	63	80	52	58
B Farmland basic construction	73	58	58	38	57	36

Notes

A dash indicates no data provided by source.

1. These survey data are from 1200 randomly selected villages in 100 counties that are designated 'rural economic information' counties. All provinces, municipalities and autonomous regions are covered except Tibet and Hainan.
2. The term 'collective' refers to Chinese term *jiti*, and 'unified' to *tongyi*. Collective and unifed activities are carried out by villages and groups, which this source lumps together using the expression *cun(zu)*.

Source: Ministry of Agriculture Economic Policy (1989) pp. 5, 12, 14.

only with those of the farmers, but also with those of higher levels of government. Moreover, certain aspects of agricultural production such as irrigation and basic construction are probably better handled collectively than by households. Nevertheless, village and other local cadres belong to formal governmental bodies, their decisions are likely to be influenced by administrative or political considerations, and they have a tradition of infringing on the decision-making rights of households. The persistence, and in some regions resurgence, of local government involvement in agriculture thus reflects administrative intervention under a new guise.

Increased use of administrative interventions has arisen because of difficulties guiding production using indirect policies. Efforts to influence farm household decisions using prices and incentives have not had the desired effects. Economic incentives continue to conflict with, rather than complement, the government's objectives for agriculture. So long as farm-level incentives and government objectives conflict, farm behaviour will diverge from that desired by higher levels, and the temptation to intervene directly in production decisions will remain strong.

6.3 PROCUREMENT POLICIES: PRICES, QUOTAS AND INCENTIVES

In the 1980s, China's policy-makers relied heavily on pricing, procurement and related measures to influence agriculture. Such policies can raise farm profits and enhance agriculture's ability to attract resources, and so spur production. The allocation of resources depends, however, not on agriculture's absolute profitability, but on the relative profitability of farming in comparison to alternative pursuits. Non-agricultural developments therefore can, and have, counteracted efforts to encourage agriculture using prices and incentives. Incentive measures have also been hindered by the continued link between pricing and the state budget. Increasing farm prices raises, while reducing prices lowers, government budgetary outlays. In a period of persistent budget deficits, the government has shown greater willingness to lower than to raise farm prices.

Reform of agricultural procurement policy began in 1978. Initially the basic structure of the procurement system remained unchanged: farm products were subject to mandatory delivery quotas at planned prices, in some cases with a price bonus or other incentive award for beyond-quota deliveries. Adjustments were made, however, in the levels of prices and incentives. In 1979 the government implemented substantial, across-the-board increases in quota procurement prices (Table 6.3). In the early 1980s, quota prices were adjusted further, and seasonal and quality price differentials were widened. By 1983, quota prices for grains exceeded their 1977 levels by 15 to 20 per cent, for oils and oilcrops by 27 per cent, for sugar crops by 26 per cent, for cotton by over 30 per cent and for pigs by 27 per cent. These price adjustments followed more than a decade of constant quota prices.

The government concurrently expanded bonuses for above-quota deliveries. Prior to 1979, grain and oilcrops had received a price bonus of 30 per cent for deliveries beyond the quota level. In 1979 this bonus

Table 6.3 State procurement prices for selected farm products (yuan per ton)

	Paddy (Indica)		Wheat		Shelled peanuts		Rapeseed		Cotton, North		Cotton, South		Live pigs
	Quota	Above quota or contract	Quota	Above quota or contract	Quota	Above quota or contract	Quota	Above quota or contract	Quota	Above quota or contract	Quota	Above quota or contract	(per 100 kg.)
1971	196.2	255.1	268.6	349.2	760.0	988.0	560.0	728.0	1869.4	1869.4	1869.4	1869.4	96
1978	196.2	255.1	272.2	353.9	760.0	988.0	560.6	728.8	2304.8	2304.8	2304.8	2304.8	99
1979	231.4	347.1	329.6	494.4	965.8	1448.7	714.6	1071.9	2765.0	3594.5	2655.2	3451.8	125
1980	231.4	347.1	314.4	471.6	965.8	1448.7	714.6	1071.9	3062.0	3980.6	2916	3790.8	125
1981	231.4	347.1	314.4	471.6	965.8	1448.7	714.6	1071.9	3062.0	3980.6	2916	3790.8	125
1982	231.4	347.1	314.4	471.6	965.8	1448.7	714.6	1071.9	3062.0	3980.6	2916	3790.8	125
1983	231.4	347.1	314.4	471.6		1255.5		929.0		3980.6		3790.8	125
1984	231.4	347.1	314.4	471.6		1255.5		929.0		3615.8		3265.9	125
1985		312.0		424.4		1255.5		929.0		3528.4		3265.9	175
1986		312.0		424.4				929.0		3440.9		3265.9	180
1987		312/342		424.4		1448.7		929.0		3440.8		3266	212
1988		312/352		454.4/464.4		1448.7		1000.4		3528.4		3528.4	313
1989		312/352								4728.5		4728.4	349

Notes:

1. For paddy and wheat, the quota/above-quota price system was replaced by a single contract price in 1985; for peanuts and rapeseed in 1985; for cotton in 1983.

2. For live pigs, prior to 1985 the price given is the planned price (*paigou jiage*); from 1985 onward all state pig procurement has been at negotiated prices. The 1985–9 prices are the national average negotiated prices.

Sources: 1971–88 except for cotton: Sicular (1990b) tables 3 and 4.
1989 prices: Almanac of China's Commerce Ed. Comm. (1990) pp. 56, 76.
Cotton prices for 1971–9: Sicular (1990b) tables 3 and 4.
Cotton prices for 1980–9: author interviews in Shandong; Almanac of China's Prices Ed. Comm. (1989) p. 140; Almanac of China's Commerce Ed. Comm. (1990) p. 76; and notes r, s and t to table 3, Sicular (1990b).

was increased to 50 per cent. Cotton, which had earlier received no above-quota bonus, now began to receive a nationwide 30 per cent price bonus for sales to the state exceeding the average quantity delivered over the three year period 1976–8. Price bonuses for other farm products were also implemented, in some cases by provincial governments. The increased above-quota bonuses were multiplied by the now higher quota prices, so that between 1977 and 1983 above-quota prices rose 36 per cent for grains, 47 per cent for oils and oilcrops, and over 80 per cent for cotton (Table 6.3).

In addition to the above price measures, the government expanded a variety of material incentive programmes under which farmers were awarded the right to purchase low-priced or scarce commodities in return for delivering farm products to the state. For example, in 1978 the central government raised the nationwide award of chemical fertilisers per 100 kg of cotton delivered to the state from 35 to 40 kg, and starting in 1979 also gave farmers in cotton-growing areas 100 to 200 kg of grain at the low, urban retail price. Similar incentive programmes applied to grain, oilcrops, sugarbeet, sugarcane, hemps and tobacco. By the early 1980s, the overall number of material incentive programmes and the quantities of items awarded had grown quite large. According to incomplete statistics, products eligible for encouragement grain awards numbered 206 at the end of 1981, as compared to only 68 in 1971. The quantity of grain supplied under encouragement sales programmes rose to a historical high of 24 per cent of total state grain procurements in the early 1980s.[9]

The price and incentive measures described above were accompanied by a gradual reduction in quota levels and in the overall scope of procurement planning. Quota levels for some products, most importantly grain, were lowered. Between 1978 and 1982, the national grain quota and tax was reduced by 20 per cent (Table 6.4).[10] Efforts were also made to adjust the geographical distribution of quotas to permit greater regional specialisation. Finally, the number of farm products subject to centrally planned procurement and distribution was reduced, while the number of products handled by lower-level governments or traded on free markets was increased.

As early as 1978, the government began to encourage the revival of rural markets. By 1980, all products except cotton were allowed on the market after state delivery quotas were fulfilled.[11] By 1982, restrictions on private long-distance trade had been lifted for all farm products allowed on markets except grain, and private individuals were permitted to specialise in transport and trade. The expansion of free

TABLE 6.4   **Marketing and state procurement of grain (million tons trade grain)**

	1 *Marketed grain:*[1]			*2*	*3*	*4*
	Total	*% to state*	*% to market*	*State procurement*[2]	*Planned quota or contract*[3]	*Share of procurement at quota/contract prices*[4] *(%)*
1977	47.67	100.0	0.0	47.67	37.75	
1978	50.73	100.0	0.0	50.73	37.75	
1979	60.10	95.8	4.2	57.57	35.00	63
1980	61.29	93.1	6.9	57.07	34.33	58
1981	68.46	92.4	7.6	63.24	30.38	50
1982	78.06	92.4	7.6	72.09	30.32	50
1983	102.49	94.4	5.6	96.74		35
1984	117.25	91.7	8.3	107.48		29
1985	107.63	84.2	15.8	90.62	75.00	
1986	115.16	83.5	16.5	96.15	60.75	67
1987	120.92	82.0	18.0	99.20	50.00	57
1988	119.95				50.00	
1989	121.38	82.7	17.3	100.40		49

Notes:
[1] Data are for the calendar year. Percentage sold to the state is calculated using data in column (2); the remainder is assumed to be sold on the market.
[2] Includes purchases by state commercial departments and supply and marketing
[3] Data prior to 1985 are for the state procurement quota and tax, and from 1985 on are for the planned level of contract procurement. These data are for the production year (April of the current year through March of the following year).
[4] 1979–84 shares are quota-price procurement as a per cent of total state procurement. 1986–87 shares are contract-price procurement as a per cent of total state procurement.

Sources: Sicular (1990a) table 5; Almanac of China's Commerce Ed. Comm. (1990) pp. 566, 571.

markets provided an alternative channel for the sale of farm products, often at prices exceeding those offered by the state.

The government participated in market trade through 'negotiated price' procurement. The state commercial system bought and sold beyond-quota farm products at the negotiated prices, which, according to central directives, were to be agreed upon jointly by both sides, to apply to voluntary above-quota deliveries, and to be decided on the basis of regional, yearly, seasonal, varietal, and quality considerations. These prices were to follow trends in demand and supply, but were in general not to exceed local market prices. Although in practice these prices were set administratively and did not fully reflect market trends, the revival of negotiated-price trade gave the state commercial system more flexibility in responding to market conditions and provided a lever for influencing the market.

The commercial reforms in the late 1970s and early 1980s successfully promoted agricultural growth, but they also led to expanding budgetary outlays on state commerce in farm products. As production grew, the government found itself buying ever increasing quantities of farm products at the higher, above-quota prices. The share of procurement at above-quota prices rose dramatically, in the case of grain from 37 per cent in 1979 to 71 per cent in 1984 (Table 6.4). Meanwhile, the government continued to sell farm products at low ration prices. State retail prices of grain had not changed since the 1960s and had already been lower than quota prices before the 1979 price increases. The combination of rising procurement costs and low, unchanged retail prices generated growing price subsidies. Attempts were made to stem these subsidies by raising retail prices for non-staple foods like meat and vegetables; however, increases in retail prices were invariably accompanied by income supplements or wage increases for urban residents, the costs of which offset subsidy reductions.[12]

By the mid-1980s, budgetary losses from price subsidies on farm products grew to a critical level. In 1984, price subsidies on grain, oilcrops and cotton had reached 20 billion yuan, equal to 12 per cent of total government revenues.[13] Similar subsidies also existed for other farm products and on foreign trade in farm products.

Growing budgetary costs prompted an overhaul of procurement policy. First, the government abandoned the two-tiered quota/above-quota pricing system and instituted a single, 'proportionate' procurement price for each crop. The new proportionate prices were weighted averages of the old quota and above-quota prices, with the weights varying somewhat by region and crop. Proportionate pricing was implemented for oilcrops in 1983, for cotton in 1984 and for grain in 1985. The new grain price was set equal to 30 per cent of the quota price plus 70 per cent of the above-quota price. Proportionate pricing stopped the upward drift in the costs of procurement as above-quota deliveries expanded. It also eliminated the incentive to evade quotas in order to receive higher above-quota prices.

Second, the Chinese government announced on 1 January 1985 that, except for a few products, it would do away with the old procurement system and no longer send down mandatory delivery quotas to farmers. For grain and cotton, mandatory quotas were to be eliminated and replaced by a combination of voluntary contract and market purchases. State commercial departments were to negotiate purchase contracts with farmers before the sowing season: the contract prices would be set at the new proportionate prices, and farmers could choose freely whether or not they wished to sign contracts with the state or dispose of their products on the market. The state no longer promised to purchase grain and cotton beyond the contract amount. Only if market prices fell below the old quota price would the state guarantee to buy additional grain, and then it would only pay the old quota price. Planned procurement of other farm products was to be gradually eliminated and replaced by market allocation.

If fully implemented, the 1985 reform would have eliminated mandatory state quotas, drastically reduced the scope of commercial planning and greatly expanded the role of markets in allocation and price determination. Together with concurrent reforms on the retail side, they would also have reduced budgetary outlays on state commerce. This budgetary objective would be accomplished both by establishing a maximum level of state outlays on the procurement of farm products, and by reducing the scope of low-priced state sales. For all farm products except grain, oils and cotton, both state purchases and sales were eventually to take place at market prices. For grain and oils, planned supplies to urban residents were to continue at unchanged, low prices, but starting in 1985, sales of grain in the countryside were to take place at the higher, proportionate procurement prices. Since in the early 1980s government resales of grain in rural areas had exceeded 40 per cent of state grain procurements,[14] the budgetary savings from raising rural sales prices were potentially substantial.[15]

Although the 1985 reforms were meant to slow growth in agricultural output and reduce government procurement of farm products, subsequent declines in crop production and deliveries exceeded expectations. Cotton deliveries fell from 6 million tons in 1984 to only 3.5 million tons in 1985, and grain deliveries from 107 to 91 million tons. These delivery levels were well below the expected amounts: contract-price deliveries of cotton were only 70 per cent, and of grain only 72 per cent, of the totals promised under contracts signed.[16]

Price and incentive reforms undoubtedly contributed to these trends. The shift to proportionate pricing, although designed to maintain the average prices paid for deliveries to the state, effectively lowered marginal prices. Previously farmers received above-quota prices for additional deliveries; now they received proportionate prices. The proportionate prices were lower than the old above-quota prices by about 13 per cent for oilcrops, 10 per cent for grains and 12 to 14 per cent for cotton (Table 6.3). The switch to proportionate pricing therefore discouraged farm production, and, together with low market prices in 1983 and 1984 due to oversupplies of farm products, adversely affected expectations about profits from farming.

Concurrent reductions in material incentive awards reinforced the negative effects of price measures. In 1985, grain incentive awards for cotton deliveries were eliminated, and chemical fertiliser awards were to apply only to within-contract, and no longer to beyond-contract, cotton deliveries. Additionally, the price of grain supplied under material incentive programmes was raised from the old quota price to the higher proportionate price.

Declines in production and deliveries led the government to back away from some of its 1985 initiatives. Voluntary contracts for grain soon became mandatory. Numerous local reports confirm that delivery contracts were indeed obligatory quotas under a new name. Problems with grain procurement also prompted greater administrative inter-vention in free markets. To ensure contract fulfilment, local govern-ments closed markets during the procurement seasons and blocked trade of farm products across administrative boundaries.

In 1987 and 1988, the central government imposed further restric-tions on markets as part of the effort to slow inflation. Measures taken included allowing local governments to set ceilings and floors on free market prices of grain, oils, animal products, vegetables, and other farm products. In some regions, the central government established responsibility systems with local governments for control of the retail price index. In 1988, the State Council issued a decision that starting in the autumn 1988 procurement season, procurement of rice would be subject to monopoly by the Ministry of Grain. Other departments, units and individuals were not permitted to supply rice.[17]

While reimposing controls on marketing, the government also took steps to improve incentives for crop production. Over the two years 1986 and 1987, the central government reduced nationwide planned delivery contracts for grain by one-third (Table 6.4). Although in part a practical step in response to the unrealistically high 1985 contract target, the contract reductions were also meant to allow farmers to sell more grain at negotiated and market prices. Furthermore, in 1987 the central government reinstituted material incentives for contract deliveries of grain and cotton. For grain, the 'three link' (*san guagou*) policy awarded cash advances and tied sales of high-grade chemical fertiliser and diesel oil at low state list prices for contract deliveries. Similar 'link' awards were instituted for cotton and certain other crops. The amounts of these material awards were increased further in 1988 and 1989.[18]

The government began to raise contract procurement prices in 1986 (Table 6.3). In contrast to the dramatic, across-the-board increases of the early 1980s, the procurement price adjustments of the late 1980s were modest, occurred gradually, and applied only to particular products in particular regions. Overall, price adjustments in 1986–8 raised grain and oilseeds contract prices by between 8 and 16 per cent over their 1985 levels in the regions where they applied. For cotton, as of 1988 the contract price in the North had recovered to its 1985 level, and in the South was 8 per cent higher than in 1985. The state implemented additional price increases in 1989, including an 18 per cent hike in grain contract prices.[19]

The intent of these quota, incentive, and price measures was to revitalise farm production and encourage deliveries to the state. Crop production and deliveries, however, were slow to respond (Tables 6.1, 6.4). One reason for the slow supply response was that local implementation of these measures was uneven. In many areas, local governments did not supply, and farmers did not receive inputs promised under the 'link' programmes. A nationwide survey of over 10 000 farm households revealed that in 1987 tied sales of fertiliser and diesel fuel for grain contracts were 20 per cent below levels promised in central directives. Cash advances were only 86 per cent of the stipulated amounts.[20] Local governments also did not pay farmers the prescribed prices in a timely way. In 1987 and 1988 local governments issued IOUs to farmers instead of paying them cash. One article estimates that in 1988 the nationwide average debt owed farmers for each 100 yuan deliveries of farm products was 20 to 40 yuan.[21] These debts often remained outstanding for several months or longer, in some cases for up to a year. Such practices seriously eroded farmer confidence in government policies.[22]

In addition, the increases in contract prices were inadequate. The 1988 price adjustments at best raised contract prices back to the level of above-quota prices before 1985. For many crops in many regions, contract prices in 1988 remained lower than the old above-quota prices. Only in 1989 did contract prices begin to exceed the old above-quota prices, and then only for some crops in some regions. While contract prices were just regaining their previous levels, market prices were rapidly rising. Inflation far outpaced contract price increases:

between 1984 and 1988 the general price level rose 47 per cent.[23] Inflation caused the gap between contract and market prices to widen considerably. Chinese sources report that by 1988, market prices for rice were over three times higher, for wheat 50 per cent higher, and for oilseeds 20 to 60 per cent higher, than contract prices.[24]

6.4 POLICIES ON AGRICULTURAL INVESTMENT

One explanation given for the slowdown in agriculture is insufficient investment. Available evidence indeed suggests that the level of agricultural investment grew slowly and that the rate of investment in agriculture declined. The causes of lagging investment are twofold: first, during the early and mid-1980s, the government reduced direct state investment in agriculture. Second, local and private investment in agriculture did not expand as hoped. In the mid-1980s, reductions in crop prices and increased off-farm opportunities drove local invest-ment funds, along with other financial, human and material resources, towards more profitable non-agricultural activities.

Table 6.5 presents data on government investment in agriculture. State annual spending on agricultural basic construction declined from levels of 5 billion yuan in the late 1970s to between 3 and 4 billion yuan in the mid-1980s, and then by 1989 rose back to 5 billion yuan by 1989. Much of the recovery in the late 1980s, however, reflects rising prices. In real terms, state investment in 1989 was only half that in the late 1970s. Moreover, agriculture's share of total government outlays on basic capital construction fell from 11 per cent to only 3 per cent

The government reduced direct investment with the expectation that pricing and incentive policies would elicit substantial local and private investment. Higher prices would increase the returns to agricultural investment, and, by raising farm incomes, also enlarge household savings which could be used for that investment. In addition, the government modified credit policies. Rural credit cooperatives, the major source of formal credit to farm households, were allowed to lend out a larger proportion of their deposits, and were in general granted more independence in their lending decisions. Informal cooperative and even private credit institutions were allowed to emerge so as to help match the supply and demand for funds.[25] Such measures were meant to increase the supply of investible funds and so promote farm investment.

Another measure meant to encourage agricultural investment was the policy of 'using industry to support agriculture' (*yigong bunong*).

TABLE 6.5   **State investment in agricultural basic construction[1] (million yuan)**

Year	Current prices	Constant 1981 prices	Share of total state basic construction (%)
1978	5334	5750	10.6
1979	5792	6097	11.1
1980	5203	5359	9.3
1981	2921	2921	6.6
1982	3412	3316	6.1
1983	3545	3296	6.0
1984	3712	3261	5.0
1985	3694	2979	3.4
1986	3666	2737	3.1
1987	4282	2950	3.2
1988	4719	2850	3.1
1989	5174	2846	3.3

Notes:
[1]   The value of expenses incurred during the calendar year on work complete or in progress, calculated using budgeted prices. Includes basic construction for crops, livestock, forestry, aquatic products, meterology, and water conservancy. Note that water conservancy, which includes hydroelectric projects not solely for agriculture use, accounts for about half of the total.
[2]   The constant price series is deflated using a construction price index as a deflator. This construction price index is calculated from data given in State Statistical Bureau (1990b) p. 82. It is an index of budgeted construction prices.

Sources: Statistical Bureau Department of Fixed Asset Investment Statistics (1987) pp. 74–5; State Statistical Bureau (1990a) p. 239; (1990b) p. 82.

Under this policy the central government urged local governments and rural enterprises to devote a share of their profits to subsidise agriculture. These monies could be contributed directly by the enterprises, or could come out of local government tax revenues from industry.[26] Some of these funds subsidised purchases of farm current inputs, and some was used for investment.

Despite these measures, local and private investment in agriculture did not increase. Profits of rural township and village enterprises used to aid agriculture declined in the early 1980s and then rose but did not recover fully. Nominal investment in agricultural fixed assets by rural collectives similarly declined in the early 1980s, and then recovered in 1987/8. Again, much of the recovery in the late 1980s simply reflects rising prices: in real terms, between the early 1980s and late 1980s both local enterprise aid to and collective investment in agriculture declined (see Table 6.6). These data suggest that government efforts to promote local and private investment were not terribly successful.

Unfortunately, available data on private investment are not broken down between agricultural and non-agricultural components.[27] Farm household purchases of fixed agricultural and non-agricultural productive assets rose substantially through 1983, levelled off at about 17 yuan per capita in 1983–5, and then rose rapidly again in 1987 and

TABLE 6.6 Statistics on agriculture investment by rural collectives and farm households

Year	Profits of township and village enterprises used to aid agriculture (million yuan)[1]		Investment in agricultural fixed assets by rural collectives (million yuan)[2]		Per capita purchases of productive fixed assests by farm household (yuan)[3]	
	Current prices	Constant 1981 prices	Current prices	Constant 1981 prices	Current prices	Constant 1981 prices
1981	1700	1700	3380	3380	2.61	2.61
1982	1400	1374	5205	5059	11.69	11.47
1983	1360	1295	3337	3102	18.44	17.56
1984	640	560	2899	2547	16.89	14.78
1985	880	735	2073	1672	18.70	15.61
1986	690	570			16.66	13.76
1987	850	656	4252	2929	20.52	15.83
1988	1160	770	4290	2597	25.14	16.69

Notes and sources:

[1] Includes all aid to agriculture by these enterprises, both for investment and current inputs. From State Statistical Bureau Department of Rural Socioeconomic Statistics (1985) p. 190, and (1988) p. 176. Deflated using the price index for agricultural inputs from State Statistical Bureau (1989) pp. 693–4.

[2] Includes investment in both productive and non productive fixed assets. Statistical Bureau Department of Fixed Asset Investment Statistics (1987) pp. 348–9, 351; State Statistical Bureau (1988) p. 641; and State Statistical Bureau (1989) p. 559. Deflated using the construction price index discussed in Table 6.5.

[3] Investment in productive agricultural and non-agricultural fixed assets. State Statistical Bureau Department of Rural Socioeconomic Statistics (1989) p. 296. Deflated using the price index for agricultural inputs.

1988. For reasons discussed below, it is likely that much of the growth in later years reflects purchases of non-agricultural assets. Holding prices constant, household purchases of fixed assets show no significant real improvement after 1983.

The data in Tables 6.5 and 6.6 thus reveal that during the 1980s neither state, nor collective, nor private investment in agriculture grew in real terms, and the sum total of these various categories of agricultural investment probably declined. Since agricultural output grew substantially during these years, the rate of investment undoubtedly fell.

Starting in the late 1980s, policy-makers responded to slowing agricultural growth by raising direct state investment. In autumn 1988, the government called for an expansion in large-scale agricultural capital construction and water conservancy.[28] In 1989, the nominal level of government investment in agriculture increased 10 per cent, and the share of agriculture in total government capital construction rose (Table 6.5). The 1990 national economic plan calls for an additional 30 per cent increase in central government investment in agriculture, and for similar increases in local government investment.[29] If carried out, the real level of state investment in agriculture will rise. Statements by the central leadership indicate that this upward trend in state investment is likely to continue.[30]

6.5   NON-AGRICULTURAL POLICIES THAT INFLUENCED AGRICULTURE

The agricultural slowdown in 1985 was not solely the result of reduced prices and incentives for farm products. A spate of concurrent changes in domestic industrial, financial and commercial policies expanded profitable opportunities outside agriculture and lowered the relative attractiveness of farming. These policies continued to detract from agriculture until 1988, when a severe economic retrenchment slowed growth in off-farm opportunities.

From agriculture's standpoint, one of the most important non-agricultural policies was the decision to relax restrictions on private rural business. Restrictions on private business had been eased gradually in the late 1970s and early 1980s, but in 1983 private business was for the first time officially condoned.[31] In 1984, rural residents were further permitted to move to small towns to set up private businesses.[32] Individuals from the countryside could now engage in urban–rural transport, set up stalls or stores in towns, and hire employees or apprentices. The attitude underlying these measures was expressed in a speech by Wan Li in December, 1984:[33]

> [Some people's] conceptual understanding of rural enterprise is incomplete. They only consider the mass-run, collectively-owned enterprises of the original townships, villages and teams to be rural enterprise, and they do not count the more recently established businesses that farmers run themselves or using pooled funds. Some people go so far as to look down on such businesses. This is incorrect . . . People should treat them equally and without discrimination, give them encouragement and support.

More generally, at this time the government implemented a range of measures to encourage the development of industry and services in the countryside. The rationale for these measures was explained in the 1984 No. 1 Document, which states that in the process of rural development more and more people must necessarily leave the land to enter into small industry and services. With these considerations in mind, in 1984/5 the government allowed, and, furthermore, mandated rural credit cooperatives to provide credit for rural industrial and commercial enterprises. Previously, the rural credit cooperatives, which were the major credit institutions at the village level and the only formal source of agricultural credit for farm households, had issued loans primarily for agricultural production. Available statistics show the resulting diversion of credit from agricultural to non-agricultural borrowers. By 1985, of total loans by rural credit cooperatives, 45 per cent went to township enterprises and household-run industry and services, and only 36 per cent went to agriculture. In 1986, the share of non-agricultural loans had risen to 51 per cent of the total, while the share going to agriculture had fallen to only 33 per cent.[34]

The diversion of funds from agriculture was further facilitated by policies on fund raising outside bank channels. At this time, rural businesses were granted permission to raise funds by selling bonds and shares. Thus rural residents who did not themselves set up businesses were given a means of investing in industry rather than agriculture.[35]

Christine Wong describes how such measures, combined with a general wave of credit expansion in 1984–5, benefited both private and collective rural enterprises. In 1984, bank credit to township and village enterprises more than doubled to 47.5 billion yuan; in 1985, net borrowings by these enterprises increased by an additional 27.8 billion yuan.[36] Growth of private rural business was phenomenal, especially in 1985: their number rose from 4.2 million in 1983 to 4.4 million in 1984, and then more than doubled to 10.7 million in 1985. By 1985 employment in rural private businesses surpassed 28 million.[37] Total employment in rural enterprises, both private and collective, increased from about 50 million in 1984 to 95 million in 1988 (Table 6.7), and by 1988 rural enterprises employed almost one-quarter of the rural labour force.

During these years, other reforms in industrial and commercial policies also detracted from agriculture. In 1983, the central government began to permit the sale of manufactured products at market prices. Extra-plan marketing of important farm inputs began in 1983 when the State Council allowed the sale of imported fertilisers at higher prices. In mid-1984, supply and marketing cooperatives and other local suppliers were permitted to purchase farm inputs independently and to sell the inputs at prices that reflected their purchase and handling costs. Fertilisers, pesticides and fuel were now increasingly sold at market prices. Since market prices were higher than state list prices, the liberalisation of commercial policies raised the cost to farmers of additional farm inputs. By 1985, chemical fertiliser prices were 43 per cent, pesticide prices 83 per cent and farm machinery prices 92 per cent higher than in 1983, and the prices of diesel fuel, electricity and water had all doubled.[38]

Although it began later, inflation further contributed to the deterioration in agriculture's status. Fiscal and monetary actions caused

TABLE 6.7   Statistics on the development of rural township and village enterprises

		Employees	
	Number of enterprises (1000s)	Number (1000s)	Per cent of rural labour force
1984	6 065	52 081	14.5
1985	12 225	69 790	18.8
1986	15 153	79 371	20.9
1987	17 446	87 764	22.5
1988	18 882	95 455	23.8
1989	18 686	93 686	22.9

Source: State Statistical Bureau (1990a) pp. 113, 399–400.

large budgetary deficits, rapid growth in the money supply, and unprecedented inflation in 1987–8. This inflation had several disadvantages for agriculture. First, as mentioned above, inflation outpaced increases in state contract procurement prices. As the differential between market and state prices for farm products grew, farmers became increasingly unwilling to sign or fulfil delivery contracts to the state. Local governments, which were responsible for ensuring contract fulfilment, responded by restricting free market trade of major farm products. Not surprisingly, such actions only increased the relative attractiveness of the many off-farm activities not subject to price and market interventions. Second, inflation exacerbated increases in the cost of farm inputs. In 1986/7 market prices for urea were 20 to 50 per cent higher, and by 1988/9 more than double state list prices.[39] Thus inflation prolonged the outflow of resources from agriculture.

The austerity programme that began in late 1988 reversed some of the policies discussed above. In order to stem inflation, the government severely restricted credit. Inflation slowed, and market prices began to level off. This permitted increases in contract prices to reduce, although not eliminate, the gap between planned and market prices.

One consequence of the economic retrenchment was slower growth in rural industry. Rural enterprises were denied new credit and expected to raise funds internally. Supplies of raw materials and energy were tightened. The government hoped that a large number of township enterprises would either go bankrupt, become accessories to state-run urban firms, or shift to production based on local resources. Private business was a particular target: the government announced in August 1989 a nationwide campaign to inspect private firms for tax evasion and illegal activities and called for the closing of a large number of private businesses. Official statistics reflect the effects of these measures. After growing at rates of 10 per cent or more per annum, in 1989 the number of rural township and village enterprises and the number of their employees both declined in absolute terms (Table 6.7). By dimming the prospects for rural industry, then, the retrenchment also certainly enhanced agriculture's relative standing: rural industry's loss was agriculture's gain.

6.6 FOREIGN TRADE AND TRADE POLICIES

China's foreign trade in agricultural products has undergone considerable change during the 1980s. This change in part reflects the consequences of the domestic policies discussed above and in part has been due to the reform of China's foreign trade policies. The reforms, however, have not lowered trade barriers sufficiently to generate substantial structural change in agricultural production. The central government continues to monopolise foreign trade in major farm products, and so domestic agriculture remains fairly insulated from international market trends.

Prior to 1980, China's international trade was highly centralised subject to plan, and carried out by state-owned foreign trade corporations under what is now the Ministry of Foreign Relations and Trade.[40] During the 1980s, the central government granted to lower levels of government and designated enterprises the authority to engage in trade directly. These lower-level participants were also permitted to retain a portion of the foreign exchange earnings from the products they exported directly or indirectly through the central foreign trade corporations. Within certain limits they could use this foreign exchange to import products of their choosing.

Although these reforms have to some extent applied to the trade of agricultural products, certain aspects of agricultural trade have not been decentralised. In particular, the central government has maintained its monopoly over the trade of key farm products. For example, exports of rice, soybeans and cotton, and imports of wheat and corn are still subject to monopoly by the national foreign trade corporations.

The trade reforms contributed to unprecedented growth in China's foreign trade. During the 1980s, the total value of China's commodity trade (imports plus exports) tripled; by 1989, the value of commodity trade was equivalent to 26 per cent of China's GNP.[41] Agricultural trade, shown in Table 6.8, also grew rapidly. Between 1983 and 1989 agricultural exports more than doubled, and imports almost doubled. (Data for agricultural trade are only available since 1983.) Agricultural trade continues to be an important component of total trade, accounting for about 20 per cent of total exports and 10 per cent of total imports.

Decentralisation has promoted the growth and diversification of trade; it has also led to unprecedented balance of trade deficits and somewhat irrational composition of trade. These problems stem from the fact that lower-level actors have faced distorted incentives. Despite devaluations in recent years, during the 1980s the exchange rate was overvalued. This encouraged imports and discouraged exports. Furthermore, price planning and other policies maintained a domestic

TABLE 6.8 China's agricultural trade (millions US dollars)

	Exports	Per cent of total exports	Imports	Per cent of total imports	Trade balance		Imports of fertiliser and pesticides
					Total	Agriculture	
1983	4,552	20.5	3,906	18.3	840	646	1,914
1984	5,233	20.0	2,753	10.0	−1,270	2,480	1,607
1985	6,280	23.0	2,446	5.8	−14,900	3,834	753
1986	7,116	23.0	2,737	6.4	−11,970	4,379	1,455
1987	8,027	20.4	3,888	9.0	−3,770	4,139	2,492
1988	9,457	19.9	5,828	10.5	−7,750	3,629	2,560
1989	9,702	18.5	6,705	11.3	−6,600	2,997	

Notes:

1. These statistics are compiled by China Customs Administration.
2. China's agricultural trade is calculated as the sum of SITC categories 0, 1, 21, 22, 26, 29 and 4.

Sources: US Department of Agriculture Economic Research Service (1990) pp. 23, 58; State Statistical Bureau (1986) p. 573; (1988) p. 731; (1990a) p. 641.

price structure that had undervalued raw materials and farm products and overvalued industrial products relative to world prices. Consequently, lower-level participants have had incentives to import manufactured goods and export farm and other unprocessed products. Prior to the reforms when trade was highly centralised, these incentives were not operative; with decentralisation, however, they have affected the level and composition of trade.

In view of the foreign exchange rate and domestic price structure, and the government's continued monopoly on wheat imports (which constitute the largest single agriculture import item), the surplus in China's agricultural trade is not terribly surprising. During the 1980s, agricultural exports grew more rapidly than imports, and the agricultural trade surplus expanded (Table 6.8). Since one objective of China's agricultural trade policy has been to earn foreign exchange to pay for imports of advanced technology and equipment, the trade policies appear to have achieved a certain success.

Yet two considerations diminish this success. First, although China's net trade in agricultural products continues to show a surplus, that surplus has been offset by substantial outlays on imports of chemical fertilisers and pesticides. On average during the 1980s, fertiliser and pesticide imports consumed 85 per cent of the agricultural trade surplus (Table 6.8).

The high level of farm chemical imports raises questions about the economic rationality of China's agricultural trade pattern. In principle, at the margin an extra dollar of fertiliser should be imported only if it generates additional farm output sufficient to reduce farm imports by at least a dollar. If this is not the case, China could benefit from reducing fertiliser imports and becoming less self-sufficient in farm products. Second, given her limited land area and large population, China should probably be a net importer rather than net exporter of farm products. To the extent that China does export agricultural products, they should be less land-intensive, higher-value items. Exports have in fact diversified in this direction: the importance of fresh and processed vegetables, fruit and meats in China's exports rose during the 1980s.

Historically, the Chinese government has used imports and exports to balance the domestic supply and demand for major farm products. This aspect of trade policy has continued during the reform period. Consequently, the domestic policies discussed above have, by affecting the level of farm production, influenced levels of trade. The effects of domestic policies on trade have been especially visible for grain and cotton, which together constitute about 60 per cent of China's agricultural imports.[42] In the early 1980s, rapid growth in the production of these products contributed to a substantial decline in agricultural imports. Meanwhile, exports continued to grow, so that the agricultural trade surplus rose nearly sixfold between 1983 and 1985. The agricultural slowdown in the late 1980s, combined with rising international prices for wheat, reversed these trends. China's large size and underdeveloped transportation system also caused regional imbalances between supply and demand. Provinces in the North-East produce surplus corn, while provinces in the South-East and South produce pigs and are short of inexpensive feed grains. The North-East exports corn; the South and South-East import corn.

6.7 CONCLUSION

During the 1980s China's leaders demonstrated an unprecedented willingness to relinquish direct control over agriculture. Central policies abolished mandatory production planning and reduced the scope of mandatory procurement quotas. Price and incentive measures became important policy tools. Restrictions on private domestic trade were relaxed, and markets were permitted to play a larger role in resource allocation. These initiatives contributed to a period of dynamic growth in the early 1980s.

Agriculture's fortunes reversed in the mid-1980s. Planned prices and incentives for farm products were reduced and market prices began to fall. Commercial reforms permitted extra-plan sale of farm inputs at high and rising prices. The government condoned the establishment of private rural businesses and adopted credit policies that diverted funds from farming to non-agricultural activities. Together, these measures caused resources to flow out from agriculture. Growth in farm, and especially crop, production slowed dramatically. This reversal was reflected in rising imports of farm products and a declining surplus in the balance of China's agricultural trade.

Steps taken in the ensuing years did little to bolster agricultural performance. Both the central and local governments increased controls over cultivation and restricted market trade in major farm products. Policies raising planning prices and material incentives were not implemented fully. Inflation increased the relative attractiveness of activities subject to fewer restrictions and of products that could be sold at market prices. Only with the austerity programme in 1989 and 1990 did agriculture's relative standing begin to improve.

Thus agriculture's slowdown in 1985 and stagnation in ensuing years can be explained largely as the result of certain domestic policies enacted in the mid-1980s. Other factors – the exhaustion of one-time gains from decollectivisation, declining and uneconomically distributed land area, uncertain land rights, and insufficient farm investment – may have contributed to the slowdown, but several considerations suggest that they were only secondary causes. First, none of these factors explains why agricultural performance declined so abruptly in 1985. Second, evidence from studies of other countries does not support the conclusion that small farms are inefficient. Third, rural residents were apparently willing to invest heavily in private non-agricultural businesses despite the fact that such activities also had uncertain prospects and little legal protection.

If the slowdown was largely the result of policies implemented in the mid-1980s, what implications can be drawn for farm policy in the 1990s? First and foremost, these findings imply that the slowdown was not inevitable, and that under certain policies agricultural growth is sustainable. Some might conclude further that government policies should sustain agricultural growth by discouraging or restricting the development of competing non-agricultural activities in rural areas. This conclusion is incorrect. Economists have long recognised that the development of non-agricultural sectors, and the flow of resources from agriculture to those sectors, is a key part of the development process. Yet resources should flow in both directions: as non-agricultural demand for labour and farm products expands, farm prices and incomes should rise. Higher prices for agricultural products draw labour and investment funds back into agriculture, and growth in farm incomes causes rural demand for both farm and industrial goods to increase.

Unfortunately, Chinese government policies, especially the planned procurement and distribution of farm products, discourage resources from flowing back to agriculture. In order to ensure deliveries at planned prices, the government prevents farmers from producing the most profitable crops and from selling their products to the highest bidder. When market prices for farm products begin to rise, a necessary precondition for the reversal of the resource outflow, the government imposes price ceilings and blocks market trade. Such actions discourage farm production and cause imbalance in the development process.

Macroeconomic policy has contributed to agriculture's unequal standing. During the 1980s, the Chinese government experienced persistent budgetary deficits. These deficits caused inflation, which, since farm prices were controlled, discouraged agricultural production and investment. Agricultural price subsidies contributed to those deficits. The central government's concern about the state budget and its desire to provide low-priced rations to the urban population have made it reluctant to raise agricultural prices and incentives. Thus the combination of budgetary pressures and urban bias have led to the continued undervaluation of agriculture. Budgetary considerations have also caused local governments to act in ways detrimental to agriculture. Local governments bear part of the financial burden of price and incentive programmes, and this reduces their willingness to carry out central directives to raise prices. So long as prices and incentives are closely linked with government finances, budgetary considerations will continue to interfere with the making of farm policy.

The effects of non-agricultural concerns on agriculture highlights the close connection between agriculture and other sectors of the economy. Non-agricultural development both competes with and complements agricultural growth. Non-agricultural policies can reinforce or detract from agricultural programmes. Effective agricultural policy in the 1990s will thus require a broad view, attention to policy coordination, and a true willingness to put agriculture on an equal footing.

7   Macroeconomics and the Agricultural Sector

P. MIDMORE and D. A. PEEL

7.1   INTRODUCTION

The study of macroeconomic linkages with the agricultural sector has become firmly established over the past two decades. Of course, agricultural economists have never been entirely parochial in their interests: real variables, as a matter of course, have always been used as explanatory variables in sectoral modelling (such as gross domestic product in demand functions, interest rates in cost functions and the valuation of farm assets). Occasionally, though, the range of interest has been more to do with macroeconomic issues themselves: in the 1960s, for example, concern with the macro issue of the balance of payments problem in the UK led to debate on the import saving role of agriculture (summarised, for example, by Hill and Ingersent, 1977, pp. 176–80); earlier, in the input–output paradigm, there had been interest in interindustry linkages (see Fox, 1963).[1]

Macroeconomic understanding is now more centrally important to the serious student, however, principally because of changed conditions in the arena of world trade. The abandonment of fixed exchange rates in 1973, and the consequent move to flexibility of interest rates combined with widespread abolition of financial controls, have facilitated the increased mobility of international capital investment. Capital flows have thus gained considerably in influence over the determination of exchange rates, relative to real trade and production conditions: the latter are crucially determined by fiscal and monetary policies. On the theoretical side, the development of the Rational Expectations approach, and the associated Efficient Markets Hypothesis has revolutionised the way in which macroeconomists think; these have filtered through into the agricultural economics discipline, and their part in the modern understanding of macro linkages with the sector is of considerable importance.

A useful point of departure of any discussion of macroeconomic linkages and agriculture is Schuh's (1974) article on the exchange rate and agriculture. This seminal contribution was sufficient, in the considerable volume of literature which it prompted, to identify the exchange rate as the mechanism which transmitted changes in fiscal and monetary policy to agriculture. We cannot hope to describe in detail the development of these insights: rather, we will attempt to develop a theoretical model which demonstrates the current state of thinking, and then briefly review some of the (supporting or otherwise) empirical evidence.

The chapter is organised as follows: the following section examines agriculture in the context of international macroeconomic events. In section 7.3 we attempt a brief synopsis of both the rational expectations hypothesis and the closely related efficient markets hypothesis. Subsequently, in section 7.4 we examine the model of 'overshooting' which has attracted so much attention recently. Because many international commodity prices are denominated in US dollars, the macroeconomic policies of the USA have external implications for agricultural prices in other countries. Section 7.5 briefly explores these implications for the European Community and for developing countries. Finally, section 7.6 provides our assessment of the relevance and validity of the most recent developments in thinking on these issues.

7.2 EXCHANGE RATES AND AGRICULTURE

Essentially prior to 1973, nominal exchange rates were fixed for long periods of time, and realignment occurred only in cases of severe external imbalance. Under normal circumstances, disciplined monetary and fiscal policies were expected to maintain parity: a balance of payments deficit which occurred if domestic inflation exceeded the external rate had to be dealt with by contractionary policies, and currency devaluation was reserved only for extreme cases of macro-economic imbalance. However, this reckoned without the reserve currency status of the US dollar, effectively the unit of account for international transactions, and the standard of measurement for other currencies. Thus the USA was able to run a current account deficit almost without exception in the years from 1950 to 1971: as a result, domestic inflation occurred, bringing about an increase in the real value of its (nominally fixed) exchange rate.

During this period, farm incomes in the United States had been under considerable pressure. The conventional explanation for this, throughout the period, was that rapid productivity increase in the face of sluggish demand, combined with immobile production factors, had caused falling prices. Schuh's originally contentious assertion (stated more comprehensively in 1976) was that part at least of the reduction in agricultural commodity prices over this period came about because of an effective export tax on the sector. In order to sustain internal balance, real interest rates were higher than they otherwise would have been, imposing a further squeeze on the capital-intensive agricultural sector. Consequently, agricultural resources were undervalued as a result of overvaluation of the dollar. Schuh also asserted that financial stress induces technical change, rather than the other way around. Price support, which effectively substituted for export demand in the earlier part of this period, led to accumulating surpluses: the change to an urban-oriented Democratic administration in 1964 shifted the emphasis of policy towards set-aside and export subsidies, most notably through the food aid programme. Artificial land scarcity further influenced the course of technical change.

Thus, from Schuh's initial contributions, the idea that inappropriate macropolicies prompt real changes in subsectors of the economy took root. Since 1973, of course, the dollar exchange rate has been at least nominally flexible, though the monetary authorities have intervened, heavily at times, to influence the level of exchange rate. At first there was considerable depreciation and domestic inflation, coinciding with a boom in agriculture, and rising real land values (see Feldstein, 1980, for an empirical treatment of this phenomenon).[2] The era of 'Reaganomics', on the other hand, reversed the dollar's decline, the result of a growing budget deficit combined with tight monetary policies. High interest rates attracted large foreign capital inflows, and it was during this period that agricultural exports again fell back, farmland values declined, and, because of the high interest component of farm costs, incomes also declined. These issues are treated more extensively in Schuh and Orden (1988), and Schuh (1989) where it is concluded that 'macroeconomic policies have an important effect on the agricultural sector . . . [and] . . . an important vehicle for that effect is the changes that are brought about in the value of the US dollar' (p. 537).

How rapidly markets adjust, and whether different markets adjust at different speeds, are crucial to the understanding of the short-run real effects which can occur in the agricultural sector as a result of monetary and fiscal policy changes. Before exploring these ideas further, it is necessary to set out some of the principles which have become of considerable recent importance in macroeconomic theory.

7.3   THE 'MODERN' APPROACH TO MACROECONOMICS

In the last few years it has become increasingly standard in macroeconomics to formulate aggregate hypotheses which have explicit microeconomic foundations. It is argued that macroeconomic models built upon such foundations may avoid inconsistencies and therefore provide a better understanding of the real world (see Barro, 1990). The microfoundations are agents, households or firms which maximise or minimise their utility or objective functions subject to the appropriate intertemporal budget constraint. Models with such microfoundations generate a key result. Current decisions by agents will in part be determined by the path of future variables (see Sargent, 1978). Because these agents will in general not have perfect information, optimal decisions therefore involve them in forming expectations of future outcomes. Here we examine two hypotheses which have become integral to the modern approach to macroeconomics, and underlie the model developed in the next section.

7.3.1   The rational expectations hypothesis

One question that immediately arises is how in aggregate should expectations be modelled. The prevalent model now employed is to assume that agents form their expectations rationally. This concept was formulated by Muth (1961) in the context of a model of agricultural supply. The essential idea of Muth is that expectations are informed predictions of future events, and are the same as the predictions of the relevant and correct economic theory. In other words, expectations are formed as if agents understood economic theory and processed all available information within the structure of the correct economic model. There are many good texts available which spell out in detail some of the macroeconomic implications, and empirical evidence, on the hypothesis (see Begg, 1982; Minford and Peel, 1983; Sheffrin, 1983; Holden, Peel and Thompson,1985). For our purposes in this chapter, it is sufficient to set out two of the properties of the hypothesis.

The first property of rational expectations is that since they correctly embody all publicly available information available at the time expectations are formed, the actual outcome (Y_{t+1}) minus the expected outcome $(E_t Y_{t+1})$ is equal to (u_{t+1}), an unpredictable (random) error.[3]

$$Y_{t+1} - E_t Y_{t+1} = u_{t+1} \qquad (7.1)$$

where Y_{t+1} is the outcome of a variable at time $t + 1$, $E_t Y_{t+1}$ is the expectation of Y_{t+1} based on information available at t.

This property is known as unbiasedness. We note immediately from (7.1) that rational expectations are not perfect forecasts. This will in general be the case due to the unpredictable element (u_{t+1}). We also note that rational expectations do not necessarily have a high correlation with the outcome. This will depend on how noisy is the environment (variance of u_{t+1}) in which expectations are being formed. The assumption of rational expectations does imply, however, that expectations will be correct on average (since u_{t+1} has an average value of zero). In addition, since rational expectations are based on the correct model the error will have the smallest variance of all available aggregate forecasts.

A second property possessed by rational expectations is that expectations of future outcomes formed at different times, or on the basis of the different information sets, should be consistent with each other. This implies that they should only differ by new information, which is by definition unpredictable, and hence implies they differ only by a random error. Another way of stating this property is that if expectations are rational, the expectation formed at a date (say, $t-1$) of the future expectation of an outcome (say, $E_t Y_{t+1}$) can be expressed as $E_{t-1}[E_t Y_{t+1}]$. For example, the rational expectation formed on Monday of the expectation formed on Tuesday of the price of sheep on Friday will be Monday's expectation. We can set this out formally in the following way.

For consistency we require (for example):

$$E_{t-1}[E_t Y_{t+1}] = E_{t-1} Y_{t+1} \qquad (7.2)$$

and

$$E_t Y_{t+1} - E_{t-1} Y_{t+1} = \text{a random error} \qquad (7.3)$$

This property of rational expectations, as we shall see later, underpins Samuelson's famous demonstration that, under certain assumptions, futures prices for commodities would exhibit the properties of a random walk (i.e. changes in the futures prices are random).

There is one other important characteristic that economic models will, in general, possess if expectations are formed rationally. This is that the evolution of all endogenous variables within such models will depend on expectations of all future values of exogenous variables, including policy-determined parameters such as tax or subsidy rates. Current behaviour implicitly depends on the current policy parameters as well as expectations of their future values.

Before considering in detail some of the implications for agricultural economics of models embodying rational expectations, it is important to note that the microeconomic assumption of rational optimising agents, which equate the marginal costs and benefits of processing and interpreting information for the purposes of improved forecasts, does not necessarily imply that expectations in aggregate are formed rationally. In particular, the optimising assumption does not imply that the representative agent has knowledge of the true structure of the economy (Figlewski, 1978; and Frydman and Phelps, 1983, develop these and other points). Notwithstanding this important point, rational expectations is now the standard method employed by macroeconomists to model expectations. Perhaps the major rationale for this is that its properties (e.g. unbiasedness and consistency) are, *a priori*, more appealing than those generally implied by mechanistic alternatives given that so much informed opinion is available to the microagents at essentially negligible marginal cost (for instance, public forecasts of major agencies, ready access to economists). Consequently, even though 'the true nature' of the scheme generating expectations in aggregate may defy easy description, the rational expectations method is the theoretical construct which currently most readily encapsulates the idea that aggregate expectations incorporate publicly available information.

Even though Muth employed an example based on agricultural economics to illustrate the concept of rational expectations, until quite recently it was standard to model expectations in models of agricultural supply in an adaptive manner (see Askari and Cummings, 1977, who list over five hundred studies), even though adaptive expectations are not in general rational expectations

The popularity of the adaptive expectations assumption was probably based in part on the fact that models embodying it were able to generate stable cyclical fluctuations in agricultural prices that are a stylised feature of agricultural markets (see Nerlove, 1958). It is useful to set out Muth's original model, which illustrates the concept of rational expectations and also how an agricultural model embodying rational expectations can also readily exhibit fluctuations in price.

We write the model as follows (all means are put to zero for simplicity):

$$q_t^d = -\beta P_t \tag{7.4}$$

$$q_t^s = \gamma E_{t-1}(P_t) + u_t \tag{7.5}$$

$$I_t = \alpha(E_t[P_{t+1} - P_t]) \tag{7.6}$$

$$q_t^d + kI_t = q_t^s + kI_t - 1 \tag{7.7}$$

where q_t^d and q_t^s are quantity demanded and supplied, respectively; P_t is price; E is the expectations operator; k, β, γ, and α are constants; I_t is a speculative inventory; and u_t is an error process.

In this model we assume that storage of a commodity is possible, and that storage, transactions costs and interest rates are negligible. Consequently, a speculative inventory exists which depends on the anticipated capital gain from holding the stock. The parameter, α, which measures the response of inventory demands to expected price changes is a function of the degree of risk aversion and the conditional variance of prices in Muth's exposition (also see Turnovsky, 1983).

Because storage can occur, equilibrium does not require that current production (supply) equals current consumption demand. Equation (7.7) represents the market equilibrium condition. A parameter k is introduced for analytical convenience: if storage occurs it is equal to unity; otherwise if we set $k = 0$ and $\alpha = 0$, we have the standard, no storage, market clearing model.

Substitution of equations (7.4), (7.5) and (7.6) into (7.7) yields the reduced form:

$$-\beta P_t + k\alpha(E_t[P_{t+1} - P_t]) = \gamma E_{t-1}P_t + u_t \\ + k\alpha(E_{t-1}[P_t - P_{t-1}]) \tag{7.8}$$

Assume initially that u_t is random or white noise.

One method of solving (7.8) involves guessing the general solution (see McCallum, 1980), substituting back into the equation and calculating the restriction on the coefficients.

If we let

$$P_t = \pi P_{t-1} + \pi_1 u_t \quad (k = 1) \tag{7.9}$$

where π, π_1 are constants, (so that $E_{t-1}P_t = \pi P_{t-1}$, $E_t P_{t+1} = \pi P_t$), we find by substitution that this will be a rational solution to (7.8).[4]

If

$$\pi_1 = \frac{1}{\alpha\pi - (\alpha + \beta)}$$

and $\tag{7.10}$

$$\pi = 1 + \frac{1}{2}\left(\frac{\beta}{\alpha} + \frac{\gamma}{\alpha}\right) - \frac{1}{2}\sqrt{\left(2 + \frac{\beta}{\alpha} + \frac{\gamma}{\alpha}\right)^2 - 4}$$

with $0 < \pi < 1$

the price solution (7.9) for this model is of great interest. Price does not fluctuate randomly around its mean even when u_t, a variable which can represent all exogenous influences, is random. The reason for this is that inventories can smooth out the effects of disturbances (shocks) to demand or supply. Consider, for instance, an abnormally good harvest due to exceedingly favourable weather. In a market without storage, the additional supply will all be absorbed into the market in the current period. However, with an inventory demand, speculators will buy up some of the harvest, since the price in the future will *ceteris paribus* be expected to be higher than today, as weather returns to its normal expected value. This procedure will generally dampen price fluctuations. In addition, the shock in the current period will have impact in future periods which in this context is another way of stating that price movements will exhibit serial correlation.

Equation (7.10) also leads to another insight, as pointed out by Muth. As the importance of inventory speculative demands dominate a market relative to flow demands or supplies (as is likely over short periods of time) and consequently α becomes large relative to β or γ, then we see from (7.10) that π will become close to one. Consequently, price will approximately follow a random walk. This is an empirical feature often noted in price series for storable commodities for high frequency data (see Kendall, 1953). We also note that in this model rational price expectations are a fixed multiple of last period's price, though the coefficient is a function of the parameters of the model. In general, rational price expectations will be a function of lagged prices, though not in the mechanistic fixed fashion implied by use of an adaptive expectations model. Muth, however, did use a special case of the above model to illustrate how adaptive expectations scheme could be rational. If we let $k = 0$ and $\alpha = 0$ we obtain the reduced form of the market clearing model given by

$$-\beta P_t = \gamma E_{t-1} P_t + u_t \qquad (7.11)$$

it is useful to write

$$u_t = \rho u_{t-1} + \varepsilon_t \qquad (7.12)$$

so that $-(\beta + \gamma) E_{t-1} P_t = \rho u_{t-1}$ which yields two interesting polar cases: either $\rho = 0$ (the disturbance term is primarily due to the weather); or $\rho = 1$ (price follows a random walk). Let us suppose the random disturbance term is described by a random walk (see Holden, Peel and Thompson, 1991, for a rationale for such modelling); taking rational expectations of (7.11), after substitution from (7.12) we obtain:

$$-(\beta + \gamma) E_{t-1} P_t = u_{t-1} \qquad (7.13)$$

If we lag (7.11) one period and substitute for u_{t-1}, from (7.13) we obtain

$$-\beta P_{t-1} = \gamma E_{t-2} P_{t-1} - (\beta + \gamma) E_{t-1} P_t \qquad (7.14)$$

If we add $\beta E_{t-2} P_{t-1}$ to both sides and rearrange, we obtain

$$(E_{t-1} P_t - E_{t-2} P_{t-1}) = \left(\frac{\beta}{\beta + \gamma}\right) (P_{t-1} - E_{t-2} P_{t-1}) \qquad (7.15)$$

Equation (7.15) will be recognised as the model of adaptive expectations. Of course, in order for 'mechanistic' adaptive expectations to be rational in this model, the coefficients of adaptation must be related to the demand and supply parameters, β and γ. We should also note that if an error structure, such as (7.12), is introduced into the storage model, then cyclical patterns of prices are possible. The Muthian model is of great interest since it demonstrates how all the stylised outcomes in agricultural markets, generated by assuming naive behaviour, can be readily generated if rational expectations are assumed.

Before we examine a model, including this assumption, of macro-economic behaviour which has particular implications for agricultural prices, it is useful to outline another hypothesis, related to rational expectations, which has been employed in the finance literature for many years.

7.3.2 The efficient market hypothesis

The essential underpinning of the efficient market hypothesis is that in asset markets such as exchange markets, futures markets, stock markets or bond markets, information is processed by the market efficiently. There have been many theoretical developments over the last decade or so (see Ball, 1989 for a good survey); nevertheless, the standard approach to efficient market modelling is based on a typology outlined by Fama (1970), who defined an asset market to be efficient when market prices fully and instantaneously reflect all available relevant information. Three types of market efficiency are distinguished, according to the extent of the information reflected in the market. A market is weak-form efficient if it is not possible for a trader to make abnormal returns by developing a trading rule based on the past history of prices or returns. For example, if a market is weak-form efficient, the analysis of the past history of sugar prices will not enable one to discover a pattern from which one can be able to predict sugar prices in order to make systematic abnormal profits. A market is defined to be semi-strong efficient if a trader cannot make abnormal returns using a trading rule based on publicly available information. Examples of publicly available information are past money supply data, weather reports and analysis in the farming press. A market is defined to be strong-form efficient when a trader cannot make abnormal returns using a trading rule based on any information source, whether public or private.

These three forms of efficiency represent a crude partitioning of all possible information systems, the precise boundaries of which are not easily defined. However, they have proved useful for classifying empirical research on market efficiency. As their names suggest, strong form efficiency implies semi-strong efficiency which in turn implies weak form.

We note immediately that the semi-strong form of efficient markets, i.e. that based on publicly available information, is an application of the concept of rational expectations, though this was not stressed in the early literature on efficiency which predates that of rational expectations. If expectations are non-rational, then publicly available information will not be reflected in asset prices which will give rise to systematic abnormal profits opportunities. In other words, the 'market' has to behave as if it knew the model governing prices in order to eliminate abnormal expected returns; if the model governing expected prices is different from that governing actual prices, there will be systematic abnormal returns available in the market.

One problem which researchers face in implementing empirical tests of market efficiency is defining what constitutes the normal rate of return (since this is required if the empirical test is to operationalise the abnormal returns part of the market efficiency definitions). This is a central topic in modern portfolio theory, and the interested reader is directed to, for example, Copeland and Weston (1983) for a full discussion. Risk averse traders will require a risk premium (see Copeland, 1989) on each asset; this premium will be included in the equilibrium expected rate of return as well as the rate of return on a safe asset (e.g. treasury bills). Tests of market efficiency must be conducted after allowance for the equilibrium rate of return. If the riskiness of an asset does not change over time (or, conversely, if its risk changes randomly over time) then, for example, weak-form efficiency implies that there should be no extrapolative pattern in the time series of returns. If there were a recurring pattern of any type, traders who recognised the pattern would use it to make abnormal returns. Given the essentially costless nature of the information, the very effort to use such patterns would, under the efficiency hypothesis, lead to their elimination.

One immediate implication of the semi-strong efficiency of asset markets is that in the absence of a time varying risk premium, futures prices for commodities will exhibit the properties of a random walk. This was demonstrated by Samuelson (1965). Arbitrage funds will imply in an efficient market that the futures price for a commodity, say, will be set equal to the rational expectation of the spot price on the closing day of the contract.

Accordingly, let $F_{t,N}$ be the futures price at time t, for future 'delivery' of a commodity at time N. We can write this assumption

$$F_{t,N} = E_t\, P_{t+N} \tag{7.16}$$

Similarly, yesterday's futures prices for 'delivery' at N is given by

$$F_{t-1,N} = E_{t-1} P_{t+N} \qquad (7.17)$$

By the consistency property of rational expectations, $F_{t,N} - F_{t-1,N} = E_t P_{t+N} - E_{t-1} P_{t+N}$, where $P_{t+N} = $ a random variable.[5]

The random walk property of futures prices for commodities is an implication of rationally formed expectations in the absence of a time varying risk premium, which in turn might seem to imply that the analysis of an agricultural market with a storable commodity is essentially the same either with or without a futures market. In fact, matters are far less simple. Muth (1961), for instance, suggested that the parameter α would not necessarily be invariant to the introduction of a futures market. In particular, if a futures market led to less risk adverse traders entering the market, then α would increase – that is, inventories would become more responsive to changes in prices (also see Turnovsky, 1983; Bond, 1984). Cox (1976) argues that the introduction of a futures model may broaden the incentives for collation of information relevant to the formation of price expectations. In other words, the futures markets give speculators incentives to gather 'private' information in the pursuit of monetary gains. Clearly, if appropriate this assumption will have implications for the actual path of commodity prices in the model. These and other themes are explored in, for example, Newbery (1983), Newbery and Stiglitz (1983), and Williams (1987).

In the last decade or so there has been a great deal of work conducted on empirical testing of the efficiency of asset markets. It is probably fair to say that the early empirical work appeared supportive of weak and semi-strong efficiency (see Pesando, 1978; Sargent, 1972). More recently, a variety of empirical work has appeared which suggests that there may be systematic departures from efficiency (Guimaraes *et al.*, 1989). One interesting empirical finding is that the prices of assets appear excessively volatile, in the sense that the underlying assumed fundamental determinants (e.g. discounted expected future dividends for a stock price or the 'exogenous' variables of demand and supply in a commodity market) are less volatile than can explain the observed volatility of the price (see Shiller, 1981).

One explanation for excess volatility is that asset markets may be characterised by temporary 'rational' bubbles. Bubbles are a phenomenon which reflect self-reinforcing movements in price away from their fundamental equilibrium level. To give some illustration of this possibility, consider once again the rational expectations solution (7.9) to the Muthian storage model. This solution was based on the fundamentals in the model. Suppose, however, that we had conjectured a solution for prices of the form:

$$P_t = \pi P_{t-1} + \pi_1 u_t + B_t \qquad (7.18)$$

where B_t is an extraneous process – a bubble.

Substitution of (7.18) into the reduced form model (7.8) (with $k = 1$) and taking expectations of (7.18), we find it is indeed a valid solution of the model for a variety of B_t processes (try, for example, $B_{t,} = eB_{t-1}$ where e is a constant).

If the bubble is given a probabilistic structure, so we suppose there is a probability a bubble will last another period, it is possible to explain rational explosive bubbles. Agents will hold an overvalued asset if there is a finite probability of a capital gain. In fact, the greater the probability that an explosive bubble will burst, the faster the asset price must be expected to rise to compensate for holding it. In a non-probabilistic structure there is no obvious rationale for a rational explosive bubble since if traders know it will come to an end, no one would hold it in the last period and, working backwards, the period before it, and so on. There is as yet no good model to explain why bubbles, if they exist, start or end (see Sheffrin, 1983, for a good discussion of the issues, also Diba and Grossman, 1988). Of course, if bubbles do occur, then this would naturally need to be evaluated in any cost–benefit analysis of the introduction of futures markets in agricultural markets or other markets.

In general, the empirical analysis is broadly supportive of the hypothesis that asset markets are weak-form efficient. One potentially important exception to this is the empirical work reported in a series of papers by Taylor (1982; 1983), and Taylor and Tari (1989). Taylor examines the prices of a number of agricultural commodities which include cocoa, coffee and sugar. His trading rules are based on a careful and relatively sophisticated statistical analysis of the past patterns of commodity prices. His analyses are certainly suggestive that there is *prima facie* evidence of the possibility of abnormal returns. However, Taylor is careful to note that his models require many years of prices for appropriate calibration and, in addition, his allowance for any time varying risk premia may not be satisfactory (see also Garcia, *et al.*, 1988). In addition, we should stress (also see Ball, 1989) that Taylor is using sophisticated statistical methods which in part he developed. It might be appropriate to consider him as having private information, in which case, his findings are not at odds with the weak or semi-strong efficiency models. From this perspective of greater interest would be the empirical finding that abnormal returns can be made in these markets using the rules suggested by him, given that they are now part of the publicly available information set.

We will now outline a model which embodies both the notions of rational expectations and efficient markets, which has been proposed as an explanation of the instability or 'overshooting' of agricultural prices in response to macroeconomic policy shifts.

7.4 OVERSHOOTING OF AGRICULTURAL PRICES

The term 'overshooting' was first coined by Dornbusch (1976) to show how, even with perfect foresight and instantly adjusting asset markets, immediate exchange rate movements may exceed their long run expected change in response to a monetary shock. It depends critically on an assumption that some sectors of the economy are fixed price sectors which respond only slowly to changes in the money supply (the fixed-flex division derives from Hicks, 1974 and Okun, 1975). The long-run effect of a one-off increase in money supply is likely to be an equi-proportionate increase in the price level, and a fall in the nominal exchange rate which maintains its real level. Given that in the short run, however, prices do not immediately react, the real money supply is also increased, and to maintain money market equilibrium, *ceteris paribus* interest rates initially need to fall. The consequent capital outflow reduces exchange rates below their long-run equilibrium level. However, a falling interest rate is associated, from the need for asset market equilibrium (the covered interest arbitrage condition see Copeland, 1989) with an *appreciation* of the exchange rate. Additionally, the increase in money supply implies that in the long run the exchange rate must *depreciate* (Purchasing Power Parity – see Copeland, 1989, on this point also). The only way to reconcile these two competing factors is for the current exchange rate to depreciate further than its long run expected value – to 'overshoot' – in order to generate expectation of an appreciation on its path back to its new long-run equilibrium value.

The foreign exchange mechanism is a market like any other, and Frankel (1986) has shown that even in a closed economy, differential adjustment speeds will lead to overshooting of prices in flexible markets in response to an unanticipated change in monetary growth. Consider an economy in which there are two types of goods, commodities and manufactures. If commodity markets adjust perfectly to changed conditions, an arbitrage condition relates the interest rate to future prices, such that there are equal returns from holding commodities or treasury bills, taking into account storage costs and ignoring risk. Formally

$$i = \dot{p}_{c^e} - sc \tag{7.19}$$

where i is the short term interest rate, $\dot{p}_{c^e}$ the expected rate of change of the commodity price, and sc storage costs. In contrast, the rate of change in the price of manufactures, $\dot{p}_m$ responds by only a proportion of excess demand over and above the secular rate of inflation, μ. In log form,

$$\dot{p}_m = \pi(d - \bar{y}_m) + \mu \tag{7.20}$$

where d is demand for manufactures and $\bar{y}_m$ potential manufactures output. Excess demand is in turn related to the relative prices of commodities and manufactures, and the real rate of interest,

$$d - \bar{y}_m = \delta(p_c - p_m) - \sigma(i - \mu - \bar{r}) \tag{7.21}$$

where $\bar{r}$ is the long-run equilibrium interest rate. From (7.20) and (7.21), the rate of change in commodity prices is functionally related to the price ratio between commodities and real interest rates,

$$\dot{p}_c = \pi[\delta(p_c - p_m) - \sigma(i - \mu - \bar{r})] + \mu \tag{7.22}$$

In the long run where no excess demand exists, the price ratio between commodities and manufactures is stable and for convenience is normalised, so that the rate of change in commodity prices settles down to the rate of inflation. Turning to the money market, a conventional demand function is used (again in log form):

$$m - p = \phi y + \lambda i \tag{7.23}$$

m being the nominal money supply, y aggregate output, and p the aggregate price level. This is a weighted average of both types of goods,

$$p = \alpha p_m + (1 - \alpha)p_c \tag{7.24}$$

Combining (7.23) and (7.24),

$$m - \alpha p_m - (1 - \alpha)p_c = \phi y + \lambda i \tag{7.25}$$

In long-run equilibrium, money demand will settle down to

$$\bar{m} - \alpha \bar{p}_m - (1 - \alpha)\bar{p}_c = \phi y + \lambda i$$

$$= \phi y + \lambda(\bar{r} + \mu) \tag{7.26}$$

Subtracting (7.26) from (7.25), assuming output to be fixed and the long-term growth rate of the money supply to be constant, we have

$$\alpha(p_m - \bar{p}_m) + (1 - \alpha)(p_c - \bar{p}_c) = \lambda(i - \mu - \bar{r}) \tag{7.27}$$

which allows all the components of Frankel's model to be combined. With (7.19) and (7.27), the expected rate of commodity price change is obtained as

$$\dot{p}_{c^e} = \frac{\alpha}{\lambda}(p_m - \bar{p}_m) + \frac{(1 - \alpha)}{\lambda}(p_c - \bar{p}_c) + \mu + \bar{r} + sc \tag{7.28}$$

and from (7.22), (7.27) and the fact that the lognormal long-run ratio of prices between commodities and manufactures is zero,

$$\dot{p}_m = \pi\{\delta[(p_c - \bar{p}_c) - (p_m - \bar{p}_m)]$$
$$\quad - (\sigma/\lambda)[\alpha(p_m - \bar{p}_m) + (1 - \alpha)(p_c - \bar{p}_c)]\} + \mu$$

$$= -\pi[\delta + \sigma\alpha/\lambda](p_m - \bar{p}_m) + \pi[\delta - \sigma(1 - \alpha)/\lambda](p_c - \bar{p}_c) + \mu \tag{7.29}$$

If expectations are formed rationally, then $\dot{p}_c = \dot{p}_{c^e}$ and so the model is closed. In matrix form:

$$\begin{bmatrix} \dot{p}_m \\ \dot{p}_c \end{bmatrix} = \begin{bmatrix} -\pi(\delta + \sigma\alpha/\lambda) & \pi(\delta - \sigma(1 - \alpha)/\lambda) \\ \alpha/\lambda & (1 - \alpha)/\lambda \end{bmatrix} \cdot \begin{bmatrix} (p_m - \bar{p}_m) \\ (p_c - \dot{p}_c) \end{bmatrix}$$

$$+ \begin{bmatrix} \mu \\ \mu + \bar{r} + sc \end{bmatrix} \tag{7.30}$$

Solving for the eigenvalues of (7.30), Frankel provides a result for the rate of change of prices of the two commodities such that

$$\dot{p}_m = -\theta(p_m - \bar{p}_m) + \mu$$

$$\dot{p}_c = -\theta(p_c - \bar{p}_c) + \mu + \bar{r} + sc \qquad (7.31)$$

where $-\theta$ is the negative eigenvalue (rejecting the positive eigenvalue for the sake of stability). This establishes a simple regressive form in the rationally expected rate of change,[6] such that, combined with the arbitrage equation (7.19),

$$\dot{p}_c = \bar{p}_c - \frac{1}{\theta}(i - \mu - \bar{r}) \qquad (7.32)$$

Thus an expansion in the rate of growth of the money supply which lowers the interest rate below its long-run value $\bar{r}$ implies that commodity prices p_c will rise above their long-run equilibrium path $\bar{p}_c$. This overvaluation of commodities is necessary in order for the expected future decline to be offset by the lower interest rate. The persistence of the overvaluation depends on the value of θ, which in turn is directly related to π, the rate at which manufactures prices respond to excess demand; slow rates of adjustment lead to a lower value of θ, and a longer persistence of the overshooting of p_c in relation to $\bar{p}_c$.

The notion that flexible prices will react more in the short run to changes in macroeconomic policy if some prices in the economy adjust only slowly (whether these are commodity prices, as in Frankel's model, or exchange rates as in Dornbusch's original formulation) has been extensively investigated. In a specifically agricultural context, two main empirical approaches have been used: either the construction of a 'structural' model in which an attempt is made to specify each of the equations which link the macroeconomy with the sector, or a non-structural method in which a set of key endogenous agricultural variables are linked directly to changes in exogenous variables, exploiting statistical qualities in time series data which can be used to answer questions about relationships: for example, between commodity prices and the money stock.

In the former category, the interaction between the macroeconomy and agriculture has been treated in a variety of ways; for example Chen's (1977) model uses manual iteration to arrive at solutions for, on the one hand, the overall economy and, on the other, the agricultural sector. Rausser *et al.* (1986) use the alternative of a fully simultaneous model to investigate the effects of different types of macro policy on agriculture. Their conclusions, amongst others, were that tight and easy monetary regimes acted as implicit taxes and subsidies, respectively, for agricultural commodity prices; however, because floor prices are established for key commodities, some producers (e.g. of cereals) would be better off under restrictive monetary policies because they would achieve higher relative prices. In their view, this suggests that support mechanisms for agriculture need to be reassessed in the light of the impact of macroeconomic policies:

> If macroeconomic policies were appropriately designed, there would be no need for sector-specific polices to address this problem. Experience in controlling business cycles, however, suggests that this is not likely to occur soon. If the normative justification for government intervention is to reduce instability, then instability from outside the sector due to monetary and fiscal policy suggests that agricultural policies may be appropriate to insulate the sector. (Ibid., p. 411)

Given, however, that there is an asymmetry in the distribution of adjustment costs (when monetary control is light, higher prices benefit farmers; when it is more stringent the burden of lower prices falls on the public sector), there is an obvious need for more flexibility in policy response. In the United States context, price supports (loan rates) imply downward inflexibility of price once they reach the publicly determined floor, and there is an unexpected increase in the cost of monetary price supports and the level of CCC stocks.

However, though structural models increasingly build in overshooting as a feature of their specification (see Bosworth and Lawrence, 1988), there is by no means a consensus that it exists or that, if it does, it necessarily always occurs in all situations. Obstfeld (1986) has shown that, under a slightly different set of assumptions, the sweeping assertion that flexible prices overshoot when some prices are sticky in the short run is unwarranted. This is reflected in the mixed quality of support for overshooting in the non-structural modelling approaches. Gardner (1981), using US data from 1910 to 1978 to regress changes in farm price levels on various indicators (including the exchange rate, inflation, and perhaps more importantly, a proxy for unanticipated inflation) concluded that no linkage existed between macroeconomic policies and events in the agricultural sector. Whilst this result was confirmed by Grennes and Lapp (1986), the opposite conclusion was reached by Starleaf *et al.* (1985); agricultural prices, on their reckoning, were significantly more variable than changes in the general rate of inflation. More complex time series methods, such as Vector Auto-regression (VAR[7]) also yield equivocal results: amongst others, Bessler (1984) used a VAR analysis to relate agricultural commodity prices in Brazil to the money stock, and found no link; yet using the same method in the USA, Devadoss and Meyers (1987) demonstrated that agricultural prices responded more quickly to monetary shocks than those in other sectors. Robertson and Orden (1990) have used a Vector Error Correction (VER) approach to show that in New Zealand relative agricultural commodity prices respond in the short run to monetary shocks, even though the theory of long-run neutrality holds. Lapp (1990) investigated, in a specifically rational expectations context, the sensitivity of relative prices in the United States to monetary shocks (unanticipated changes in the growth of the money stock) using quarterly data from 1951 to 1985. Prior to 1973, only unexpected monetary growth had a positive impact on agricultural prices: 'The estimated effect is quantitatively small and does not explain an economically meaningful portion of the variation in the relative price of agricultural commodities' (ibid. p. 629).

As with so many other controversies in economics, the issue has become dominated by discussions concerning econometric evidence, and views also tend to be coloured by whether one leans towards either the new classical or the neo-Keynesian view of the way in which markets adjust to equilibrium. What is clear, however, is that since the dollar has been allowed to float, its exchange value against other currencies has been highly unstable (Krugman, 1989). Because world prices of agricultural commodities are denominated in US dollars, this has implications for the external trade of all other countries as well, and it is to this subject which we turn in the next section.

7.5   THE DOLLAR AND WORLD AGRICULTURAL MARKETS

An appreciating dollar raises the export price for countries outside the USA when it is expressed in their domestic terms; and, of course, vice versa. This, in turn affects world demand in the short run, so that, *ceteris paribus*, world prices expressed in dollars will respond inversely to movements in the dollar exchange rate.[8] The impact of this on different countries varies according to the degree of government intervention in agricultural markets, and the relative volume of agricultural commodity exports. Before concluding, we briefly discuss two of the more important cases: that of the European Community and that of developing countries which are predominantly primary commodity producers.

7.5.1 The case of the European Community

Discussion of exchange rate and monetary influences on the agricultural system in the EC is predominantly within the context of the complex tax-subsidy system which governs trade between member states. Before exchange rate flotation, common agricultural prices were set in terms of the European Monetary Unit, equivalent to the IMF's SDR. However, with floating exchange rates, prices set centrally in a common unit of account could fluctuate when translated into national currency terms; in 1973 the immediate effect of flotation was an appreciating Deutschmark relative to the French franc, reducing the relative institutional prices in Germany. This difficulty was overcome by the evolution of agricultural representative or 'green' exchange rates which were invariant with respect to market exchange rates; the difference between traded border prices occurring as a result of the latter has been compensated for by a system of taxes and subsidies known as monetary compensatory amounts (for further details, see Parris and Peters, 1983; or Beattie, 1988). Thus agricultural markets have been effectively internally insulated from movements in exchange rates; externally, exports to third countries have been subsidised by a system of export restitutions, which together with monetary compensatory amounts (whether positive or negative) have bridged the gap between the domestic and the world price. The magnitude of European Community surplus production is a potent political issue (Burrell, 1987), and one of the consequences of open-ended commitment to price support through intervention measures is that the size of the export restitution element has grown considerably: see the first and second columns of Table 7.1. This element of price support is also, obviously, crucially affected by the relative US dollar/ECU exchange rate; a weak dollar implies an increasing gap, in ECU terms, between the EC and world prices of products, and of course, vice versa.

Many popular commentators (e.g. *Agra Europe*, various issues) argue that it is the strength of the US dollar which has allowed the budget to remain within the restraint guidelines set for it by the summit

TABLE 7.1   The European agricultural budget and dollar/ECU exchange rate 1978–89

	Total EAGGF expenditure	Export refund expenditure	US$/ECU exchange rate
1978	8672.7	3749.6	1.274
1979	10440.7	4981.8	1.371
1980	11315.2	5695.0	1.319
1981	11141.1	5208.5	1.118
1982	12092.5	4764.2	0.981
1983	15919.7	5559.7	0.891
1984	18371.9	6619.1	0.790
1985	19707.0	6716.1	0.762
1986	22079.2	7409.2	0.981
1987	23176.0	9374.9	1.154
1988	27554.8	9929.0	1.183
1989	25840.0	9714.0	1.102

Sources: IMF (various issues); Commission of the European Communities (various issues).

meeting of Community leaders in 1986, rather than the stabiliser mechanisms and other output-limiting controls which have been subsequently imposed. Supporting evidence for this is provided by the third column of Table 7.1, which juxtaposes US dollar/ECU average annual exchange rates against the budgetary expenditures as a whole. Export restitutions have been higher in value (both in relative and absolute terms) when the dollar has been relatively weak; this is brought out even more clearly by Figure 7.1, which plots the percentage share of export restitutions in total expenditure, on the right hand axis, against the dollar/ECU exchange rate on the left hand axis.

   Thus although exchange rate movements are not a direct mechanism by which the effects of monetary and fiscal policy are transmitted to the agricultural sector in the European Community, the overall level of support and its variation through time are at least in part affected by international macroeconomic events – particularly as the USA is such a weighty actor in these affairs. The influence of macroeconomic policy on the agricultural sector and the issues of commodity price instability are likely to have a greater weight in future in the agricultural economics literature in Europe as a consequence of policy reform and any commitments made in the agricultural negotiations in the Uruguay Round of the GATT.[9] Thus, ongoing policy reforms will be

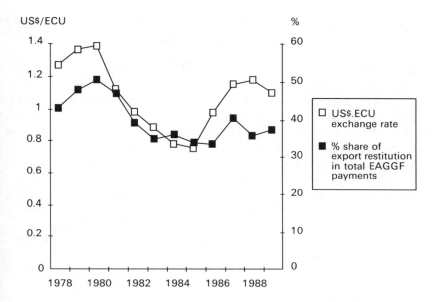

FIGURE 7.1   The dollar/ECU exchange rate and per cent share of European Community export refunds in total EAGGF expenditure, 1978–89

Sources: IMF (various issues); Commission of the European Communities (various issues).

likely to reduce the inflexibility of domestic commodity prices and make them more responsive to world market forces.

7.5.2   The developing world

It is extremely difficult, even insulting, to lump together developing countries in a single generic group. Nevertheless, provided the differences between them are acknowledged, there are common identifiable features among sufficient of them with regard to macro-economic policy and primary commodity markets. For example, agricultural production is far more important in most developing countries than in the industrialised countries, in terms of its contribution to output, export earnings and food security. Most developed countries experienced faster growth during the commodity boom in the 1970s, but experienced difficulties in sustaining this as a result of the second oil price shock and emerging recession in industrialised countries at the end of the decade. Falling world prices of commodities reduced export earnings, but many developing countries were unwilling, for a variety of reasons, to allow the exchange rates to depreciate to compensate. Predominantly this was because of socio-political factors; the experience of a real rise in incomes could engender expectations among the population that this would be sustained, and given the fragility of many governmental structures it is perhaps understandable that remedies other than deflation were sought. Another important reason for maintaining parity of exchange rates was the effect on the manufacturing sector; industry in many developing countries at the time of the commodity boom had been affected by the Dutch Disease phenomenon,[10] and was subsequently treated relatively favourably. For the most part, this sector is highly dependent on imported inputs, and thus would be assisted by an overvalued exchange rate. The exchange rate has been maintained at its official level by capital inflows, either of aid or borrowing (exacerbating the 'debt problem'), though a variety of other devices, such as multiple exchange rates and currency conversion controls have also been used.

Considerable domestic inflation has occurred as a result of this mixture of policies, and of course the effect of the overvalued exchange rate has been to impose an effective tax on the (predominantly exporting) agricultural sectors in developing countries, as discussed earlier in section 7.2. A considerable amount of evidence has been collected throughout the developing world, demonstrating the impact of macroeconomic policies on the real level of protection afforded to agriculture: see, for example, Krueger *et al.* (1988) for an overview, and Bautista (1987, 1989), Garcia (1989), Oyejide (1986,1989) and Tshibaka (1986) for continental examples.

One further interesting point which needs to be made in this context concerns the relationship between the official exchange rate (measured in terms of the local currency price of US dollars), and the real exchange rate of the dollar itself, effectively determined by the ratio of tradeable to non-tradeable prices within the US domestic economy.[11] Real prices can be doubly distorted, first by overvaluation of the local currency, and secondly through the influence of the USA via its monetary and fiscal policies' influence. If the dollar is itself overvalued in real terms (as it mostly has been, throughout the past decade), then the potential exists for even lower prices for agricultural prices for producers in developing countries than production conditions, *ceteris paribus*, would dictate. If in addition, as the model and some of the evidence explored in the previous section suggests, world prices are inherently unstable as a result of the overshooting phenomenon, then the arguments marshalled by, among others, Rausser (1985) for domestic stabilisation policies for agriculture would also apply in global terms. That is, that the restructuring policies advocated by the World Bank are not in themselves sufficient to reverse the dramatic decline in productivity in third world agriculture which has occurred in the 1970s and 1980s.

7.6   CONCLUSION

It should be clear to the reader that our purpose in this chapter has not been to review all of the various linkages between the macroeconomy and agriculture. Rather, we have focused on the way in which the related hypotheses, rational expectations and efficient markets (now standardly employed in modern macroeconomic analysis[12]), can provide insight into how macroeconomic policy changes influence the course of economic events in the agricultural sector. At a minimum, we believe that investigation of these linkages should incorporate an analysis of the sensitivity of the assumption that the economy embodies the two hypotheses.

Thus we have only provided a starting point; those wishing to explore further, beside pursuing the citations which we have provided in the main body of the text, could also refer to the volume of papers edited by Grennes (1991) (but, for a cautionary introduction, see also the review by Stallings, 1991). Evidence of the dilution of North American dominance of both theoretical and practical investigation of this area is sparse, but see, for example, Peters (1991), and also the section on 'Macroeconomic Linkages and Agriculture' in the volume of invited papers to the Twentieth International Conference of Agricultural Economists edited by Maunder and Valdes (1989, pp. 519–612).

128-204

8 Economics of Agricultural Research and Biotechnology

W. LESSER and D. R. LEE

8.1 INTRODUCTION

The issue of the level and source of funding for agricultural research has received considerable attention following the pioneering studies by Griliches in the 1950s (Griliches, 1957, 1958) and cross-country comparisons by Ruttan and colleagues beginning in the 1970s (Ruttan, 1982; Hayami and Ruttan, 1985; Binswanger and Ruttan, 1978). These and subsequent studies have shown social returns to public investment in agricultural research of over 100 per cent in some developing countries, with typical returns exceeding 30 per cent. Since these returns are far higher than can typically be expected from other investments, the argument can and has been made for major increases in public funding of these endeavours. While these results are most dramatic, and pertinent, for developing countries, they also apply to developed countries where agricultural research continues to be heavily supported by the public purse.

Nothing of course is so simple, especially in the dynamic environment of agriculture. Over time a number of additional considerations and interpretations of the returns to publicly funded research have arisen. Methodologically, researchers have raised questions about data and estimation procedures as well as the appropriateness of extrapolating past results to the future, all of which are elements of the debate about under- versus over-investment in this area. Others have re-evaluated the apportioning of returns to the several factors of production as well as the distribution of benefits and have questioned the high returns.

Most topically, the development of biotechnology within the past generation has raised an entirely new and promising area of research which is attracting both public and private research support. This, along with the gradual impoverishment of national treasuries across a wide spectrum of countries, has led to more privately funded agricultural research. The extension of patent and patent-like protection to an ever broader array of agricultural products including, in the USA, animals, is a further component in the shifting of sources and levels of agricultural research funding. Some decry these changes while others see them as not only necessary but desirable.

The objectives of this chapter are first, to review the current status of public and private agricultural research worldwide, and second, to assess the current state of knowledge about the returns to this research. One aspect of that effort is a partial mediation between the strongly held positions of the over- versus under-investment camps. A secondary objective is the use of historical research to generate insights into forms and levels of the 'new' agriculture, soon, according to some, to be dominated by biotechnological developments.

The chapter begins with an overview of the current data on public and private investments in agriculture worldwide, and then proceeds to a conceptual evaluation of the ramification of private versus public investment. Section 8.4 evaluates the existing literature on the returns to agricultural research and lessons for the appropriate level of funding. The next to last section applies the lessons learned to the emerging issue of biotechnology and its interaction with 'traditional' research. We reserve the final, or sixth, section for the conclusions and implications.

8.2 INVESTMENT IN AGRICULTURAL RESEARCH

The principal objective of research in agriculture is to increase agricultural productivity. This can be accomplished in a number of ways (Arndt and Ruttan, 1977). First, research increases the returns from productive inputs by increasing output or lowering the costs of production. Second, research reduces the risk and uncertainties associated with agricultural production in an environment where many sources of uncertainty exist (Anderson, 1991). Third, research results in improved quality of both outputs and inputs, and, in some case, wholly new products. Improved output quality may be reflected in several ways, through increased economic value, enhanced nutritional status of consumers, or improved product characteristics which facilitate further transformation through processing. Improved input quality is typically reflected in improved system productivity.

By most estimates, the record of agricultural research in generating sector productivity growth has been outstanding. Agricultural productivity growth, due to research and other factors, has been highly variable across countries, but in some cases has been consistently high. For example, agricultural productivity in the USA increased about 2.3 per cent annually between 1970 and 1983 (Capalbo and Vo, 1988). Estimated productivity growth in UK agriculture has been slightly less in the post-war period, about 1.9 per cent annually (Harvey, 1988), while Canadian agricultural productivity growth measured around 1.4 per cent annually between 1962 and 1984 (Veeman and Fantino, 1988).

8.2.1 Public investments in agricultural research

Research-induced improvements in agricultural productivity have been a function of both public and private sector investments. In most countries, the former far outweigh the latter. In addition, data on public agricultural research expenditures are typically more easily accessible than comparable data on private sector research and development expenditures. The recent ISNAR study reported in Pardey *et al.* (1991) provides the most comprehensive estimates to date of public agricultural research expenditures worldwide over the past two and a half decades. The discussion in this section is based on data reported in that study.

Globally, public agricultural research expenditures (measured in terms of 1980 purchasing power parity adjusted US dollars) increased from an average of $3.2 billion in 1961–5 to $8.4 billion in 1981–5 (Table 8.1). The developing country share of these totals increased from 33 per cent in 1961–5 to 43 per cent in 1981–5; however, there was considerable variation in real expenditure growth across specific developing country regions. Research expenditures in the Asia and Pacific region (excluding China) increased the most rapidly – averaging 6.7 per cent annually between 1961–5 and 1981–5 – while growth in Sub-Saharan Africa was the slowest, 4.7 per cent annually. Research expenditures in developed countries grew at an annual rate of roughly 4.0 per cent over the same period, albeit from a substantially larger base.

The available data on recent trends in developing country agricultural research provide some cause for concern (Pardey *et al.*, 1991).

TABLE 8.1   Average annual public agricultural research by region, 1961–85 (1980 PPP millions of dollars)

Region	1961–65	1966–70	1971–75	1976–80	1981–85
Sub-Saharan Africa (43)	149.5	227.2	276.9	359.1	372.3
China	271.4	296.2	485.4	689.3	933.7
Asia & Pacific excl. China (28)	316.7	475.4	651.5	928.3	1159.6
Latin America & Caribbean (38)	229.1	355.1	486.6	679.3	708.8
W. Asia & North Africa (20)	126.9	249.7	300.8	341.2	455.4
Less developed Countries (130)	1093.6	1603.7	2201.0	2997.3	3629.8
Japan	404	573	781	891	1022
Australia & New Zealand	161	209	290	259	313
Northern Europe (5)	90	122	135	156	182
Western Europe (8)	454	714	980	1059	1135
Southern Europe (4)	88	97	142	190	317
North America (2)	994	1342	1399	1617	1845
More developed Countries (22)	2191	3057	3726	4171	4813

Notes
Number of countries in each region indicated in parentheses.
PPP = Purchasing Power Parity.
Source: Pardey, Roseboom and Anderson (1991).

Comparing average annual growth rates for 1971–5 to 1976–80 with those between 1976–80 and 1981–5, only in the Asia and Pacific region (excluding China) did the rate of growth in research expenditures exceed the growth rate in research personnel. This means that most regions had, on average, declining levels of real resources per researcher. In addition, comparing the same time periods, with the exception of the West Asia and North Africa region, average annual growth rates in research expenditures declined as well. These declines were especially sharp in Sub-Saharan Africa, Latin America and the Caribbean.

Additional insight into investment trends in agricultural research can be gained from Table 8.2, which presents a number of relative measures

TABLE 8.2   Relative measures of agricultural research expenditures, GDP groupings, 1971–85 (percentages)

Income group[1]	1971–75	1976–80	1981–85
	Agricultural research intensity ratios[3]		
Low (13)[2]	0.42	0.44	0.60
Lower-middle (18)	0.64	0.65	1.04
Middle (12)	0.56	0.52	0.63
Upper-middle (12)	0.62	0.77	0.95
High (15)	1.63	1.88	2.13
Total sample (17)	0.79	0.88	1.00
	Percentage of agricultural research expenditures in total government expenditures		
Low (13)	0.82	0.72	0.67
Lower-middle (18)	0.67	0.50	0.58
Middle (12)	0.52	0.39	0.36
Upper-middle (12)	0.22	0.20	0.17
High (15)	0.29	0.24	0.24
Total sample (70)	0.52	0.42	0.42
	Percentage of agricultural research expenditures in agricultural expenditures		
Low (13)	7.8	6.5	7.1
Lower-middle (18)	9.7	8.4	8.4
Middle (12)	8.3	7.3	7.7
Upper-middle (12)	6.7	6.3	5.9
High (15)	5.6	6.6	7.0
Total sample (70)	8.2	7.8	7.9

Notes:
All data represent simple averages across all countries in each income class.
[1] Countries assigned to income classes based on 1971–75 per capita GDP averages where low, < $600; Lower-middle, $600–1500; Middle, $1500–3000; Upper-middle, $3000–6000; and High, > $6000.
[2] Bracketed figures represent number of countries in each income class.
[3] Measures agricultural research expenditures as a percentage of agricultural GDP.
Source: Roe and Pardey, 1991.

of agricultural research expenditures based on the same ISNAR data set (Roe and Pardey, 1991). Agricultural research expenditures as a proportion of agricultural GDP ('agricultural research intensity ratios') demonstrate a generally upward tendency between 1971 and 1985, particularly during the latter part of that period. As a percentage of total government expenditures, however, agricultural research has typically declined over time for most country income groups. As a proportion of total expenditures in agriculture, no clear trend is evident. Other evidence suggests, though, that agricultural research expenditures relative to total government transfers to (and from) agriculture are strongly and positively correlated with per capita country income levels (Lee and Rausser, 1992).

Given the long lags between the development of technical innovations in agriculture and the impacts of those innovations on agricultural productivity, any effects of declines in public agricultural research expenditures would not be evident for many years. The above evidence on trends in research expenditures is mixed; absolute levels of research continued to increase through the mid-1980s, while several relative measures indicate a deterioration in governments' commitments to agricultural research. It is imperative that this situation continue to be monitored so that any further evidence of declining (relative or absolute) public investment in agricultural research be recognised well in advance of any unfavourable effects on productivity growth. At the same time, it is important to remember that public investment in agricultural research is only one part of the story; private sector investment is another important component.

8.2.2   Private agricultural research

Private sector agricultural research is both more limited and less well documented than that done by and for the public. This is especially true of the less developed countries. Available data are presented in Table 8.3. Compared with the figures for the public sector from Table 8.1, the private sector contributes 28 per cent for developed countries but below 2 per cent of total agricultural R & D in developing countries. Data on *trends* in expenditures are even more limited, but indications are that they have been increasing at 2–3 per cent annually, or just below increases in public funding (Pray and Echeverria, 1991).

TABLE 8.3   Estimates of private sector agricultural research expenditures, selected countries and years, 1985–9

Country	Year of estimate	Coverage	R & D expenditures (millions US $)
More developed countries			
Australia	1986–7	Agriculture	7.2
France	1986	Agriculture	122.0
UK	1987	Agriculture	370.0
USA	1984	Agriculture	1400.0
Less developed countries			
India	1985	Agriculture	16.7
Indonesia	1985	Agriculture	2.0
Malaysia	1985	Agriculture	10.0
Pakistan	1985	Agriculture	0.8
Philippines	1985	Agriculture	4.4
Thailand	1985	Agriculture	4.3
Chile	1984	Seed	0.2
Argentina	1989	Seed	10.0

Source: Pray and Echeverria (1991) table 10.4.

Pray and Echeverria (1991, table 10.5) used a survey of twenty-seven major multinational companies to gather both a more detailed geographic and product breakdown of R & D investments in developing countries. Results indicate that most private funding is directed to plantation crops (especially in Indonesia), plant breeding (with Latin America leading) and, a distant third, pesticides. The division of research between local firms and multinationals varies by region, due no doubt to variations in national foreign ownership and intellectual property laws, among other factors. As examples of the extremes, most private plant breeding in India is done by locally owned firms while in Latin American multinationals are the dominant players. Considering only maize, Echeverria (1991, table 11.5 and p. 376) found that 85 per cent of developing country seed (and 92 per cent of hybrid maize) is supplied by private firms. Hybrids are especially attractive for private companies because of their 'built-in' protection from on farm seed propagation, which arises because the hybrid vigour of seed retained on the farm rapidly deteriorates. However, while the farms are responsible for the breeding work, the pure (inbred) lines are largely supplied by the public sector.

8.3   PUBLIC VERSUS PRIVATE INVESTMENT

Farmers, while often seen as maintainers of traditional values, are also major adopters of new technologies. Developed country agriculture has increased in productivity between 1.4 and 2.3 per cent annually in recent years (see section 8.2 above). Within the developing world, India moved from a major food *importer* in 1960s to an *exporter* within a generation. These enormous advances in agricultural productivity are attributable to both cheap energy, which allows mechanisation and fertilisation, and to improved varieties which simultaneously are more resistant to pests and diseases and produce a more usable product per hectare.

The sources of investment funds which led to the development of these two classes of technology are quite distinct, with private sources heavily responsible for the mechanical products and public funding for the crop-based developments. What explains these differences? This section examines that question, beginning with the theoretical treatment of the role of public enterprises in market economics.

The public goods nature of research is a principal argument for its public financing. But the same theory applies to many forms of non-agricultural research, few of which are traditionally publicly funded. Why is agriculture treated so differently? Two other criteria are applied to differentiate agriculture. These are the ubiquity of food consumption, meaning that the benefits will apply across a population, and the particular relevance of food expenditures to low income consumers; that is, as income rises, food purchases become an increasingly smaller portion of total expenditures. A reduction in the cost of food made possible by increased production efficiency is therefore an effective and efficient means of redistributing income to lower wealth groups, while the universality of food consumption allows broad public support for those expenditures.

Additional more practical matters come into play. Farming in most countries, and until quite recently in the developed nations, provides the bulk of the population with income and employment so that agriculture receives considerable political support. In developing countries, governments strive to placate urban groups by maintaining low food prices. Research is a component in that process (Hopkins, 1988). In developed countries, the preservation of the 'family farm' has broad public support, the prevention of corporate monopoly control over the food supply being but one reason (Strange, 1988). As those family entities are too small to conduct research efficiently, the government assumes that role. All in all, the public support of agricultural research has a broad base.

The public good nature of agricultural research is not pertinent to private firms if non-paying users can be excluded from access. Certainly hybrids are excludable; protect the pure lines and access is barred even if the crosses are widely known. This in fact is done and hybrids are widely privately produced. Preventing access to self pollinated varieties is not feasible physically, and until recently standardised legal means were unavailable. As a result research support had been exclusively public for such varieties.

That changed in 1961 with the drafting of the International Convention for the Protection of New Varieties of Plants (UPOV) which provides patent-like protection for plants, so-called Plant Breeders' Rights, or PBR. As a result of the ability legally to exclude access, private investment in plant breeding increased as predicted by economic theory. The response is best documented in the USA where PBR is associated with increases in private funding and acreage planted to private varieties (Butler and Marion, 1983; Perrin, Hummings *et al.*, 1983; Brim, 1987). Investment is however uneven across crops with soybeans leading (Knudson and Pray, 1991). To date no developing country is a member of UPOV, although six, Argentina, Chile, Mexico, Peru, Kenya (not operationalised) and Uruguay, have similar national laws. Some documentation of experiences in Chile and Argentina indicates private responses not unlike the USA (Pray, 1989; Gutiérrez, 1991). India has also in recent years experienced an increase in private hybrid breeding activity, but that is due to a relaxation of a national prohibition (Agrawal, 1990). As a result of these legal changes, many countries are experiencing mixed public and private activity in the agricultural research realm. This is compelling many countries to consider the advantages and disadvantages of private versus public funding systems.

Despite its theoretical superiority, publicly supported research necessitates a budgetary allocation process, which is difficult, conceptually and practically, for governments. Private firms typically use financial return analysis with simple decision criterion such as the 'highest returns' or 'all positive returns' for budget setting and project selection purposes. Of course the process is not so simple, for different methods of analysis can yield differing rankings while competing projects may not be separable/independent (see Herbst, 1982; or Brigham and Gapenski, 1991). But in the main the process is straightforward. That is not so with public investments, for three reasons.

1. The prices used for the analysis may be distorted so as not to reflect relative scarcity. At a minimum, prices are partially controlled by government policy – tariff levels for example – so the process is interactive. In a related fashion, the existing distribution of income affects prices so they may not be a good guide to social welfare.
2. The public sector must explicitly consider externalities. Many externalities are negative, but some may reflect a seepage of benefits outside the target area, such as plant varieties useful in neighbouring countries. How are those benefits to be quantified and incorporated into the analysis?
3. Governments must often choose between economic efficiency (the project with the highest return) and practicality (the use of a project as an income redistributing device when other approaches are infeasible) (see UN, 1972).

The use of financial ratios in such cases makes further assumptions about the equality between private and public benefits and the efficiency ('competitiveness') of the market. Since these conditions are frequently not met, alternative approaches have been proposed for public resource allocation and goal setting (review in Ruttan, 1982, ch. 11). Yet as Barker (1988) correctly points out, the more complete models place excessive demands on data availability and analytical skills. Not the least of these complexities is the difficulty of measuring the impacts of past projects, as discussed below. As a result, unsystematic methods are likely to be used, including annual adjustments to existing budgets, leading over time to allocations which are not related to social needs. Indeed, when the recipients of the benefits (farmers in the case under discussion) are involved in the allocation process, funding levels are certain to be distorted from the social optimal (de Gorter and Zilberman, 1990).

Private firms can avoid the internal complexities of allocation decisions identified above, although the level of difficulty for private firms should not be underestimated. What is problematic from a societal perspective is the impact of the private goals on the public. One aspect is the 'distorted objectives' of private breeders (Simmonds, 1990), which can refer either to a short- rather than a long-term focus or the development of varieties lacking real productive merits (as opposed to advertised ones) or requiring socially undesirable inputs, like herbicides (Schmid, 1985). Of special concern to some is the 'fine tuning' of public varieties (including those from the international breeding centres) and the capturing by private firms of all the economic benefits (Fowler and Mooney, 1990, ch. 9). That concern, however, applies only where there is little competition; otherwise, the private breeder commands only the small marginal value of his/her contribution. Experience has indicated that farmers are risk averse selectors of seed varieties (Butler and Marion, 1983, p. 61). Under such conditions, the fear of overpaying for private varieties is often misplaced.

Private investment leading to private gain has been associated with placing a monetary value on germplasm, which in turn raises concerns that free exchange will be hampered. Prior to private firm plant breeding activities, germplasm was described as being freely exchanged among public breeders, something considered essential to continued advancements. Private firms, however, have an economic incentive to protect certain materials, possibly slowing the exchange. Property rights in particular are implicated, but the situation is not limited to them (see Kloppenburg and Kleinman, 1988; Fowler and Mooney, 1990). Available surveys have not documented a substantial problem (Butler and Marion, 1983, ch. 3), but germplasm owners increasingly request a signed agreement giving some renumeration in the event of successful commercialisation. It will be some time before procedures are standardised and the long-term implications become clear.

Germplasm exchange is but one example of how interactions among the public and private sectors are evolving. Some observers decry these changes which typically involve the commercialisation of public agricultural research, such as by university faculty members operating private companies, universities patenting inventions and new varieties, and joint public/private research. These contracts are seen as possibly distorting the public role as well as reducing its perceived impartiality by the public (Kenney, 1986).

Despite the expressed (but not well documented) concerns about the inroads of private firms into agricultural research, numerous researchers suggest that the most productive system will involve a combination and collaboration between the private and public sector (Butler and Marion, 1983, ch. 4). There are several reasons for this recommendation, including the problem of assuring responsiveness within purely public systems. This has been noted in developing countries, where public systems are notoriously poor at seed propagation and distribution (Echeverria, 1991, p. 372). Private sector involvement in breeding is seen as beneficial if it contributes to those activities. A second, and even more pragmatic justification, is the sheer availability of funds. With numerous countries struggling under a debt load, public activities are facing ongoing budget cuts, in real if not nominal terms. Private funding provides one means of maintaining research programmes near required levels. Moreover, the obvious economic failures of the communist countries in the USSR and Eastern bloc have contributed to a renewed recognition of the role of private enterprise. For these reasons the private share of agricultural research is likely to trend upwards for the foreseeable future. What is equally clear is the ongoing role of public efforts in this area, not the least of which must be directed to preserving competition in the central activity of food production.

8.4 ASSESSING THE RETURNS TO INVESTMENTS IN AGRICULTURAL RESEARCH

Although economists have in the past devoted considerable attention to the evaluation of agricultural research investments, recently this attention has divided over allegations that current funding is too low or, for others, too great, to maximise social welfare. These debates have been applied to national and international agricultural research systems in developed as well as developing countries. Many of these debates revolve around analytical approaches employed in the economic evaluation of publicly sponsored agricultural research programmes and their effects. In large measure, the critical factors leading to divergent results relate to analytical assumptions, external and often unmeasurable factors, as well as fundamentally different theoretical approaches. The purpose of this section is to examine the multiple criticisms that have been raised with respect to the standard approaches to agricultural research evaluation.

8.4.1 Traditional approaches

Two major approaches to the *ex post* estimation of returns to agricultural research investments have been employed in the economic literature: an economic surplus approach and one using econometric production functions. Both approaches, as well as numerous applications utilising each, have been reviewed previously in the literature

(Peterson and Hayami, 1977; Norton and Davis, 1981; Echeverria, 1990).

The *economic surplus approach* involves estimation of the underlying consumer and producer surpluses generated by shifts in the agricultural supply function which result from research-induced unit cost reductions or productivity enhancements. Figure 8.1 illustrates the basic case. Farmers' adoption of a research-induced agricultural innovation is assumed to shift the aggregate supply curve from S to S'. This shift reflects the unit cost savings involved in producing any given level of output (say, Q_1), or alternatively, the additional output produced at any given price level (P_2, for example). In general, the gains from research are equal to the area $P'ABP''$, which represents the net change in total economic surplus resulting from a gain in consumer surplus (P_1ABP_2), and the change in producer surplus from P_1AP' to P_2BP''.

A host of variations in the assumed shapes and shifts in the underlying supply and demand functions have been hypothesised in the literature under widely differing sets of assumptions. Research has

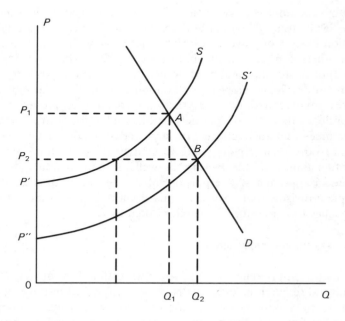

FIGURE 8.1   Welfare gains from research-induced supply function shift

shown that estimates of the returns to research using the economic surplus approach are indeed highly dependent on these alternative assumptions, particularly regarding the nature of the supply shift induced by research (Lindner and Jarrett, 1978; Rose, 1980; Wise, 1984). However, a number of researchers conclude that while different assumptions could reduce the estimated return, the essential case for agricultural research is unchanged (references in Wise, 1984, p. 30).

The *econometric production function* approach has also been used widely to generate estimates of economic rates of return to agricultural research. This approach is based on the estimation of a production function for agricultural output in which research expenditures are included as one of several inputs; for example:

$$Q = \beta_0 X_1^{\beta_1} X_2^{\beta_2} \ldots X_k^{\beta_k} R_1^{\alpha_1} R_2^{\alpha_2} \ldots R_n^{\alpha_n} e^{\mu} \tag{8.1}$$

where: $Q =$ value of agricultural output;
$X_i =$ non-research inputs $(i = 1, \ldots, K)$;
$R_t =$ research input in year t $(t = 1, \ldots, n)$;
$\beta_i =$ coefficients of non-research inputs $(i = 1, \ldots, k)$;
$\alpha_i =$ estimated coefficients of research inputs;
$\mu =$ disturbance term.

Based on estimates of α_i's , the partial (or total) coefficient(s) of research, a two-step procedure is then used to estimate the marginal internal rate of return (Davis, 1981). First, the (total or partial) value marginal product (VMP) of research is determined by multiplying the estimated coefficient(s) by the average product of research. Second, the internal rate of return is calculated by equating the discounted stream of benefits from research with discounted research costs. If it is assumed that research benefits accrue in an 'inverted-V' fashion (Evenson, 1967) – that is, benefits lag expenditures in such a way as to be symmetrically distributed around an intermediate midpoint year following a research innovation – then the marginal internal rate of return (r) can be calculated from:

$$VMP \left[\sum_{i=1}^{n} W_i / (1 + r)^i \right] - 1 = 0 \tag{8.2}$$

where the individual weights (W_i) pertain to each *ith* period through to the last period, n, in which research has an effect (Davis, 1981).

Numerous studies of agricultural research returns based on versions of these two approaches, and other less common approaches, have been completed over the past three decades. Echeverria (1990 lists over 120 such studies for a variety of individual crops and crop aggregates in numerous developed and developing countries. The estimated rates of return to agricultural research range between negative 48 per cent for wheat in Bolivia to positive 438 per cent for forestry research in the United States. Only two reported estimates are negative, however, while estimated annual rates of return to crop research are commonly in the 30–50 per cent range.

High economic rates of return typical in the literature have led to the common policy prescription that national governments, international development organisations and donors should be spending more on agricultural research (Evenson *et al.*, 1979; Ruttan, 1982). Results from the recent ISNAR study cited above indicate that proportional expenditures on agricultural research, in fact, did increase between 1975–9 and 1980–5 for virtually all countries studied (Pardey *et al.*, 1989). Yet despite this, the estimated returns are so high that public agricultural research expenditures continue to be lower than socially optimal. One possible explanation is that the estimates are inflated and actual expenditures are close to the true social optimal.

8.4.2 Sources of bias in rates of return estimates in agricultural research

Objections to the consistently high rates of return to agricultural research reported in much of the literature have been raised over the past decade by a number of researchers from conceptual, methodological and political economic standpoints. Central to these critiques has been the demonstration of various sources of analytical bias which may lead to underestimation or, more commonly, overestimation of returns to research. The economic surplus methodology has been a particular target of these critiques.

Among the potential determinants of *underestimates* of returns to research are misspecifications of supply function shifts and the difficulties of accounting for 'spillover' effects of research. The importance of correctly specifying the initial shape and subsequent research-induced shift in the *agricultural supply curve* has been the subject of much recent attention in the literature (Lindner and Jarrett, 1978; Rose, 1980; Wise and Fell, 1980; Norton and Davis, 1981). Lindner and Jarrett, for example, posit four different types of supply shifts which stem from agricultural research: 'divergent' shifts (of both 'pivotal' and 'proportional' types) which lead to greater average cost reductions for marginal compared to inframarginal firms; 'convergent' shifts, for which the opposite is true; and parallel supply shifts. Pivotal supply shifts commonly assumed in the literature have been shown to underestimate the cost-reducing benefits of research to producers compared to parallel shifts.

Spillover effects refer to benefits from research which are excluded from calculated rates of return due to estimation and measurement problems. These effects can be of several types. Intertemporal spillovers of research benefits occur when anything less than the complete stream of research impacts is included in rate of return estimates. The impacts of agricultural research can persist for up to thirty years (Pardey and Craig, 1989), so it may be difficult to measure adequately the full complement of effects over this period. Cross-commodity spillover effects occur when research on one commodity or on a general input such as a management processes, generates unit cost decreases or productivity increases in another region or commodity, which are not captured in the estimated benefits from research into the first commodity.

Finally, geographic spillover effects occur when research in one region or country generates benefits in other regions or countries. These effects are particularly important since many crops are produced in widely varied locations and the results of publicly sponsored research are widely disseminated. Whether the incorporation of international spillover effects leads to a policy prescription of greater or lesser investment in research for a specific commodity will depend on whether that commodity is imported, exported or a non-tradable and whether the benefits from research are assumed to generate welfare gains at a global or solely national level (Edwards and Freebairn, 1984).

Other sources of underestimates of rates of return to agricultural research may be identified as well, particularly if inappropriate decisions are made by the analyst with regard to the many methodological choices necessary in estimating rates of return to research. However, much greater attention has been given in recent years to the numerous potential sources of upward bias in returns to research estimates, often in attempting to explain the high rates of return typically estimated. Studies using the economic surplus approach which incorporate *misspecifications of supply function shifts* may generate overestimates, as well as underestimates, of returns to research (details are given in Lindner and Jarrett, 1978; Norton and Davis, 1981; and Wise, 1984). Similarly, assuming a demand function characterised by *inappropriately high price elasticity of demand* will overestimate gains to producers by underestimating the output price reduction resulting from a research-induced supply shift.

The situation is further complicated if spillover effects also exist, specifically for exportable commodities (Edwards and Freebairn, 1984). In this case, research benefits estimated for the exporter may be overestimated if the excess demand curve facing the exporter does not reflect the long-term cost reductions and enhanced competitive position of competing exporters.

As with other public sector investments, publicly funded agricultural research may suffer from an *excess burden* – that is, deadweight losses resulting from distortions in factor and product markets – introduced from the tax collection system (Fox, 1985). Fox assumes that this excess burden amounts to 30 cents on each tax dollar, meaning that the rates of return estimated for publicly sponsored agricultural research should be reduced by a similar proportion. However, Dalrymple (1990) has recently argued that since agricultural research is both productivity enhancing and complementary to private research, Fox's estimate may be unrealistically high. Moreover, it may not be appropriate to single out this one type of public investment without considering the benefits accruing to alternative forms of public expenditures.

One of the primary assumptions of most rate of return studies is that variable factors of production released through cost-reducing, productivity-enhancing research instantaneously find full employment in alternative uses. As demonstrated by the well-known case of the mechanical tomato harvester (Schmitz and Seckler, 1970), this is not necessarily a realistic assumption. To the extent that research-induced technological change results in *unemployed or underemployed resources*, even if only temporarily, the benefits of research must be appropriately discounted. This problem may be particularly acute in developing countries where agricultural labour made redundant by mechanical or other innovations may have few alternative employment opportunities.

Estimates of the benefits of public sector research must also account for *private sector research inputs* so as not to attribute all resulting productivity effects solely to the former. This is extremely difficult to do in a consistent manner as data on private sector research expenditures are limited (Pray and Neumeyer, 1990). *Ad hoc* adjustments are typically made, such as incorporating private sector research at the same level as public sector research inputs. However, these types of adjustments may become increasingly inadequate as private sector research accounts for a greater share of the total. A related but more fundamental issue is whether private and public sectors fund complementary or substitute research activities. Evenson (1983) argues that the former is typically the case, as the public sector focuses mostly on basic science and 'pre-technology' innovations, while the private sector focuses in a complementary manner on 'prototype' and 'usable' technology development.

Partial evaluations of publicly funded agricultural research which neglect the *interactions between research programmes and other government interventions* in agriculture may also lead to overestimates of research benefits. Simultaneously accounting for the effects of government programmes such as those which link producer benefits to quantities produced – output subsidies and deficiency payment programmes, for example – will tend to alter the estimated effects of research programmes. Studies by Oehmke (1988) and Alston *et al.* (1988) demonstrate the varying conditions under which the evaluation of research benefits under market-distorting farm programmes will alter the distribution and net benefits stemming from research. Key determinants of these outcomes include the precise form of government programmes and the trading status of the country for the products in question.

Many other sources of upward bias in estimated returns to agricultural research have been identified. Some of these factors pertain to costs of conducting research and extending research results that may be ignored or only partially incorporated into rate of return estimates. These include administrative research costs, the costs associated with research failures (what Hertford and Schmitz, 1977 call 'dry holes'), extension programme costs, and other costs associated with conveying information regarding research innovations to producers. Farmers themselves experience costs in the process of experimenting with and testing new innovations and in the adaptation and adoption of these technologies.

The large number of studies which have estimated high rates of return to agricultural research for many different crops and in a wide variety of settings would appear collectively to provide compelling evidence of the research underinvestment thesis. Yet, it is also apparent that many potential sources of error exist in estimating economic returns to research, and that many of these factors are more likely than not to lead to upward biases in these estimates. Given these circumstances, comparative studies such as those of Lindner and

Jarrett (1978), Davis (1981), and Wise (1984, 1986) are particularly valuable because they evaluate the sensitivity of estimated returns to research under explicitly stated alternative assumptions. These studies make it clear that different sets of assumptions regarding the most appropriate estimation methodology, the hypothesised shapes and shifts in supply functions, elasticities of demand, the temporal distribution of research impacts, inclusion (or not) of spillover effects, resulting unemployed productive inputs, size and degree of complementarity of private sector research, and many other factors will predetermine, in large part, the nature of the estimated rate of return to public sector research.

Although the dependence of estimated rates of return to research on analysts' assumptions may render the resulting estimates 'highly subjective' (Arndt and Ruttan, 1977, after Ulbricht), it would be going too far to suggest that these estimates are purely arbitrary. Circumstances surrounding specific research programmes on particular crops in individual countries may differ significantly, and the most appropriate analytical assumptions must be adjusted accordingly. In such cases, the use of standardised 'recipes' for generating rate of return estimates would be inappropriate. Hence, the methodological debates among research analysts evident in the literature are to be expected.

Considering the myriad of studies as a group rather than individually, there is reason to believe the estimated returns are on average overstated. There are several reasons for drawing this conclusion, but perhaps the most significant ones are (i) assumed demand elasticities, (ii) the implicit expectation that released resources will be re-employed instantaneously, and (iii) the assumption of costless education and transfer. None the less, there is no evidence that the estimates are so overstated as to change the basic conclusion: the social return to agricultural research is 'high', suggesting that additional funding would enhance public welfare.

8.4.3 The political economy of agricultural research underinvestment

Assuming that returns to agricultural research are as high as often estimated, an obvious question is 'Why'? Why do governments not invest more in agricultural research, generating greater benefits over time and driving down the estimated marginal rates of return? A number of factors have been identified as leading to the current situation. The more commonly identified are as follows:

- Agricultural research competes with numerous other potentially more supportive government programmes.
- Agricultural research may be too risky even though average returns are high (Anderson, 1991).
- Spillovers and other causes of non-appropriability may make it impossible for governments of single countries to allocate socially optimal levels of funding (Roe and Pardey, 1991).
- The time frame of returns from more basic agricultural research may place it outside the time horizon for political planning.

One difficulty experienced by government policy makers is the resistance of producers to new efficiency-enhancing technologies which lead to lower prices, and in some cases, fewer farms. In such cases, the support of producers can be secured by government subsidy and transfer programmes. It has been demonstrated that such redistribution policies can be welfare increasing if otherwise non-supported productivity-enhancing programmes are made possible (Rausser and Foster, 1990). This suggests that rather than being a source of upward bias in estimates of research benefits, agricultural subsidies may be complementary with agricultural research programmes. Research underinvestment may still exist, but the degree of underinvestment may be less than it would be in the absence of subsidies (Gorter *et al.*, 1990).

8.4.4 Sustainability and agricultural research

The current emphasis on 'sustainability' carries important implications for agricultural research. Partly this is definitional in nature as there is not broad agreement on what the term implies. Batie (1989) and Graham-Tomasi (1991) identify several commonly included elements, as follows:

- *system stability*: the ability of a system to respond to and recover from shocks;
- *discounting and intergenerational equity*: the use of discount rates which adequately reflect the costs and benefits accruing to future generations;
- *incorporating externalities*: internalising in current decisions the external effects from economic activities that arise from market and institutional failures.

Moreover, concepts of agricultural sustainability contain some reference to notions of natural resource conservation and maintaining environmental quality on a long-term basis (see also Lynam and Herdt, 1989).

But whatever the operational definition may be, it is clear that the concept of sustainability incorporates more elements than agricultural research as traditionally defined. This in turn suggests that more funds will be required, at least in the short term, to maintain past levels of productivity increases. A related factor is the added complexity of measuring the output of a multifaceted research programme. This will require additional, and costly, data collection (Herdt and Lynam, 1992).

A second implication of sustainability criteria for agricultural research is the need for *appropriate technologies* across a wide variety of diverse agro-economic and bio-physical conditions (Wilken, 1991). Technologies and management practices developed for large-scale homogeneous agronomic conditions will, in many cases, not meet more stringent sustainability criteria applicable to heterogeneous farming systems.

Finally, since agricultural research occurs within the broader socio-political setting, greater attention must be devoted to the general institutional, regulatory and policy environment facing agriculture. Thus, although agricultural technologies and management practices may be efficient and 'sustainable' from a purely technological standpoint, they must also make sense within the general social system to be adopted and incorporated into long term agricultural practices. Consequently, the emphasis on sustainability suggests the need for changes in research funding and practices.

8.5   BIOTECHNOLOGY AND AGRICULTURAL RESEARCH

8.5.1   Overview of developments

Agrobiotechnology has been receiving a tremendous amount of attention, especially in the popular press. Like any complex issue there are supporters and detractors but, viewed dispassionately, agro-biotechnology is one source of optimism that the sustainable agriculture goals of reduced inputs can be achieved. Thus agro-biotechnology is an inherent component of current discussions of agricultural research programmes. Separating 'traditional' from 'biotech' research, or as some would have it the 'old' and 'new' biotechnology, is difficult conceptually but one convenient distinction is to note that the conventional research focus has been on the level of the *organism*, the entire plant or animal.

The 'new' biotechnology, the subject of this section, refers to research on *parts* of organisms, particularly the cellular and molecular levels. Typically, the new biotechnology relies on the old for the development of commercial products; the altered gene must be introduced into a viable plant or animal to realise its benefit. What has changed is the ability to act at a more basic level within an organism to achieve the previously impossible or to accelerate what was formerly slow.

Agricultural applications with short-term commercialisation potential are summarised in Table 8.4. More distant developments, while exciting, are simply too fanciful to discuss in any detail at this time.

TABLE 8.4 Areas of near term applications in agriculture biotechnologies

Technological	Area application	Reference
Tissue culture (direct production, virus free)	Oil palms	OECD, 1989, p. 89
Embryo transplants (genetically superior individuals)	Cattle	OTA, 1986, ch. 2
Biopesticides (introduce genetic potential)	Cotton	Perlak *et al.*, 1990; *Natural Resources Journal*, 1990
Genetic resistance (herbicides and viruses)	Tobacco, potatoes	Streber and Willmitzer, 1989; Segelken, 1990
Disease resistance	Livestock mastitis	OTA, 1986; Miles, Lesser and Sears, 1991
Diagnostics	Livestock	Persley, 1990, ch. 3
Somatropins (growth stimulants) (genetic potential)	Milk, pigs Livestock	Soderholm *et al.*, 1986 Hansel, 1990

Global overviews of agro-biotechnology are given in Persley (1990) and OTA (1991).

8.5.2 Funding levels and sources

In 1985 an estimated $US 4 billion were invested worldwide in research on the 'new biotechnology' with two thirds coming from private sources and only 7.5 per cent invested outside the major developed countries. Of the total $US 4 billion, nearly a quarter was related to agriculture (Table 8.5).

Within agriculture the major emphasis (67 per cent) is related to seeds and but a third to microbiology. This is in accord with the expectation that seeds will be the major delivery mechanism for agricultural biotechnology. In total, agricultural biotechnology funding represents but only 10 per cent of the $8.4 billion spent worldwide on agricultural research (Tables 8.1 and 8.5).

8.5.3 Lessons for biotechnology research

With the advent of agricultural biotechnological products, it is instructive to draw comparisons with traditional products. In terms of a baseline comparison, the agricultural biotechnology market in the year 2000 is estimated to be $US 10 billion, of which 70 per cent is seeds, 2 per cent veterinary products and the remainder microbial products (OECD, 1989, table 1; Persley 1990, p. 47). By way of

TABLE 8.5 Estimated 1985 worldwide R & D expenditures on biotechnology and allocations to agriculture ($US millions)

| | Total biotechnology | | | Agriculture | |
	Private	*Public*		*Microbiology*	*Seed*
USA	1500	600	Private	200	350
EC	700	300	Public	100	250
Japan	400	200	Total	900	
Other	100	200			
Total	4000				

Source: OTA data, reprinted in Persley (1990) tables 5.1, 5.2 and 5.3.

comparison, the worldwide seed, fertiliser and chemical market was $US 113 billion in 1987.

Despite the comparatively small projected near term market, the new agriculture is attracting proportionately far greater private investment than the old. This is true both in the developed and developing countries (Table 8.5). One causal factor is the higher potential value of genetically engineered plants and animals. For example, herbicide resistant maize is estimated to have a net social return in the USA of up to $US 3.5 billion over five years (Tauer, 1989, table 6). Seed producers traditionally recover a quarter to a half of that amount (Butler and Marion, 1983). In developing countries, biotechnology lacks the governmental prohibitions which have inhibited private involvement in seed breeding in such countries as India for many years (see Agrawal, 1990).

From the private investment perspective, the value of a product is of no consequence if that value cannot be appropriated. Microbial-based inventions are widely protectable using such legal devices as patents in developed countries but far less so in developing ones (Beier, Crespi and Straus, 1985; national details in WIPO 1988). The link between private R & D and Intellectual Property Rights (IPR) has been difficult to substantiate and widespread disagreement remains (supportive evidence in Sherwood, 1990; Siebeck, 1990; Lesser, 1991). Opinion in developing countries, where protection remains far more limited, appears to be moving slowly towards greater intellectual property rights (UNCTAD, 1988). The OECD countries are pressing for stronger IPR under the General Agreement on Tariffs and Trade (GATT) (overview in Siebeck, 1990).

The substantial level of private funding of agricultural biotechnology research is the basis for much further discussion about the indirect ramifications of private involvement in what has long been a public preserve. Of particular concern are (i) private–public (especially university) interactions, (ii) basic versus applied research at public institutions, (iii) sharing of benefits between the public and private sectors, and between developed and developing countries, (iv) allocation of research between the developed and developing countries. Space prevents a detailed treatment of these often emotive matters, but some ramifications for future research can be identified.

First, the potential private profitability of biotechnology-based inventions compared to other forms of agricultural research will continue to attract private investment. Because many of these developments are easily copied, private investors will depend on legal protection to recover their investments. Available protection is now quite extensive in the developed countries, but not in the developing world where revisions are currently under broad review. Current trends suggest greater IPR protection and, hence, more private investment worldwide.

Second, biotechnology products are facing a degree of regulation well beyond that of more traditional agricultural products for countries in which such regulations exist. Regulations apply to environmental release of genetically engineered plants and animals and to the food security of those products and other food stuffs treated by them (Fessenden MacDonald, 1989, 1990; Geisow, 1991). The form and degree of regulation will impact directly upon biotechnology research, its level and location. Developing countries are in a transitional stage with regulations ranging from stringent to non-existent. Enforcement also varies (Hall, 1991).

Third, biotechnology at this time is more human capital than equipment intensive. This means a number of developing countries including India, Indonesia and Brazil with trained scientists but limited research infrastructures can become major contributors. On the other hand, research to date has, through necessity, had a large basic component which works against developing country involvement with its traditional applied focus. The role of developing countries in agricultural biotechnology research is undergoing active debate at this time (ibid.). Industry–university collaboration is a pragmatic compromise for many, but universities have not resolved the balance between applied and basic research and among several competing interest groups (Kenney, 1986).

Altogether, at this point, it is difficult to determine the eventual form of biotechnology research. A number of technical factors and governmental decisions could alter matters rapidly. However, the private sector, both alone and in collaboration with the public sector will seemingly be more involved in agricultural research than in the past. More private involvement will require a reinvestigation of the returns to this research as well as the means by which scarce public funds are allocated.

8.6   CONCLUSIONS AND IMPLICATIONS

Agricultural research is a worldwide endeavour with funding exceeding $US 8 billion in purchase-adjusted dollars. The developed/developing country split is a relatively stable 57/43 per cent, although a per capita comparison would be much more divergent. Expenditures have been growing at an inflation-adjusted rate of between 4.0 and 6.7 per cent leading to some concerns that productivity advancements will not continue into the future.

A more basic issue has been the debate about general over- and under-investment in agricultural research. The debate appears, in its essence, to be based on the very high estimates of social returns from that investment. Estimated returns from some 100 studies completed to date fall in the 30–50 per cent range but with some figures of 100 per cent and above. That has prompted two related questions. The returns are so high, is there a possibility of error? And, if the returns are indeed so great, why is funding not increased? The simple answer to the first question is yes in that numerous potential errors have been identified and debated in the literature. Some issues are methodological but most relate to assumptions underlying the analysis. Conceptually, the identified limitations could lead to either over- or under-estimates, but over-estimation seems the more likely. Particular contributing factors are assumed demand elasticities, assumptions about the use of released productive factors, and the costlessness of technology transfer. These and other pertinent factors tend to be very crop and country specific so that analysis must be done with care and close consideration of the particulars of each case. Certainly, a standardised approach using similar data sets is not adequate. None the less, when taken as a whole, there is no evidence that past estimates are so inflated as to invalidate the basic policy prescription that agricultural research investment is suboptimal.

Why has that condition been permitted to exist? Political economy explanations are incomplete but do identify such national concerns as seepage (benefits not realised within the funding country) and time horizon-returns occurring beyond the planning period of politicians. Recent work has also clarified another point – the complementarity of research expenditures and agricultural support programmes. While support payments reduce returns to new technology, they may lead to a Pareto optimal result if effective in ameliorating producer resistance to those technologies.

The analysis of research returns has concentrated on public expenditures which dominate funding. For conventional research the public sector funds 98 and 72 per cent of research in developing and developed countries respectively. However, that situation has begun to change, for several interacting reasons. A key factor is the emergence of agro-biotechnology which promises higher returns than conventional methods and thus attracts greater private capital. A related factor is the expansion of patent and other forms of intellectual property rights which give a legal means of appropriating benefits. Such rights are relatively broad in developed countries and limited, but expanding, in developing ones. As a very pragmatic matter, the impoverishment of public institutions worldwide has created a need for the attraction of more private investment. All these factors interact and point to the inescapable conclusion that private investment will be more important to agricultural research in the future.

The entrance of the private sector into what has been largely a public preserve does and will take much planning and accommodation. Budgets must be rethought and responsibilities apportioned. The outlook based on experiences to date, however, indicates that collaborative public–private projects when properly organised are more efficient and effective than for either sector operating independently.

9 Environmental Economics and Agricultural Policy

DAVID COLMAN

9.1 INTRODUCTION

Growing awareness of environmental costs associated with many systems of agricultural production has been paralleled by increased breadth and sophistication in environmental economics. In North America and Western Europe, in particular, this has led to steps to incorporate measures to control environmental externalities into policies for the support and regulation of agriculture; a measure of 'greening' has taken place in agricultural policy. In many less-developed countries (LDCs) environmental issues relating to land use are even more pressing than in the industrial nations, but, as a generalisation, the central focus of concern is at a different end of the range of problems. For whereas in the industrial countries of the temperate zones, the problems of large-scale erosion and destruction of the land base are generally less pressing,[1] these are urgent issues in some LDCs. On the other hand, in industrial countries there is more concern about the external costs of agriculture associated with pollution of water systems, insecticide residues, and with the degradation of the 'wild' environment as land is managed ever more intensively for agriculture and forestry. In addition, there is serious pollution of agriculture from the by-products of industry and urban living, particularly by 'acid rain'.

One of the concepts which has moved to centre stage is that of sustainability in relation to agriculture and forestry as well as to all economic and social systems. This will be briefly reviewed, after first considering issues of relating property rights in land to the control of environmental damage and natural resource depletion. This leads on to a discussion of economic principles for environmental and resource management, followed by a brief review of methods and problems in valuing environmental costs and benefits. In the light of the theoretical issues raised, an illustration of some policy options is presented, drawing upon UK experience. Before embarking upon these, the next section presents a brief overview of environmental problems associated with agriculture.

9.2 EXTERNAL COSTS OF AGRICULTURE

As the dominant, most widespread land-using activity, agriculture has profound interactions with and consequences for the environment. As settled agriculture encroaches further into forested and fragile areas, whole ecosystems are destroyed with universally acknowledged adverse impacts on all forms of wildlife. Deforestation is already held to have caused irreversible damage in some areas, and its continuation to portend ecological disaster in many tropical areas.

Agriculture's multifaceted interactions with the hydrological system are outstandingly important and sensitive. Removal of forest cover reduces water-holding capacities, leading to flash floods, soil erosion, and exacerbation of dry season water shortages downstream. At the same time, agriculture is the dominant user of water in irrigated areas; in the USA, agriculture, which accounts for only 3 per cent of GDP, uses 83 per cent of the water supplied, whereas manufacturing industry while contributing 27 per cent of GDP consumes less than 6 per cent of the water (Rogers, 1985, p. 282). In Asia, over 90 per cent of water supplies are directed to irrigation. Since, also, in temperate latitudes agricultural land is a major component of water catchment areas, it is evident that much of the world's water supplies 'pass through' agricultural systems and may become contaminated with natural salts, animal wastes, and agrochemicals before being used by urban and industrial consumers (as well as by downstream farmers). There is a clear link here with Pearce and Turner's (1990, p. 39) criterion for sustainability, that any wastes discharged into the environment (e.g. a water system) should not exceed its natural capacity to assimilate wastes and thereby cause conversion of 'what could have been a renewable resource into an exhaustible one'.

As the farmed area in the less developed countries (LDCs) continues to expand into the next century, to help meet the food needs of growing populations, pressure on the environment will increase the need for appropriate policies to reduce external costs from agriculture. FAO

(Alexandratos, 1988, pp. 127–33) estimates that something less than half the potential arable land in the developing countries is currently (and will be by the year 2000) under cultivation, and that further expansion will occur. However, most of the reserves, which are mainly in Latin America and Sub-Saharan Africa, are more marginal than land already in use. Much of the 'reserve' is in tropical forests and grazing areas with unreliable rainfall. At the least, expansion into such areas will require significant investment in infrastructure plus intensified use of fertiliser and other chemicals to compensate for low fertility. Increasing the irrigated area is viewed as being imperative, because of the high yields; however, the capacity to do this is constrained by water availability: 'Water rather than land is the binding constraint for almost 600 million ha. of potentially suitable arable land' (ibid., p. 132) in developing countries. Moreover, there are widespread problems of waterlogging and salinity in irrigated areas.

At the worst, continued expansion of the cultivated area in some LDCs could, if not carefully managed and controlled, lead to a self-reinforcing process of economic and social decline rooted in the degradation of natural and cultivated areas of forest and grassland. The estimated current rate of loss of forest in LDCs, at over half a per cent a year (Spears and Ayensu, 1985), is generally perceived as jeopardising the 'sustainability' of the whole pyramid of systems for human support which are based on the non-exploitation of plant cover. Spears and Ayensu indicate a range of possible courses of action and programmes which might reduce the rate of decline and improve the productivity of forest and woodland systems. These courses of action reflect actual experience ranging from development of communal fuelwood lots (Nepal, Korea), large-scale settlements based on agroforestry (Malaysia), state managed forestry (Senegal, Zambia), and large-scale private forestry (Chile). Underlying this diversity is the common factor that in each case rights to use the land were, or became, sufficiently well defined and secure to enable a system of management, whether communal, state or private to succeed. The existence of such rights does not automatically lead to success, and there will undoubtedly be many instances of project failure, but it is a crucial factor in so far as the most damaging forms of exploitation occur where there is an absence of enforceable rights, such as in the tropical forests of Latin America or the marginal and forested lands of Sub-Saharan Africa.

In the industrialised developed countries, land rights are generally well defined, with ownership and right of sale largely in private hands (either of individuals, companies or trusts). On some of this land, use rights are transferred to tenants with considerable security of tenure. In addition, there are public lands, such as those in the western USA and Alaska, which are well protected against unauthorised use. There are the murky issues of common land in the UK, where threats now exist to historic communal status and use rights. This is a minor issue, however, which reveals some of the difficulties in enforcing common rights against continued pressure to appropriate them for private gain.

Private ownership is not a guarantee of environmentally sound management, despite the in-built incentive owners have to protect the value of their land for the longer term. Potter (1991, pp. 4, 45) cites estimates of others to the effect that 'about 9 per cent of the agricultural area of England and Wales has suffered from significant wind and water erosion in the recent past' and that 'for each bushel of corn produced on the rich lands of the Corn Belt, two bushels of soil are lost'. The main environmental problems here are seen to be associated with the progressive intensification of agriculture, particularly of arable farming, although intensive livestock production with its problems of manure disposal and pollution of water courses with silage and other effluents is high on the agenda in EC countries.[2] In addition to these external costs imposed upon suppliers and users of water, are problems of chemical contamination of foodstuffs which cannot be detected directly by consumers themselves, and of transformation of the visual appearance and biological diversity of the countryside as agriculture responds to new technological possibilities and pressures to increase the private profits and efficiency. As the burden of external costs rises so the pressures to counteract these leads to policy measures to internalise them back into agriculture. The rights of others assert themselves against those of agriculturalists.

9.3   PROPERTY RIGHTS ISSUES

Where environmental damage occurs attention focuses upon the rights of both those causing the damage and of those who suffer it. With natural biological resources, damage is also often 'self-inflicted' by those who are responsible for the primary economic activity, examples being overgrazing, soil erosion, waterlogging and salinisation, deforestation and overexploitation of fish stocks. In a period where macroeconomic and structural adjustment policies favour privatisation, in many instances the source of the problem is identified as residing in prevailing systems of common property rights (as in the case of pastoralism and communal tenure systems of land holding) or of open access (the classical case of which is with ocean fisheries). Where the problems are associated with land use a prescription often given is for the establishment of private land ownership and titles. This is clearly over simple, as a number of works indicate (Ciriacy-Wantrup and Bishop, 1975; Runge, 1981; Livingstone, 1986; Bromley and Cernea, 1989), and it is important to review briefly the issues which have been raised because policies for environmental management essentially involve adjusting systems of rights and of regulating and enforcing them.

Bromley and Cernea distinguish four separate types of property regime (i) State, (ii) private, (iii) common, and (iv) the open-access case in which the concept of property loses meaning. In the first two cases, rights of ownership and of use may be separated by means of a tenancy agreement between owner and user. By incorporating appropriate conditions into the agreement, land use can, if the owner chooses, be restricted to that which is environmentally friendly, provided there is enforcement. Policy mechanisms exploiting this possibility are discussed below in relationship to the UK, and would *a priori* appear to have considerable relevance to the debate in Eastern Europe concerning agricultural reform on State land.[3]

Common property is the case of private property for a group (since all others are excluded from use and decision making) in which individuals have (not necessarily equal) rights and duties. Following Ciriacy-Wantrup and Bishop, Bromley and Cernea emphasise that common property regimes are not an invariant recipe for overexploitation of land and that, as Runge explores, it is inappropriate to assume that all individuals within the group act individually to maximise their own benefit; rather, common property regimes can and do exhibit the capacity for sustainable existence and sound environmental management. They may, however, like other property regimes, be blown off course by external pressures such as technical progress, new socioeconomic relations with other groups, or natural disasters. These authors emphasise that it is a grave error to confuse common property with open access and thereby to assume that the 'tragedy of the commons' is likely to be visited upon common property regimes. It may do so if the group is unable to enforce and regulate its rights to the exclusion of others; for open access is defined as a situation in which there is no property, which may arise because rights had never been assigned or where previous rights systems have failed to be enforced or become unenforceable.

While the issue of property rights is important in relation to the probability that land use will be managed in such a way that the flow of services from land is not diminished or destroyed, so too are issues relating to the rights of land users to inflict external costs on others. Concern here attaches to two particular classes of externalities; (i) chemical residues on food, and water pollution, and (ii) damage to wildlife and the landscape. A succinct exploration of changing perceptions, and of policy in relation to these rights issues in UK agriculture is presented by Hodge (1989).

In the UK there is an asymmetry between the rights of farmers and the rights of urban dwellers and property owners. This arises from the exclusion of agriculture from the powers of the 1947 Town and Country Planning Act which Hodge describes as 'nationalising development rights so that subsequent to the Act, any development would require planning permission and no compensation had to be paid for refusal'. The exclusion of agriculture from these provisions has meant that (with very limited exceptions) landowners and farmers only accept development restrictions on a voluntary basis, and that often voluntary compliance is purchased by means of compensatory payments of various types.[4]

Hodge argues, however, that there is a changing public perception of the threat to wildlife and landscapes as these have been degraded, and also to agricultural pollution in its various forms. This is leading to an increasing degree of control being placed on agriculture and action to curtail farmers rights to externalise social costs. This is transparent in terms of regulations to control discharges and effluents into water catchments and over chemical residues in foodstuffs, as it is also in protecting wildlife and landscapes.

Hodge states that according to Batie (1984) similar changes are also occurring in the USA 'with a shifting view of the farmer as "praiseworthy yeoman of the soil" towards a "corporate business person"'. As a consequence, the rights to use land are being constrained in relation to the impacts of land use on other values.

The State has various means of changing the rights structure. It can try to restrict the rights of private land owners. It can encourage privatisation or conversely it can purchase or rent certain rights leaving land users only a restricted set of rights. All these approaches are employed to promote environmentally sensitive management of agriculture, and will be discussed further below.

9.4 SUSTAINABILITY[5]

The concept of optimal sustainable yield in relation to exploitation of fish stocks has had a firm place in natural resource economics for many years (Gordon, 1954), and sustainability in a broader philosophical sense may be traced back to Malthus[6] in concerns about the balance between agriculture and population dynamics, and beyond. What is new, however, is the extension of concern from individual species or ecological habitats to the sustainability of man's current demands upon the environmental system as a whole, and to the incorporation of economic, social, institutional, political and technological factors into concepts of sustainability.

There are many alternative definitions of sustainability, with the annex in Pearce, Markandya and Barbier (1989) identifying at least twenty-four. A much quoted definition is that from the Bruntland Commission (WCED, 1987): 'Sustainable development is development that meets the needs of the present without compromising the ability of future generations to meet their own needs.' Other, more complex definitions, can be seen as complementing this, in that they become more specific and address different aspects of this general statement such as the nature of 'development', 'needs' or the time scale involved. However, the strength of this definition lies in its emphasis on maintaining intergenerational welfare over time.

Abstracting from the more general aspects of sustainability to focus specifically upon agriculture, land may be accepted as the key resource. In terms of classes of resource McInerney (1976) defines land as a non-destructible, non-renewable stock with renewable service flows. Some of the service flows, such as space for building may be seen as indestructible and unchangeable over time. Nevertheless, withdrawal of land from agriculture for, say, building inevitably reduces the annual flow of productive services to agriculture and renders them costly to renew even in the longer run. As regards land in agriculture or forestry, it is self-evident that the current level of use of its productive services may cause depletion of service flows in future periods and may threaten the capacity for regulating them.

Indeed, it is not just the flows of land services for agricultural production which are of concern. In addition, following Pearce and Turner's typology of services delivered by the environment generally, land provides (i) services as a waste sink (e.g. for disposal of manure from intensive livestock production), (ii) as a source of existence values for landscape and wildlife, and (iii) a source of resilience to external shocks which helps cushion human welfare from various disturbances through the biodiversity supported by existing land use. Agricultural pressures on the supply of all three of these classes of service are currently the source of issues on the policy agenda. The EC, following the lead of the Netherlands, is considering controls on the disposal of livestock slurry in order to control water pollution; new policies are proliferating to protect habitats and landscapes threatened by changing agricultural methods; halting the reclamation of wetlands and the destruction of tropical forests are issues rising up the political agenda.

Technological change has made agriculture increasingly dependent upon purchased chemical and mechanical inputs. This has led to new forms of wastes and externalities, to which legislation continuously responds in order to control use and emission (e.g. on fertilisers, disposal of liquid wastes, on use of insecticides and growth hormones). In other words, changes in agricultural technology through dependence on manufactured inputs, are increasingly perceived as threatening wider economic and biological systems. The dichotomy of 'internal' and 'external' resources has been suggested as being important for identifying those practices which will lead to sustainable agriculture. Thus Francis (1988) states: 'Sustainable agriculture builds its foundations on the resources which are renewable on the farm and its immediate area'. It is on this basis that there is growing espousal of 'organic farming', agro-forestry and other more closed, self-sustaining, self-regenerating forms of agriculture. Policy-makers are cautiously encouraging this type of approach, while economists try to assess the relative profitability of 'organic' as opposed to 'inorganic' farming and the extent to which producers of the latter type would need to be forced to internalise more of the external costs before the balance switches to the former.[7]

9.5 PRINCIPLES OF ENVIRONMENTAL MANAGEMENT FOR LAND USE

As Pearce and Turner (1990, ch. 4) emphasise, the optimal level of pollution associated with agricultural or other productive activity is non-zero. To the extent that associated natural systems have a capacity to assimilate wastes without impairing their regenerative capacities, a positive element of pollution may be accepted as giving rise to zero external costs. Only beyond a certain level does human welfare[8] become impaired and external costs arise. Some such external costs will be tolerated where the transactions and enforcement costs are high relative to the costs which might be saved by taking action to reduce pollution.

9.5.1 'Optimal' pollution levels

The basic principles enunciated by Pearce and Turner, and by others, rest firmly on the standard propositions of welfare economics, which generally include that the monetary value of benefits and costs of all interested parties are given equal weight. In a static analytical framework this enables issues of the optimal level of pollution to be explored, starting with the proposition that this is where the marginal net private benefit from production is equal to the marginal external cost of pollution caused ($MNPB = MEC$).[9]

Where property rights are well developed and transactions costs are negligible, Coase's theorem (1960) suggests that bargaining between polluters and those bearing external costs may reduce any departure from the optimal position and help restore 'equilibrium'. Where polluters do not possess rights to pollute, and where their $MNPB > MEC$, they have a basis for negotiating with those who own the rights to compensate society for increases in production and pollution up to the point where $MNPB = MEC$. Conversely, where the sufferers do not possess property rights over the polluted resources they employ and where $MEC > MNPB$, they may be able to negotiate successfully compensation to the polluter to reduce production and pollution. Generally, the conditions for such private bargaining to regulate pollution adequately do not exist and there is market failure; nevertheless, there are examples, in relation to agriculture, of groups completely buying out farmers rights in order to eliminate the risk of pollution from a change of private land use (see below).

9.5.2 The case for regulatory policy

The distribution of rights and the market conditions are what generally militate against success of private bargaining in achieving anything like Pareto optimal levels of externality generation in agriculture. Thus government intervention and regulation is widespread. There are several characteristic situations, all of them applicable to agriculture, in which governments may need to act to regulate pollution levels. These are where:

- The external costs are visited on such large numbers of people, and through such complex routes of transmission, that the transaction costs of individuals trying to seek redress would be excessive and prohibitive.
- Pollution is the product of numerous cumulative actions (as may be the case with small farmers), and where those bearing the external costs would be unable to attribute them to any one of numerous polluters (e.g. deforestation effects upon plains dwellers and water users). This is a situation where it is difficult, even impossible, to ensure that 'polluters pay'.
- A significant burden of the external cost falls on the State in the form of expenditure on public goods such as health services or flood control.
- Where polluters have economic and political power, such that affected individuals acting separately have little prospect of winning compensation for the external costs imposed upon them.
- Where the external costs are so high or so uncertain that tight control or outright prohibition needs to be imposed (e.g. as with control of agro-chemicals and animal drugs).

9.5.3 Mechanisms for controlling pollution

It is possible to enter into theoretical debate about the relative efficiency of alternative instruments such as taxes, subsidies and standards reinforced with penalties as means of achieving optimal levels of pollution and economic welfare. In reality the optimal levels are incapable of accurate definition, given that the $MNPB$ and MEC curves required for that purpose are imperfectly known or even impossible to estimate, and that notions of Paretian optima are diminished by their dependence upon acceptance of a particular (usually the existing) distribution of income and wealth. Nevertheless, examples of the applications of all these instruments to agriculture are to be found and deserve brief discussion in the context that the policy agenda accepts that current levels of agricultural pollution in key areas exceed the indefinable optima (i.e. that $MEC > MNPB$) and should be reduced. This entails introducing policies to reduce the pollution caused by existing enterprises operating with installed technology, and to stimulate new enterprises and technologies which are environmentally more friendly.

Irrespective of whether pollution taxes, quotas, or standards are used, a regulatory authority is required plus means to measure the output of pollutants. Whether the accuracy of monitoring and measurement needs to be of the same quality in each case is not entirely clear; intuitively it would seem that where a tax or charge is levied on each unit of pollution that measurement precision is required, but that where standards are imposed with penalties for transgression there might be the less demanding requirement of establishing whether an incident has occurred. This may explain why pollution taxes are uncommon, but why regulation by standard is proliferating (e.g. quality of water discharges from farm drains) despite the case based on Baumol and Oates (1988) that taxes are more economically efficient than standards both statically and dynamically. Clearly, measuring the pollution-outputs from myriads of farms is a daunting task, and is unlikely to be cost effective. It is more feasible to identify farms and locations which are more at risk from pollution (e.g. where there are large intensive farms close to water courses or human settlements) and to establish standards, monitoring and regulation for these.

In fact, rather than taxes on pollution outputs, the taxation of inputs associated with the generation of externalities is more widespread and easily manageable through points of sale. Taxation of fuel is the norm, reflecting both the need to provide public goods in the form of roads and (somewhat ineffectively) the need to reduce fuel use and pollution.[10]

Subsidies for pollution reduction are judged on theoretical grounds (Pearce and Turner, 1990, pp. 107–9) to be inherently less efficient than taxes.[11] Subsidies are used to provide incentives for the development and adoption of environmentally superior technology, and in that dynamic context they have an important role to play.

An alternative pollution control instrument is through the setting of maximum pollution quotas overseen by a regulatory authority. By allowing for marketable quotas, firms which can generate greater private benefits per unit of pollution are able to buy or lease quota from less efficient enterprises at prices which adequately compensate the sellers. This helps promote efficiency, and it also allows environmental groups to purchase (and lock up) quota thereby demonstrating that external costs exceed private benefits, since the quota purchase price will be less than or equal to the net present value (NPV) of the external costs which would have been borne by the group but greater than the NPV of the private benefits willingly surrendered by the seller.

As referred to in section 9.7 below, pollution quotas are beginning to be introduced in agriculture, a development aided no doubt by the spread of production quotas for such commodities as sugar and milk which have a similar rationale in that they control production.

9.6   VALUATION OF ENVIRONMENTAL DAMAGE AND AMENITY

External costs attributable to agriculture cover the full spectrum from identifiable market costs to far less transparent costs in terms of amenity and other values. Examples of market externalities would be where public authorities incur costs to control the effects of soil erosion, where firms incur costs to alleviate pollution of their water supplies, or where damage to freshwater fish stocks impairs or destroys the livelihood of fishermen. While it is often not straightforward to account fully for these costs, the rules of measurement are well developed; thus they and the problems of measurement will not be discussed here.

What has posed a challenge, which has been embraced enthusiastically by agricultural economists, is measurement at the non-market end of the cost spectrum. One category of these costs is loss of recreational (and other use) benefits, such as might arise because a particular much visited park is converted into an industrial estate. Another category (Hanley, 1989, p. 246) is in terms of what

> The early contingent valuation literature [of] such non-use benefits [classified] as option value, existence value and bequest value. Option value was seen as an insurance premium that prospective users, unsure of their future use of a good would be willing to pay to retain the option of future use; that is, an excess over expected consumer surplus. Existence value arises when individuals value an asset even though they [may] never see or use it directly. Bequest value was a benefit derived from knowing the resource could be passed on to future generations.

The methods used for measuring 'non-market' goods fall into two categories:

1. There are what Young and Allen (1986) call 'interdependent demand approaches'. The essence of these methods is to estimate the implicit values of non-market goods from observable market behaviour; recreational values are revealed from expenses incurred in recreation, and locational values from property values. The approaches used include the *hedonic pricing* (*HP*) and *travel cost* (*TC*) methods.
2. Alternatively, there are direct approaches employing direct questioning to elicit estimates of (i) 'willingness to pay' to prevent

the loss of or obtain access to some amenity, or (ii) 'willingness to accept' compensation for the loss of some amenity or right. These are known as *contingent valuation* (*CV*).

9.6.1 Hedonic pricing

Hedonic price analysis seeks to estimate the value or price assigned to particular characteristics embodied in traded goods or assets which possess a (large) number of quantifiable and qualitative features. Thus, for example, it is possible statistically to assess the effect on house prices of such environmental features as the presence/absence of views over open countryside, cleanness of the air, access to woodland, or proximity of heavy industry and traffic; this would be done simultaneously with estimating the effect upon price of quantifiable variable costs such as the age of house, number of bathrooms, etc. In this way, it is sometimes possible to estimate the value put upon certain environmental existence values by buyers and sellers of goods and assets influenced by such characteristics. However, such measurements can only be partial, in so far as it is not only house owners who are influenced by and place an existence value upon a park, for instance; there are also all the actual and potential users of the park. Thus as Young and Allen (1986) conclude, hedonic pricing methods are of only limited applicability, in addition to which there are a number of methodological issues to be confronted before confidence can be placed in such estimates of environmental values.

9.6.2 Travel-cost method

This also is a method suited only to selected valuation problems, limited as it is to sites which are visited for recreational purposes. The cost which visitors incur for each visit can be surveyed (along with details of relevant variables) and may be assumed to be their minimum willingness to pay (WTP) for the recreational services obtained. By regressing the number of trips per visitor (or the number of trips by zones of origin) upon the travel cost incurred, and upon other variables such as the cost of visiting other substitute sites, and the socio-economic characteristics of visitors, a demand function for visits can be estimated. The area under the demand curve provides an estimate of the consumer surplus of visitors, and the function can be used to estimate the effects of imposing or changing entry fees upon demand for use of the site. Inevitably the method gives rise to a variety of methodological difficulties (e.g. as discussed by Anderson and Bishop, 1986), but it is increasingly widely used as the economics of rural tourism assumes ever greater importance in countries at all stages of development. In this context it helps estimate the implicit value of the tourist resource to those who visit it, but omits the option and existence values to the larger number of people who are not visitors.

9.6.3 Contingent valuation

CV is a key method in experimental economics, whereby estimates of values and behaviour are obtained by eliciting respondents' reactions to hypothetical questions. Thus it is possible to obtain estimates of respondents' willingness to pay, to prevent, say, a road being built through a National Park, or of their willingness to accept compensation in the event that the road should go ahead. Either way,[12] estimates of the external cost of the road to the respondents is obtained, even for respondents who do not live close to the National Park. CV is therefore a valuable procedure for trying to estimate values which cannot be inferred from market behaviour, and there is no valuation problem which a questionnaire 'experiment' could not attempt to assess (including those to which indirect methods can be applied).

The design of CV experiments is critical to the usefulness of the outcome (Loomis, 1987); it is widely recognised that respondents' answers may contain forms of bias which depend upon what if any actions may be taken as a result of their answers (Schulze *et al.*, (1981);[13] and careful sampling is required to enable the sample results of the experiment to be raised to valuations for the whole population. Nevertheless, this is a highly flexible and versatile tool with which to attempt more difficult valuation exercises.

9.7 ENVIRONMENTAL AND CONSERVATION MANAGEMENT INSTRUMENTS FOR AGRICULTURE – ILLUSTRATION FOR THE UK

The range of instruments for environmentally sensitive management in the UK has expanded rapidly within the framework of the Common Agricultural Policy, and others have been considered. While there are undoubtedly other measures deployed elsewhere, UK policy provides a basis for illustrating some of the possibilities.

9.7.1 Instruments to influence the application of existing user rights

Taxes

Given the difficulties already discussed of monitoring agricultural pollution it is not surprising that there are no taxes per unit of pollution. What has been the subject of analysis, however, is the possibilities of taxing the use of nitrogen fertilisers, that is of an agricultural input, in order to reduce the amount of nitrates passing into waterways and the consequences thereof. The potential success of such a tax depends upon the price elasticity of demand for fertiliser of which there have been many studies (Burrell, 1989, provides a summary). According to Burrell's own estimate that the elasticity lies between 0.1 and 0.3, taxes equivalent to 100 per cent to 33 per cent of the price would be needed to reduce usage of fertiliser by 10 per cent. This has not generally been judged feasible, and in view also of the considerable doubts about the impact of reduced fertiliser use on water quality (House of Lords, 1989), it is perhaps not surprising that no tax on usage has yet been implemented.

Subsidies

A wide range of subsidies is available to promote more sensitive environmental management, and for investment in pollution abatement, but there is none of the textbook type which provides a subsidy per unit by which pollution is reduced below some target. Most of the subsidies are to cover part of the costs of capital works such as to install manure handling systems, to renovate traditional buildings, or to plant trees. For these purposes subsidies are particularly well suited, and the rate of subsidy can be increased where the works produce little commercial benefit but are judged to provide external benefits.

A somewhat unusual form of subsidy is available in the form of fixed annual payments to farmers in environmentally sensitive areas (ESAs), who sign a five-year contract to manage land according to a given set of restrictions. In some cases, no change of management is required to meet the restrictions, in which case the payment may be seen as a subsidy to ensure protection of the landscape and farming system against the damaging effects of changed management and to support what is seen as good practice. In other cases, qualification for the payment does require a switch to less intensive farming, something farmers may be assumed to volunteer for only if the payments exceed the private benefits foregone.[14]

Proposals emanating from the Commission of the EC indicate increasing support for introducing the USA policy of *cross-compliance* into EC agricultural policy. In this, subsidies for production are used as a lever to encourage environmentally sensitive farming by making such payments conditional upon a contract to increase the output of public goods and reduce external costs.[15]

Standards with charges

An example of this in the UK relates to milk where all deliveries to the Milk Marketing Board are tested for antibiotics and other contaminants. Automatic penalties are applied for any deviation of standards.

Another example is provided by the powers of the National Rivers Authority to prosecute farmers who discharge effluent exceeding specific standards into waterways. In this case, the problems of monitoring and of legal process make it more difficult to ensure that the polluter pays than in the case of milk.

Permits

As yet there is no instance of pollution permits in UK agriculture, but such a policy has been introduced in the Netherlands for animal wastes and the basis for such a policy appears to have been established in the UK with the creation of a Code of Good Agricultural Practice (MAFF/ WOAD, 1991). This sets out recommended maximum volumes of manure or slurry which may be applied on high risk sites, as well as the recommended maximum nitrogen equivalent of that which can be spread. It would be a simple step from there to grant farmers a permit for a quantity of manure (and its nitrogen equivalent) to be spread on their own land, and to calculate the expected output from their livestock. As in the Netherlands, the policy would operate by requiring farmers to obtain certificates to show that the excess of estimated over 'permitted' manure output had been disposed of by approved means. This might be by transporting it to the fields of farmers whose permitted levels exceeds the output of their own livestock, or to a sewage treatment plant. Clearly, disposal by these means might well entail costs to the livestock farmer (certainly in the second case), in which case he/she would be forced to internalise some or all of the external costs.

9.7.2 Policies of acquiring or changing user rights

Public land purchase and ownership

The most secure way of conserving land in a particular use and of obtaining control in order to change use is for the public sector to buy it from existing private owners, and either to manage it directly or rent it subject to strict conditions of use. Powers to do this in the UK are available to the English Nature Council (ENC),[16] National Park Authorities (NPAs) and Local Authorities (LAs). Both the ENC and NPAs have been slowly adding to their land stock where this has enabled them to protect what are seen as key sites from a landscape, wildlife, geological or archaeological standpoint. The ENC by 1989 had purchased some 52 000 hectares for protection as National Nature Reserves and the NPAs owned 39 760 hectares. The importance of this is supported by analysis[17] which suggests that public land purchase is often a cheaper way of securing the desired form of management than an alternative involving paying a private owner to undertake it.

At the same time as limited land purchases have continued to be made by the ENC and NPAs, government has been putting pressure on LAs, the Forestry Commission and the Ministry of Defence to dispose of parts of their large landholdings, including some which have special conservation status. When added to the effects of privatising the formerly public Water Authorities, with their significant moorland and forest holdings, a pattern of policy emerges which entails reducing the public sector role in managing conservation land and key sites, but placing increasing reliance on voluntary bodies (VBs) which have diverse conservation interests. This switch is supported by ensuring where designated conservation land is sold by public bodies, that legislation gives VBs the first opportunity to buy.

Transfer of ownership to voluntary bodies

UK policy supports this to a limited extent by making funds available through key statutory authorities to grant-aid (subsidise) the VBs in purchasing the land. Among the VBs with significant land holdings are the National Trusts (240 000 hectares), Royal Society for the Protection of Birds (38 000 ha.) and the Royal Society for Nature Conservation (20 000 ha.). The majority of these holdings have been willed to these bodies or bought wholly with their own funds. Even where public grant-aid has been used, it is frequently only modest in proportion to the full purchase cost. This, of course, is the very attraction of the role of the VBs, for the bulk of their holding is acquired at the expense of their members, and any continuing management costs will likewise be met by their members [18] This may be interpreted as reflecting a situation where the willingness to pay of the conservationists exceeds the willingness to accept of private owners, thus permitting bargains to be struck whereby land ownership passes to the VBs. It has the additional merit that where public funds are used to subsidise the purchase it is usually much cheaper in public costs than other policy options.

Renting user rights

Opportunities for achieving environmental objectives through land purchase occur at random and somewhat infrequently. Moreover, there is considerable feeling against a heavy-handed approach, which might be considered as creeping land nationalisation despite any virtues that might have (Bateman, 1989). There is a very strong political ethos in favour of voluntary action secured by means of incentives. Certainly this is the mainstay of UK policy efforts to secure environmentally friendly management.

Even where policy adopts its most regulatory stance, which is where the NCC has designated key areas as Sites of Special Scientific Interest (SSSIs), compliance with the required management system is essentially voluntary. Owners of SSSIs have to notify the authorities of certain proposed changes and if the authorities feel these will damage the scientific interest they must enter into negotiation and offer a payment to compensate owners from abandoning their plans. There are many complexities to the procedure, very fully discussed by Whitby *et al.* (1990), but since agreement is almost always obtained with the owners it would appear that this voluntary system is successful, and at a modest cost.

9.8   FINAL COMMENTS

There can be no doubt that any review of current issues in agricultural economics has to give due weight to environmental economics. Neither the policy nor the methodological issues involved are transient ones, but they have risen progressively in importance in the last two decades to the point where they occupy a major, even central, place in the current research agenda. Work in this area has opened up new impetus for multidisciplinary interaction with environmental biologists, geographers and others. This is a reflection in itself of the way that the expansion and intensification of agricultural production has exerted ever increasing strains upon the environment in the ways outlined above. In order that further expansion of output globally can take place acceptably, there will be a continuous policy process of reacting to new evidence of external costs by seeking new technologies and by applying both incentives and restrictions. Concern with environmental issues also complements the agenda for agricultural policy reform in the context of the GATT negotiations.[19] Payments to farmers for the production of what may be called environmental goods may prove to be an acceptable substitute for commodity price supports as a means of supporting agriculture. Provided that such measures are judged not to stimulate commodity output or distort trade they may be classed as 'decoupled' and assigned to the 'green box' of acceptable support measures. Thus policies to reduce output by support for conversion from intensive to extensive or organic farming, or for set-aside and cross-compliance are likely to prove acceptable. Certainly, such measures are part of the reforms of the Common Agricultural Policy proposed by Commissioner Ray MacSharry and are the subject of many proposals for new measures.[20]

10   Less Favoured Areas and Rural Decline

K. J. THOMSON[1]

10.1   INTRODUCTION

For many years, much attention has been paid to the role of agriculture in regions with longstanding socio-economic difficulties. However, this is only one of a larger and more complex set of issues concerning the rural economy in areas with a disadvantaged economic base. With a specific focus on the role of agriculture, this chapter discusses some of these issues from an economic viewpoint under a number of headings: definitions, classifications, theories, demography, development and policy. Its title, in concentrating on less (rather than more) favoured areas and on rural decline (rather than growth), can be interpreted as reflecting both the political fact that difficulties attract more public attention than opportunities, and the economic fact that change occurs 'at the margin'.

The attention paid to agriculture's role in rural development can in part be explained – and criticised (Wibberley, 1981) – by a number of factors. First, agriculture's relative economic decline to an average of about 3 per cent of GDP in industrialised countries (OECD, 1991) has regional implications: it appears that the technological changes behind the supply side of this phenomenon tend to favour the more central regions with better production conditions and this has implications for both agriculture's share of regional output, and for the development of upstream and downstream sectors. Second is the 'bias' towards agriculture in the political economy (see Chapter 2). Third, farming, as a longstanding and still-important industry in many areas, and one with well-developed organisations and statistics, offers an obvious and easy area of analysis. Fourth, large amounts of public expenditure on agriculture naturally prompt questions of effectiveness in promoting regional economic growth. Finally, some of the more recent concerns over rural environmental issues (see Chapter 9) have important regional aspects. Thus, agricultural issues continue to play a prominent role in debate over rural affairs despite the growing importance of other sectors such as tourism and public services.

10.2 DEFINITIONS

While issues of rural decline can be discussed in general terms, practical economic analysis cannot proceed very far without clear definitions and corresponding numbers. In the present context, the first problem to be met is what is meant by *rural*, and to what extent it should include elements other than 'pure' countryside, for example, small towns, coastal areas, isolated factories or mountain tops. Negative definitions, such as 'non-metropolitan' or 'unbuilt-up', help a little, but there seems no hope of establishing a single comprehensive definition, and even less of seeing this reflected in official statistics, which are presently collected in a wide variety of ways. Yet without such a definition, it is difficult to reach general conclusions.

Two escapes may be sought from this impasse. One is to accept the diversity of rural areas (a feature which is stressed by all observers), and to agree to gather information and to interpret results in the recognition that universal truths are unlikely to be found. If the problems of rural areas require fresh thinking and the creative adaptation of ideas from elsewhere, this approach has much to commend it. An alternative is to classify rural areas, so as to isolate the features that distinguish each type from others and from non-rural areas. This is explored in the next section.

The term *less favoured* needs to be interpreted with some objective or subjective concept of comparability in mind. At one level, the variability of terrain, climate and other conditions of agricultural production is too obvious to require much further comment. Clearly, attainable yields per hectare can differ widely even within countries, and where low may render farming only marginally profitable. However, as the section below on economic theories will indicate, there are a number of alternative approaches to marginality, including the rather naïve one that all resources will find their optimum use, and that equivalent factors will be equally rewarded wherever they are located.

Rural *decline* is another problematic concept. A straightforward economic definition would be an absolute or relative decrease in the output of the region concerned, measured in gross or net (product) terms. However, given the difficulties of defining 'rural' for statistical purposes, and the additional problem of allocating the increasingly important service elements of economic activity to a specific region, it is not surprising that this approach does not get far in practice. It is easier to analyse changes in the structure of rural economies, which allows the (contentious) corollary that falling shares of certain characteristic industries such as agriculture indicate a malaise in the region as a whole.

Social indicators offer another set of measures through which 'rural decline' may be detected: falling population levels are an obvious example, or perhaps more specialised variables as unusual ratios of age, class or occupation, or endangered standards of education or health. Or, 'decline' may be assessed by the changing nature of people's lives, through indicators of rural poverty (McLaughlin, 1985), the abandonment of traditions, or rising levels of crime and anti-social behaviour in rural areas.

The environment offers yet another set of potential measures of 'rural decline'. The appearance of the landscape has been altered by farming and forestry in ways which many regret. The physical consequences of an industrial national economy – overhead wires, intercity highways, standardised building materials, waste disposal facilities – also introduce alien landscape features. Widespread concern is also expressed over the effects of agricultural development, and over the quality of river and lake water. In some areas, deliberate moves are made to suppress overt economic activity for the purpose of environmental enhancement, such as in the National Parks of the United States, and to promote 'natural' features of the landscape: is this properly labelled as 'decline'?

Despite these difficulties it is generally accepted (though not by all) that government policy should promote economic activity in rural areas, especially those considered to be suffering 'rural decline'. This leads to the question of '*rural development*'. Two major reviewers of the literature have defined rural development as

the overall improvement in the economic and social well-being of rural residents and the institutional and physical environment in which they live. (Jansma *et al.*, 1981)

and as being concerned with

the welfare of rural residents and with policies aimed at improving the potential of rural areas both to provide them with satisfactory incomes and access to a broad range of services, and to use rural resources in a manner consistent with the demands of urban residents. (Hodge, 1986).

These definitions certainly identify the major concepts ecompased by 'rural development'. However, it may be better to distinguish relatively objective goals (economic well-being, environment, welfare) both from methods aimed at improving these (institution[s], policies) and from less observable (and/or less economic) features (social well-being, potential, use . . . consistent with . . . demands). In line with the literature on developing countries, it also seems useful to distinguish more general economic growth (a rise in average incomes per head) from the more dynamic development (a change in the economic structure of resource use and/or output mix). However, Hodge's extension to the interests of urban residents appears justified when one considers the increasing importance of environmental and other externalities. Also, the references to institutions and policies by the two source authors are reminders of the efforts made by governments and others to implement improvement or accelerate the process of rural development in many regions.

The role of agriculture in the above definitions and reviews is played down, partly no doubt because of the already low, and still falling, proportion of output and employment accounted for by farming in most developed country regions, and partly to emphasise the more comprehensive approach taken more or less deliberately by modern investigators. Nevertheless, the 'less favoured area' (LFA) is an official designation of the Common Agricultural Policy (CAP) of the European Community (EC), and this *agricultural* interpretation of the term is commonly adopted.

10.3 CLASSIFICATION

The classification of rural regions, into 'less favoured' and 'other' areas or of different types of less favoured areas such as 'urban fringe' and 'remote', could occupy a chapter in itself. Most developed countries have defined, more or less roughly, a number of problem rural regions, such as the EC's LFAs to which special administrative arrangements and/or additional funding apply. These sometimes offer convenient if not always very suitable units of analysis, for comparison with 'normal' conditions elsewhere. However, there are often several such categories drawn up by various authorities for different purposes, and there are usually awkward changes in coverage over time as the underlying policy focus is adjusted.

A considerable amount of academic work has been directed at the objective classification of rural areas. Such classification can be done simply, but perhaps not satisfactorily, by placing areas on a scale, using an indicator such as population density, or rate of economic growth. Alternatively, more sophisticated multivariate methods, statistical or judgmental, may be used. Usually, a number of agricultural variables are employed in such analyses, including farming's share of total employment or population, its structure (size and type of farms), and sometimes farm income levels. However, because policy interest (if not expenditure) has shifted to non-agricultural development and environmental conservation, several other variables are frequently used, including indicators of population and land use. In any case, questions arise as to the appropriate size and delineation of the areas so classified.

Cloke (1977) has developed an index of rurality in England and Wales, based on several census variables at district level, combined via principal component analysis. Revell (NEDC, 1990) has employed cluster analysis to identify ten types of LFA regions within the UK as a whole. Matthews (1986) reports a number of exercises for Ireland. Von Meyer (1990) has recently examined about sixty EC regions in terms of both Gross Value Added per inhabitant (as a measure of regional development) and Agricultural Income per farm work unit, and finds that these can be grouped into three main geographical areas, each with a 'centre' and 'periphery'. He concludes that 'the economic importance of natural conditions . . . is growing rather than declining', and that agricultural incomes tend to rise with regional development, though less so at higher average regional incomes.

10.4   ECONOMIC THEORY

A number of economic theories, some general, some specific, have been put forward to aid economic analysis of differential rates of regional development, often with agriculture in mind. Only a selection of the most prominent can be given here, and then only in outline. The classical Ricardo–Mill principle of comparative advantage attempts to explain production patterns and trade flows by pointing to the gains to be made by specialising on the basis of opportunity costs. Where resources such as land and labour have different relative technical productivities in different regions, they will be allocated to different production patterns assuming price signals are not distorted to avoid this. Thus areas with difficult soil and climatic conditions, such as the hills and uplands, are largely devoted to grazing systems and the easier farmed lowlands to cropping, even though grass yields are higher in the latter. Marginal land will be brought into production, and generate non-zero rent, according to whether receipts will cover the costs of doing so.

A more modern and deeper explanation is the Heckscher–Ohlin proposition that comparative advantage depends on relative factor endowments among regions and on different factor intensities among productive processes. According to this theory, regional agricultural development proceeds according to the land, labour and capital requirements of alternative farm enterprises. Technological change, and shifts in consumer demands, therefore have regional impacts over time, and factor incomes in certain areas face long-term pressure where product prices are static, and where alternative uses elsewhere offer higher rewards to factors. Over the long run, of course, all factors except land can shift in location, but the theory retains value in relation to the geographical patterns of natural resources and of slowly adjusting levels of population and fixed investment. It also offers pointers to the regional effects of technological change, which alters factor intensities, and promotes unequal regional economic growth.

An alternative group of more explicitly spatial theories stems from von Thünen's early consideration of land use patterns, later to be complemented by the ideas of Weber, Lösch and Christaller on industrial and settlement location (Alonso, 1964; Whitby and Willis, 1978). Focusing attention on transport costs and economies of scale, these theories have had a powerful effect in shaping regional economic policies, as embodied in 'growth poles', the 'push' and 'pull' instruments of expansion controls and regional subsidies respectively, and in the improvement of communication infrastructure.

Twentieth-century efforts at the quantitative analysis of regional economies led first to the concept of the 'economic base' of an area and the associated 'multiplier' effects of changes in exogenous demand, and later to the more comprehensive input–output and mathematical programming models. Some of these have focused on agriculture alone, or on agriculture and associated industries (Johns and Leat,

1986), while others have adapted macroeconomic techniques to regional applications (Jensen, Manderville and Karunaratne, 1977). Though often formulated as somewhat simplistic models of economic behaviour, such as linear production relationships, these methods have offered numerical coefficients and output and employment estimates so that the effects of agricultural adjustment on regional economies can be better assessed.

Finally, an alternative group of theories about regional economic development, particularly in terms of differential effects, may be constructed from Marxist-inspired notions of capital accumulation processes in central and peripheral regions (Petit, 1981; Lowe, Marsden and Munton, 1990), possibly combined with analysis of rent-seeking behaviour by relevant interest groups who attempt to adapt public policy to private benefit.

Clearly, these theories both compete with and complement each other, depend on a wide range of explanatory factors, and focus attention on a number of alternative outcome indicators. The next two sections group several of these indicators under the headings of demography and rural development, reflecting, respectively, the social and the economic aspects of rural problems.

10.5 DEMOGRAPHY

Historically, rural decline is associated closely with depopulation. Outmigration from the countryside to the towns and cities, or to new countries, in response to perceptions of better working and living conditions, was the dominant rural demographic feature noted by observers over the centuries. Absolute reductions in the rural population have been somewhat less common, partly due to the general excess of birth over death rates, partly to relatively higher birth rates in rural areas, and partly to counterflows (of which more below). However, there is no doubt that in many parts of Europe and even in North America, particularly in the upland and remoter areas, substantial losses in population have been experienced, with differential outmigration leading to imbalances in age, sex and social class profiles. In some cases, there has been almost complete abandonment of the land by the indigenous population, as exemplified by the Scottish Highland clearances of the early nineteenth century and the modern-day 'desertification' in the Massif Central in France.

Another aspect, less easily measured by census but nevertheless central to the decline issue, has been the concentration of workplaces and service points. While people may still reside in rural areas, less of their economically active time is spent there. Improved transport links and higher income levels encourage commuting on a daily or weekly basis, the rise of the supermarket militates against local shopping, and larger schools and medical centres serve much wider areas. Some of these trends reflect general social developments – towards increased leisure time and home-based recreation, for instance – but others stem from deep-seated technical and economic factors which have geographical consequences. Amongst these factors are scale economies in manufacturing and, related to the provision of services, improvements in communication, changing relative prices of goods and services within the general economy, and rising real household incomes.

In recent decades, changes and reversals of these trends have been observed. Counter-urbanisation, in various forms – inner city depopulation, suburbanisation, the dispersal of employment to smaller settlements, a search for 'nature', second homes – has led to marked increases in the population of many non-urban areas (Table 10.1). Some of this is due to statistical construction (urban boundaries not

TABLE 10.1   Rural population change in the United Kingdom

	Period	Population change: people per thousand per year		
		Natural change	Migration	Net change
England and Wales	1971–88			
Overall		1.2	0.2	1.5
Mixed urban–rural		2.7	4.5	7.0
Remoter, largely rural		−0.6	9.5	9.4
Scotland	1981–89			
Overall		0.5	−2.7	−2.1
Rural		0.1	3.4	3.3
Northern Ireland	1981–89			
Overall		—	—	3.7
Rural		—	—	5.1

Source: House of Lords (1990), from OPCS, etc.

keeping pace with expanding metropolitan areas), but most is undoubtedly due to wider dispersion of households. Some technical advances, such as specialist manufacturing and leisure services, containerisation and 'telecommuting' (working at home or at a distance, using telecommunications), mitigate against older forces of concentration. Convergence in the socio-economic behaviour of urban and rural people reduces barriers to household mobility. However, detailed investigations in the more rural areas (Whitby, in House of Lords, 1990) suggest that remoteness is still a factor tending to depress population levels in areas without strong tourist or retirement attractions. In this sense, the older forces still operate, often in stages via movement into local rural settlements, which in turn act as staging post for migration to other regions.

Agriculture plays several roles in these population changes and movements. Many of the various mechanical, chemical and biological technological advances in farming, along with rising real incomes outside the industry, have tended to displace labour from farm businesses. Agriculture's share of the national workforce is now below 10 per cent in most developed countries, and down to 2 per cent in heavily urbanised countries such as the United Kingdom, where even in rural areas the proportion is rarely over 20 per cent. Both workers and managers (farmers), but especially the former, have left agriculture for alternative occupations, and this usually involves a change of residence. However, new technologies and institutional arrangements, such as cooperatives and contracting, seem more than capable of sustaining aggregate production.

Another obvious role for agriculture is as a resource base for rural development. Land is required not only for extensive uses such as forestry and golf courses, but also for urban-related development such as housing (which expands much faster than population due to the formation of smaller households). In controlling this process of resource transfer, different countries impose various forms of development control to protect better quality farmland, the United Kingdom and the Netherlands being amongst the strictest, but in recent years chronic food surpluses and a more liberal political ideology have tended to loosen these constraints. Annual growth rates in agricultural yields of 2 or 3 per cent have been more than sufficient to compensate for losses of farmland of well under 1 per cent per year. Nevertheless, there are a number of often localised concerns, such as interferences with, and 'planning blight' (land degradation while permission to develop is awaited) on, urban-fringe farming. Moreover, environmental problems are thrown up by new crops and farming techniques, and by land improvement.

Farmers are often involved in population movements in a number of other, less direct ways. Though declining in number, farm workers sometimes require new housing in areas where national policy discourages building. On the other hand, buildings no longer required for farm purposes can be rented or sold to incomers, often to great financial advantage. Increasingly, a more dispersed non-farming population with growing environmental sensitivities is taking a closer interest in farming operations such as crop spraying and field enlargement. Public intervention in the technical activities as well as the structural pattern of farming is on the increase.

Though it is now generally accepted that the industry cannot be expected to alter greatly the magnitude of national population movements, farming's role is not entirely a passive one. Part-time farming and pluriactive (multiple job-holding) farm households provide a meeting-ground for agricultural and non-agricultural activities. In some countries, such as West Germany and the United States, the bulk of farming, measured by population or household income, already exists in this form. Much research and debate is currently focused on this area (Gasson, 1988; Hill, 1989; Shucksmith and Smith, 1991), some with policy implications in mind.

10.6 RURAL DEVELOPMENT

The timing and pace of rural development appears highly dependent on a mixture of structural factors, including the land tenure system, the development and location of other industries, and the agricultural policy pursued by governments. However, it seems generally true that with economic diversification, the differences between urban and rural economies are becoming progressively smaller in many countries. Bauwens and Douw (1986) go so far as to claim that, in a narrow sense, rural development is a minor problem in the Netherlands.

In most countries, however, rural development is an important economic issue, and one that provokes considerable discussion. A neat encapsulation of three different distributional perspectives – originally suggested by Leven (1965) – is given by Jansma *et al.* (1981, pp. 294–5) in the context of a problem of outmigration. A 'self-interest' group representing the industrial and commercial segments of the regional economy try to oppose outmigration, in an effort to maintain aggregate regional income and expenditure, by exploring new resources and technologies and by stimulating local and inward entrepreneurship. The advocates of 'equity', more interested in raising per capita incomes of the regional population, try to remove the cause of outmigration – generally seen as caused by a chronic investment deficiency by public or private sectors, in roads, education, productive capital, etc. The advocates of 'efficiency' – who aim at identifying and reducing barriers to national economic performance – tend to encourage outmigration, in order to increase per capita incomes for both leavers and stayers. A similar analysis might be relevant to regional questions of, say, nature conservation or technical performance in agriculture.

Turning more directly to the place of agriculture in the economics of rural regions, the main issue once again is the importance of the industry in the general level of economic activity. In urban fringe areas, agriculture is clearly highly marginal, in several senses (Giessübel and Spitzer, 1986; Thomson, 1981). In remote areas farming occupies a more important role, and with a paucity of other alternatives it may offer more rewarding returns to policy intervention than, for instance, afforestation or manufacturing (HM Treasury, 1972).

In Ireland, an agrarian country with considerable problems of rural development, Matthews (1986) identifies five broad themes in the academic literature – first, the restructuring of agriculture and its implications for demography and land use; second, diversification of the rural economy; third, service provision in rural areas; fourth, conflicts between alternative rural land uses (agriculture, forestry, mineral extraction, nature conservation, and urban expansion); and fifth, institutional development. With reference to the first of these themes, land tenure patterns and public policies in Ireland have led to the accumulation of holdings in relatively unproductive hands, with extensification and even dereliction as the result.

A further theme in agrarian rural development is the issue of part-time farming, already noted under Demography above (Gasson, 1988). A distinction may be made (de Benedictis, 1986) between 'active' and 'passive' part-time farming. Active part-time farming involves employment of farm family individuals in numerous and diffuse small- and medium-size industries in order to benefit from the higher and regular wage levels obtainable. Passive part-time farming involves rather precarious employment outside the farm simply to maintain an acceptable level of farming income. Higgins (1983) and Cawley (1983) report that part-time farming in Ireland is associated with younger landholders whose farming performance is comparable with full-time systems.

Whatever its form, it is now generally accepted that part-time farming is not necessarily, or even mainly, a stage in the exodus of farming operators from the industry, but a stable and growing component of agriculture capable of generating sizeable economic and social benefits at the micro (farm and family) and at the territorial level. Furthermore, analysis of farming systems now encompasses 'the entire family, which becomes the relevant elementary unit where fundamental decisions about labour allocation, income production and distribution are taken' (de Benedictis, 1986).

10.7 POLICY

Against the number and complexity of the issues raised above, it is not surprising to find that there is no clear set of government policies addressed to the problems of rural economic decline. Even if there were, the complexity of the task has been termed 'the first obstacle in the way of governments' efforts' (UN, 1979). Historically, agricultural policy, directed at the core of the rural economy, has been the primary vehicle of public intervention, but the provision of infrastructure in such forms as railways, road improvements and electrification, and the supply of postal, educational and other services, has often been pursued with public funding, and contributed to the pace and nature of rural development. In some areas, and for some functions, non-agricultural policies have been introduced. Regional economic support has often been directed primarily at urban or large-scale industries, but there have been specialised rural development agencies, often in the remoter regions, and these have channelled funds to local enterprises in the hope of sustaining employment. Environmental policies have had a strong rural component in promoting wildlife conservation or recreational resources. To analyse the interaction of these various policies amongst themselves, and against a shifting background of general and local socio-economic forces, is clearly a formidable task, and one not helped by hierarchical and overlapping areas, both functional and geographical, of responsibility among the various agencies involved.

In the European Community (EC), there has been continuing discussion about these difficulties and on how to handle them, coloured by arguments over the Community's policies and budget. As is well known, the EC's Common Agricultural Policy (CAP) has dominated the latter, with the European Agricultural Fund taking up around 60 per cent of the total EC budget for many years, nearly all accounted for by its market-supporting Guarantee Section. By comparison, the Structural Funds – the Agricultural Guidance Section, and the Regional Development and Social Funds – together account for under 20 per cent of the total, and much of this is directed at non-rural targets.

Within the CAP, the less favoured areas (LFAs) have been established since 1975: in the case of the newly joined United Kingdom this replaced the post-war hill farming regions. Two main types of LFAs were set up. 'Mountain areas' higher than 600–1000 metres above sea level possess short growing seasons and/or steep slopes. 'Other' less favoured areas are characterised by infertile land, low financial returns to farming relative to the national average, and a low or dwindling population endangering regional viability. With modifications over the years – primarily their extension, so that LFAs now cover about 40 per cent of the total agricultural area of the Community – these have attracted extra Community and national support for farming 'in order to ensure the continuation of farming, thereby maintaining a minimum population level or conserving the countryside' (Commission of the EC, Official Journal L128/3, 1975).

The main Community instruments in the LFAs have been the 'horizontal' compensatory allowances paid directly to all eligible farmers on the basis of livestock units or crop areas, and a number of special or enhanced investment schemes, some in restricted regions. The compensatory allowances are payable subject to a number of limitations on holding size and intensity which severely restricted their applicability to an estimated 27 per cent of LFA holdings in the EC-10 in 1985 (Commission of the EC, 1990, p. 29). The allowances are partly financed directly by member states (50 per cent in Ireland and most of the south of the Community, 75 per cent elsewhere), and in total accounted for almost 550 million ECU in 1985; by 1988, it is estimated that this had increased by over 50 per cent. Nevertheless, and even adding other LFA scheme expenditures, these amounts were dwarfed by market-support spending from the Guarantee Section of the Community's Agricultural Fund (28 billion ECU in 1988). In the mid-1980s, efforts were made to integrate Guidance Section funds with other sources in special development programmes, primarily in the Mediterranean.

The differences between farming in the EC LFAs and in 'normal' regions have been examined in an analysis of the 1985 EC farm structure survey data (Commission of the EC, 1990). The LFAs (both 'mountain' and 'other') of the Community of Ten (i.e. excluding Spain and Portugal) accounted for 41 per cent of all EC farms, and 39 per cent of the utilised agricultural area, but for only 25 per cent of the total EC-10 standard gross margin (a measure of economic potential). Not surprisingly, therefore, the standard gross margin per labour unit in the EC-10 LFAs was only about two-thirds that in 'normal' areas. Thus the issue arises as to whether this differential is due to differences or deficiencies in LFA farming structures, or to other causes such as regional distortions in factor or product markets.

Another issue on which the structural survey throws some light is the pattern of the farm labour force, which might be expected to vary according to different cost structures and returns. Family labour, which comprises the bulk of agricultural workforce in all member states (even the United Kingdom at 59 per cent of the workforce overall), was notably more important in the LFAs (around 90 per cent of total labour in most countries, and 77 per cent in the UK LFAs). Although part-time farming was more common in the LFAs than in 'normal' areas, 'other gainful activities' were only noticeably more frequent than the Community average (of 23 per cent) in the non-mountainous LFAs. 'Apparent underemployment', measured by the proportion of part-time farmers without other main occupation (and therefore aggregating both the 'real' unemployed, and semi-retired farmers), was somewhat higher in the LFAs (especially mountain areas) than elsewhere.

In addition to these descriptive issues, questions of structural policy suitability and effectiveness can be addressed via the same analysis. The EC analysis identified five groups of LFA regions where the impact of various structural measures was expected to differ :

1. LFAs in Italy and Greece where the average farm holding area is low and there is a high proportion of farmers aged over 55. Here, early retirement and land consolidation schemes offer hope, though possibly at the risk of desertification (land abandonment) in some places.
2. Other Greek and Italian LFAs, where the age balance is close to the Community average, but farm size is comparatively low. In

such areas, the provision of alternative non-farming jobs and/or direct structural aids appear the only solutions.

3. Most of the German LFAs, where relatively young farmers occupy holdings of average size, and where group farming and equipment-sharing might improve competitiveness.

4. French and some British regions where the LFA farm size is higher than average, and structural conditions appear better.

5. Other British LFAs with extensive farm holdings, but with problems of rural depopulation.

Amongst full-time farms, those in LFAs tend to have considerably lower levels of productivity than those in normal areas, whether measured per labour unit, per hectare, per farm capital (machinery, buildings, livestock, etc.) or per unit of purchased inputs such as feed (intermediate consumption). The consequence is lower levels of farm income on LFA farms, even with direct subsidies taken into account. Such subsidies ran at rates 2 to 6 times higher on LFA farms than elsewhere, and accounted for a significant proportion of LFA family farm incomes – up to 33 per cent in most cases, and nearly 100 per cent of UK LFA family farm income in the years around 1985 (Commission of the EC, 1990).

In 1988, the EC Structural Funds were more firmly coordinated, with the establishment of a number of priority objectives, of which Objective 1 was directed at 'less developed' and often mostly rural regions, and Objective 5(b) at rural areas in general. Not only did this involve a rebalancing of Structural Fund expenditure towards the poorer countries and regions in the Community, such as Ireland, Portugal and much of the Mediterranean members, but smaller geographical areas were chosen with the aid of objective socio-economic criteria, and support was to be channelled through specific programmes. This may go some way towards remedying the inefficiencies inherent in the previous more widespread and unco-ordinated system.

A major recent event has been the publication of *The Future of Rural Society*[2] (Commission of the EC, 1988), which contains a general analysis of rural problems in the Community along with proposals for tackling these.

In this document, the Commission identified three types of standard problem areas, and for each type a basic strategy:

- Areas 'suffering from the pressures of modern life' (essentially the urban fringe), where protection of the environment should receive priority, in order to maintain a natural ecological and recreational resource. Agriculture should contribute to this by avoiding fragmentation of holdings and by adopting environmentally friendly techniques.

- Areas 'suffering from rural decline' where agriculture is still important but employment opportunities are inadequate. In these areas job creation is the major task, based on local resources, and involving mutually reinforcing clusters of processes and services, probably concentrated in intermediate centres. Agriculture can play a role in providing raw materials for processing, preferably of quality and regional character.
- Very remote 'vulnerable' areas with declining populations and fragile economies. Here the remaining population should be encouraged to remain, with assistance to providing infrastructure and sustaining tourist attractions. Agriculture will require income support, but this can be differentiated by need and to encourage environmental qualities for ecological and touristic purposes.

The application of this thinking in terms of widespread and integrated policy instruments is not yet far enough advanced to see if such approaches can help to resolve some of the longstanding problems of agriculture in less favoured areas and of rural regional development in general. If the pace of agricultural policy reform quickens, perhaps under the influence of biotechnological advances (see Chapter 8), conclusions will be the more difficult to arrive at. The nature of such reform – towards more liberalised markets, which may make the economic conditions of farming in less favoured areas even more adverse, or towards supply controls, which may be tailored in such a way as to advantage LFA agriculture (as was done with the EC dairy quotas) – will heavily influence the outcome.

What does seem certain is that the interaction between agricultural change and regional economic development (or decline) will continue to throw up issues of widespread concern and interest. Since multiple objectives, however necessary or desirable, tend to complicate matters, public and professional discussions will be assisted by clearer ideas about the most appropriate roles for land in agriculturally less favoured areas, whether in the urban fringes or in upland or remote regions. This, in turn, depends on wider social, cultural and political developments well beyond agriculture itself.

End-Notes

CHAPTER 1

1. Argentina has actually had export taxes.
2. The *gross* PSE measures the assistance provided to producers by market price support, direct government payments to producers, subsidies on inputs, taxation concessions and other support measures. The *net* PSE is the gross PSE adjusted for additional feed costs imposed on livestock products as a result of market price support. The percentage (gross or net) PSE is the value of the PSE expressed as a percentage of the value of total farm receipts. For further details see OECD (1991) p. 16.
3. The countries are Australia, Austria, Canada, EC, Finland, Japan, New Zealand, Norway, Sweden, Switzerland and the USA.
4. The total monetary transfer arising from agricultural policies are somewhat higher than those included in PSE calculations and amounted to some $300 bn. in 1990: see OECD (1991) p. 137.
5. Average figure for USA, EC and Japan in 1986/7 (Roningen and Dixit, 1989).
6. See, for example, D. Gale Johnson (1973 and 1991).

CHAPTER 2

1. I am grateful to David Colman and Tony Rayner for encouragement and for comments on an earlier draft, and to Vicki Winters for typing.
2. Social choice theory – for example, Mueller (1989) shows the impossibility, except through luck, of aggregating individuals' preferences to obtain a consistent social ordering.
3. While the idea is an old one, I believe this term originated in Winters (1987).
4. An alternative mechanism for achieving social rationality would be that governments which are inefficient maximisers eventually lose power. While true of the big issues – e.g. the fall of Communism – it is not a plausible view of agricultural policy.
5. See Hillman (1988) for more on social insurance arguments.
6. Both studies also claim to identify other determinants of protection. Honma and Hayami find smaller agricultural sectors more heavily protected, arguing, incorrectly, that the smaller the sector, the smaller per head of non-agricultural population is the burden of protecting it. (The argument is incorrect because it ignores deadweight losses – i.e.

consumer losses that do not increase producers' incomes.) Gardner finds factors affecting the ease of lobbying important and that price declines greater than average tend to 'win' protection.

7. Imagine an industry with a given demand curve for protection facing a monopoly supplier of protection with a given marginal (political) cost curve for providing protection and which is alternatively run by either politicians or bureaucrats. If politicians control the latter they seek to maximise the political profits from protection and hence set the tariff so that the marginal costs and marginal (political) revenue of the tariff are equal. If bureaucrats are in charge, on the other hand, they ignore political profits but pay regard to the amount of activity they are undertaking or the amount of revenue they can collect, and in both cases provide marginal units of tariff that would be unprofitable for the politicians. (The analogy of this argument is the simple monopoly supplier of, say, fish. The profit-maximising monopolist constrains supplies even though at his optimum point he could both earn higher revenue and sell higher output.)

8. The meat farmers were hit first by the Payments-in-Kind scheme, which raised feedstuff prices, and then by a significant glut of meat products as surplus dairy herds were slaughtered.

9. Very crudely these might be thought of respectively as 'conspiracy' and 'cock-up' theories of politics.

10. These are only tendencies. Australia and New Zealand, for example, penalise agriculture by supporting manufacturing more heavily than agriculture, while many developing countries support their import-competing sectors – see Krueger, Schiff and Valdes (1988). Balisacan and Roumasset (1987) offer a similar analysis to Anderson's.

11. Farmers earnings (value added) are given by

$$v = q \, (p - ak)$$

where v is value added, q output, p price, k the cost of inputs and a the volume of inputs required per unit of output. A little algebra shows that the elasticity of v with respect to p (holding a and k constant and writing the supply curve as $q(p)$) is

$$dv/dp \, . \, p/v = p/(p - ka) + p/q \, . \, dq/dp$$

Clearly this rises as a rises.

12. This argument presumes that dead-weight losses – losses to consumers that are not mere transfers to producers – are not too large.

13. France had several agricultural policies prior to 1936, but it was in that year that direct government intervention was introduced with the formation of the Office National Interprofessional de Ble – see Tracy (1989).

CHAPTER 3

1. The chapter by Alan Winters in this volume discusses in more detail the political economy of farm programmes.

2. See Krueger, Schiff and Valdes for an in-depth discussion of Agricultural Policy Developments in several developing countries over the period 1960–85.

3. The resolution of the OECD ministers in May 1987 went furthest in this regard (OECD, 1987).

4. The chapter by Rayner, Ingersent and Hine in this volume discusses in more depth the issue of trade policy reform in the GATT.

5. For more detail on the policy process and the changes described here, see Moyer and Josling (1990).

6. For a discussion of this debate, see USDA (1989).

7. Farm programmes existed in the member countries before the creation of the EC and the adoption of the CAP (see Tracy, 1989). They still exist, though mainly in the area of structural investment, farm labour legislation, and health and safety rules. The discussion here will focus on the CAP, which has responsibility for market price support.

8. Sheepmeat regulations remained national until 1980, when a common regime was introduced employing a 'basic' price, intervention buying and storage subsidies. Most imports enter under concessional schemes such as that with New Zealand.

9. The OECD does not calculate the efficiency of the policies in achieving their aims. To do this one needs to make further assumptions as described below. Therefore, the calculations shown should not be attributed to the OECD.

10. The triangle represents the integral of the marginal cost schedule over the quantity change (the extra costs incurred) less the value of that output at the non-subsidised price. If the world price is expected to rise as the subsidy is removed, the value of the additional output will have to be adjusted accordingly. This is done by calculating the terms-of-trade gain from the subsidy and subtracting this from the loss due to production distortion.

11. The OECD study contains a set of elasticity coefficients used in the part of the exercise that estimates world price impacts of policy removal.

CHAPTER 4

1. The contracting members of the GATT agree to conduct trade according to certain key rules :

   (i) no discrimination in trade arrangements between GATT members;
   (ii) protection to be provided by tariffs at rates fixed by international agreement;
   (iii) trade disputes to be settled by GATT mechanisms;
   (iv) regular negotiations to be held under the auspices of the GATT to reduce protection on a reciprocal basis.

2. PSEs are defined as the net assistance provided to agriculture through market price supports and government expenditures, expressed as a percentage of total farm receipts. The PSE estimates in the text were compiled by the OECD.

3. 'Global expenditures on domestic farm programs nearly doubled during the first five years of the 1980s. In 1986, the USA and the EC each spent nearly $25 billion on farm programs' (Roningen and Dixit, 1989a, p. 1).
4. The Cairns Group members are Argentina, Australia, Brazil, Canada, Chile, Columbia, Fiji, Hungary, Indonesia, Malaysia, New Zealand, the Philippines, Thailand and Uruguay.
5. For a full discussion, see Hathaway (1987) ch. 5.
6. The long-term trend in agricultural export prices relative to those of manufactures – the net barter terms of trade – is more controversial. Tyers and Anderson (see Tyers, 1990) demonstrate a declining trend for real international food prices (temperate zone products), 1900 to 1987; O'Connor *et al.* (1991b) find a declining trend for real international wheat prices, 1945 to 1990. MacBean and Nguyen (1987) pp. 55 and 64 show that the existence or otherwise of a trend depends on the time period and commodity grouping under consideration but find a generally declining trend for the period 1950–81.
7. See Winters (1990) and Chapter 2 of this book.
8. The absolute size of the agricultural labour force declines although agricultural production, under the influence of a high rate of technological change, expands over time in the developed economy.
9. The core elements of the agricultural transformation process are explicable in terms of two-sector closed economy growth models; see for example Anderson (1987) or Antle (1988) . The latter author also explains the process in the context of a three-sector open economy.
10. Schultz (1945, p. 82) called this a 'chronic disequilibrium adverse to agriculture' such that 'agriculture is constantly burdened with an excess supply of labour'.
11. For an account of agricultural policies in the USA and EC in an historical context see Josling Chapter 3 of this book, Tracy (1989) and Ingersent and Rayner (1993).
12. For an analysis of the demand for and supply of rent seeking activity in the context of trade protectionism, see Frey in Greenaway (1985). Rausser (1982) has labelled the rents from political lobbying as political economic seeking transfers (PESTS).
13. Implicitly, we are referring here to farmers in industrialised countries who consume a small or negligible fraction of their production. Note also, that the risk benefits do not accrue from price stabilisation *per se* but from a reduction in income variability. For further elucidation, see Newbery and Stiglitz (1981).
14. Domestic production of the commodity is assumed to fluctuate randomly as a result of the vagaries of weather,pests and diseases. The instability of gross income from the commodity depends on the variance of output , the variance of price and the covariance between output and price. For the small trader, the covariance term may be assumed to be unimportant.

   Formally, let q be domestic production, p be the international price and y be domestic producer gross income. The variance of the log of income is:

   $$\text{Var}(\log y) = \text{Var}(\log qp) = \text{Var}(\log q) + \text{Var}(\log p)$$
   $$+ 2\,\text{Cov}(\log q, \log p)$$

but with full price stabilisation:

$$\text{Var}(\log y) = \text{Var}(\log q)$$

For the small country, the covariance term is negligible so that price stabilisation reduces the instability of income. In the case of the large country, whose trade volume affects the international price, the covariance between domestic production and world price is negative and the benefits from an insulating policy are reduced. It is assumed in this analysis that the introduction of price stabilisation has no effect on the variance of production.

15. Food security, identified with self-sufficiency, is a dominant component of Japanese agricultural policy. For a full discussion, see Hillman and Rothenberg (1988).

16. For theoretical analyses of such mechanisms, typically in a partial equilibrium setting, see, for example, Greenaway (1983), McCalla and Josling (1985) or Houck (1986). For surveys of the use of the instruments by different countries see ABARE (1985 and 1989), McCalla and Josling (1985), World Bank (1986), IMF (1988), Colman and Young (1989), Sanderson (1990), Hillman (1991). The OECD also carries out regular surveys of national agricultural policies.

17. Partial equilibrium (PE) analysis is referred to below; for general equilibrium (GE) analyses see, for example, Stoeckel *et al.* (1989) or Burniaux *et al.* (1990). GE analysis takes account of the effects of agricultural protection on other trading sectors and on the non-traded sector by accounting for intersectoral competition for resources. In general, GE studies suggest that the welfare costs of agricultural protectionism are much higher than is implied by PE models.

18. For other studies, see for example, ABARE (1985), World Bank (1986), IMF (1988), Tyers and Anderson (1988), ABARE (1989).

19. See, for example, the studies reported in the World Bank (1986, ch. 6).

20. For further discussion, see Tyers and Anderson (1988).

21. Essentially, domestic price insulation increases world commodity market instability by making excess supply and demand schedules (export supply and import demand functions) more inelastic; see Johnson (1975) and McCalla and Josling (1985) ch. 2. Insulation of the internal price by one or more countries through trade devices increases the burden on price and trade adjustment placed on the rest of the world; see Johnson, op. cit., McCalla and Josling, op. cit., and Rayner and Reed (1979). Note also that insulation reduces the effectiveness of stock policies for absorbing sudden supply and demand shocks; see World Bank (1986) ch. 6.

22. See Hathaway (1987) p. 4.

23. Hathaway (1987) ch. 4, Hine, Ingersent and Rayner (1989) and Josling Chapter 3 above provide succinct accounts of the development of agricultural policy and the pressures for reform in the EC, USA and Japan.

24. Note that these results are presented for illustrative purposes only; other studies give differing quantitative estimates. A particular contrast between

the Tyers and Anderson (T&A) study and that by Roningen and Dixit (R&D) is that T&A show a gain to US producers from multilateral liberalisation whilst R&D show a loss.

25. Let the net economic gain from liberalisation by all industrialised countries be an approximation to the gain from joint liberalisation by the USA and the EC. Then the payoff matrices from US and EC strategies are:

	EC payoffs ($ billion)		US payoffs ($ billion)	
	USA (N)	USA (L)	USA (N)	USA (L)
EC (N)	0.0	−1.9	0.0	3.3
EC (L)	21.4	17.6	1.7	3.1

where each player has two pure strategies; namely, do nothing (N) or liberalise (L). The Nash equilibrium in this game is for both players to liberalise, this being the dominant strategy for each country. Note that if the self interest of each country was perceived in terms of producer welfare then, using the data in Table 4.3, the Nash equilibrium is for both countries to retain protection. For further discussion and an analysis of trade strategy within a game theory context employing the Nash equilibrium concept see Harrison *et al.* (1989).

26. Note that there are gains and losses within the US agricultural sector: it is likely that the highly protected dairy and sugar sectors would lose. The US position on agriculture in the Uruguay Round, described later in this chapter, appears to have been driven largely by the 'gainers', i.e. large-scale grain producers and traders with a major interest in expanding exports.

27. The identification of non-distorting decoupled payments, 'green box' policies, did not emerge until a later stage of the negotiations (see Table 4.6).

28. For a review of the agricultural negotiations up to and including the Geneva Accord, see Hine, Ingersent and Rayner (1989b).

29. In Brussels, the Swedish Minister of Agriculture, Mats Hellstrom, who chaired the negotiating group on agriculture, tried to forge a compromise solution. Hellstrom informally proposed an agreement based upon cuts of 30 per cent over five years from 1991 to 1995 in each of the three areas of internal support, border protection and export subsidies. But this proposal failed to gain unanimous support as the basis for continued negotiations.

30. The US position as presented by Bush was similar to the Hellstrom proposals as summarised in note 29.

31. 'Development and the Future of the CAP': Reflections Paper of the Commission CEC, COM (91) 100 Final.

32. Denmark, the Netherlands, the UK, Ireland, France and Italy took this position at the meeting of farm ministers on 27 January 1991.

33. See, for example McClatchy and Warley (1991) and O'Connor *et al.* (1991a) and (1991b).

34. This section draws on McClatchy and Warley (1991).

CHAPTER 5

1. This chapter draws on Csáki (1983, 1985, 1989, 1990, 1991) and Csáki and Varga (1990). Other useful sources are Wadekin and Brada (1988), Braverman and Guasch (1990), Nello (1990), Wadekin (1990), World Bank (1990), Brooks (1991), Brooks, Guasch, Braverman and Csaki (1991) and Gelb and Gray (1991). This chapter was completed prior to the break-up of the Soviet Union and the formation of the Commonwealth of Independent States (CIS) and it refers to the Soviet Union throughout.
2. For further discussion see Gelb and Gray (1991) annex 3.
3. In Eastern Europe, the value of land cannot be found in the registry of agricultural capital. The price of land is not calculated in the list of various expenses either.

CHAPTER 6

1. The author would like to thank Ti Zhongwang and Ye Qiaolun for their assistance in preparing this paper, and David Colman, Flemming Christiansen and Nicholas Lardy for their very helpful comments. Financial support from the Rockefeller Brothers Fund; the Committee on Scholarly Communications with the People's Republic of China with funds from the US Information Agency; the American Council of Learned Societies/Social Science Research Council with funds from the Andrew W. Mellon Foundation; and the National Science Foundation under grant no. SES-8908438 is gratefully acknowledged.
2. The discussion in this and later sections of the paper draw heavily on a wide range of Chinese sources, many of which are not cited here. References to the original Chinese sources can be found in Sicular (1990a).
3. See, for example, Kojima (1988).
4. See Bardhan (1973); Berry *et al.* (1979); Carter (1984); and Sicular (1989b).
5. For an example of a household contract in 1989, see Crook (1989a, 1989b)
6. Author interviews, Zouping County, Shandong Province.
7. See, for example, discussions in Oi (1986). Author interviews and observations in Shandong and Hubei also revealed this.
8. It is possible that villages draw up plans but do not seriously enforce them. Even before the reform period, however, village cadres were known not to carry out the official plans.
9. See Sicular (1990a) p. 10.
10. Producers also faced obligatory above quota deliveries, but information is not available on the level of or changes in these obligations.
11. Substandard cotton was permitted on the market in the early 1980s, but prohibitions on grade cotton remained.
12. Sicular (1989a).

13. Official statistics for government revenue include government borrowing. Also, in the early 1980s price subsidies were subtracted from government revenues rather than counted as expenditures. Western budgetary data do not count government borrowing in revenues and count price subsidies as an expenditure. In calculating this percentage, I have therefore subtracted government borrowing and added price subsidies to the official revenue data. The relevant price subsidy and budgetary data can be found in State Statistical Bureau (1990a) pp. 229, 232 and 244.

14. Some portion of these sales was probably at negotiated prices.

15. Sicular (1990a) p. 14.

16. Table 6.4, and Sicular (1990b) pp. 20–1 and footnotes 55 and 56. Note that these percentages overstate the degree of contract fulfilment, as some beyond-contract procurement occurred at contract prices.

17. The government monopoly on rice has reportedly been carried out more strictly in rice exporting localities than in rice importing localities (author interviews, Sichuan, 1990).

18. The national 'three link' programme for grain awarded 6 kg good quality fertiliser, 3 kg diesel oil, and a 20 per cent interest-free cash advance for each 100 kilograms contracted grain. In 1989, fertiliser awards were reportedly raised to 15 kg per 100 kg for contract deliveries of paddy and soybeans, and to 10 kg for wheat and corn. In 1988, cotton began to receive 5 kg diesel oil per 100 kg deliveries. See Sicular (1990a) pp. 16–17.

19. Sicular (1990a) p. 17.

20. Central Rural Policy Res. Off. Rur. Sur. Off. (1988) p. 49.

21. The estimates of debt owed farmers are from 'Pay up' (1989).

22. The actions of local governments often reflected real obstacles at the local level. In the case of 'link' incentive awards, for example, the central government apparently did not give local governments supplies of inputs sufficient to meet their 'link' obligations.

23. This is calculated using the national retail price index. State Statistical Bureau (1990a) p. 250.

24. Market price data for rice and wheat were provided by the Chinese Academy of Social Sciences; other data are from Table 6.3 and Sicular (1990a) p. 19.

25. For a detailed discussion of credit policies and related developments, see Tam (1988), Watson (1989), and West (1990).

26. Sicular (1990b) pp. 6, 23.

27. These numbers also exclude in-kind investment such as investment with unremunerated labour.

28. He (1990) p. 26.

29. Zou (1990) p. V.

30. See, for example, CCP (1990) p. VI.

31. Christiansen (1989) pp. 78–91.

32. Christiansen (1990) pp. 23–42.

33. New China News Agency (1988) pp. 270–1.

34. Chinese Finance and Banking Studies Association (1988) pp. 111–30. Unfortunately, statistics are not available for 1983 and 1984.

35. See Wong (1988) pp. 11–12.

36. Ibid., p. 11.
37. Ibid., p. 12.
38. Sicular (1990b) pp. 19–20, and Duan (1986) p. 37.
39. See Sicular (1990b) table 7.
40. The foreign trade corporations primarily responsible for agricultural trade have been the China National Cereals, Oil and Foodstuffs Import and Export Corporation; China National Native Products and Animal Byproducts Import and Export Corporation; and China National Textiles Import and Export Corporation.
41. State Statistical Bureau (1990a) pp. 20, 641. Increase in the level of trade is calculated using trade measured in US dollars; the comparison with domestic GNP uses trade measured in yuan.
42. This is also true for sugar, production of which has been fairly volatile during the 1980s.

CHAPTER 7

1. The latter interest continues: see, for example, Penson and Talpaz (1988) or Midmore (1991). However, for reasons of space mathematical programming approaches are not explicitly dealt with here.
2. Besides inflationary effects, Feldstein also investigates the influence of tax policy on land prices. The important influences of the latter on the agricultural sector are largely neglected by the theoretical exposition attempted here: but the interested reader is referred also to, for example, Alston (1986) and Burt (1986); and Leblanc and Hrubovcak (1986) who discuss macroeconomic influences on the level of investment in the agricultural sector.
3. Strictly we are assuming the decision-maker's cost function is quadratic in forecast errors, so that positive and negative forecast errors are penalised equally (see Granger, 1969) for analysis with a non-linear objective function).
4. This can be shown as follows: if $k = 1$, $E_{t-1} P_t = \pi P_{t-1}$, $E_t P_{t+1} = \pi P_t$ and $(-\beta P_t + k\alpha(E_t[P_{t+1} - P_t]) = \gamma E_{t-1}P_t + u_t + k\alpha[E_{t-1}[P_t - P_{t-1}])]$

then

$$P_t = \frac{(\gamma\pi + \alpha\pi - \alpha)}{\alpha\pi - (\alpha + \beta)} P_{t-1} + \frac{1}{\alpha\pi - (\alpha + \beta)} u_t$$

setting

$$\pi = \frac{(\gamma\pi + \alpha\pi - \alpha)}{\alpha\pi - (\alpha + \beta)}$$

and dividing both sides by α implies

$$\pi^2 - \left(2 + \frac{\gamma + \beta}{\alpha}\right)\pi + 1 = 0$$

5. As an example of this, we could suppose that the storage model for the agricultural commodity we analysed earlier embodied a futures market. In these circumstances the price given rational expectations follows the process defined by equation (7.9). Consequently,

$$P_t = \pi P_{t-1} + \pi_1 u_t$$

A little elementary algebra gives

$$F_{t,}N = E_{t-1} P_{t+N} = \pi^N P_{t-1} + \pi_1 u_t$$

and

$$F_{t-1,}N = E_{t-1} P_{t+N} = \pi^{N+1} P_{t-1}$$

so that

$$F_{t,N} - F_{t-1,N} = E_t P_{t+N} - E_{t-1} P_{t+N} = \pi^N u_t = \text{a random variable.}$$

6. The possibility of regressive expectations being rational is not a general result and depends on the particular structure of the model under consideration. The finding is analogous to the special result demonstrated earlier that adaptive expectations could be rational in certain model structures (see equation (7.15) above).
7. See Holden *et al.* (1991) for an introduction.
8. It will also, of course, be affected by real shocks and technological change. A specific example, though, illustrates the point: between 1986 and 1989 the correlation coefficient between the IMF's (various issues) monthly multilateral dollar exchange rate index and the FAO (various issues) world price series for wheat (USA hard winter no. 2, fob) was -0.56108; for the former and maize (USA yellow no. 2, fob) was -0.40143.
9. For discussions of the agricultural negotiations in the Uruguay Round of the GATT, see Rayner, Ingersent and Hine, Chapter 4, in this volume.
10. The deindustrialisation effect associated with large terms of trade swings brought about by export booms. See Corden and Neary (1982) for a theoretical description.
11. See Snape (1989) for a careful and comprehensive analysis of the relationships between real interest rates, real exchange rates and agriculture.
12. One other crucial development in macroeconomics in the last few years, flowing principally from the work of Engle and Grainger (1987), has been the importance of non-stationary integrated variables (which many economic variables such as real income, exchange rates, prices, etc., appear to be) for the manner in which empirical relationships are estimated. These developments are beginning to have impact on estima-

tion practice in Agricultural Economics (see Hallam (1991), Holden *et al.* (1991) or Lloyd and Rayner (1991) for an introduction).

CHAPTER 9

1. Although erosion and salinity of irrigated soils remain significant issues in the USA and Australia.
2. See, for example, Dubgaard (1990).
3. Indeed, as Csaba Csáki notes in Chapter 5, leasing land is one of the main options for 'reprivatisation' of agriculture in Eastern Europe.
4. In particular the Environmentally Sensitive Area and Sites of Special Scientific Interest policies operate in this way.
5. This section leans heavily on the work of my colleagues Trevor Young and Michael Burton (1991).
6. Malthus's work was republished in 1973 in an edition with an introduction and critique by T. H. Hollingworth.
7. See, for example, Vine and Bateman (1981).
8. Human welfare should here be defined to include human concerns for pollution effects on animal and plant species, and upon other existence values. Certainly, this is important in the agricultural context.
9. The definition used in that MNPB represents private returns to producers. That being so MEC should be adjusted for changes in consumer surplus arising from changes in output levels.
10. However, farmers in the UK are specifically exempted from fuel taxes in the same way that fertiliser and irrigation water are frequently underpriced in other countries.
11. This arises from the peculiarly artificial assumptions made about their mode of operation. This is that it is assumed that a subsidy could be paid on each unit by which firms reduce pollution below a new standard which is itself below their current level of pollution. Because this will only be effective if it makes firms more profitable by acting to reduce pollution, and because it is assumed that this is achieved by shrinkage of plant sizes, the theory of the firm predicts a net expansion of output *(and in resulting pollution)* in the long run due to an increase in the number of (smaller) plants. This is not the way subsidy policy is operated.
12. In general (e.g. Coursey, Hovis and Schultz, 1987), it has been found that estimates of 'willingness to accept' exceed those of 'willingness to pay', and the issue of which is to be preferred is a subject of debate (Hanley, 1989, p. 243).
13. Answers may well be different if respondents believe they may actually end up paying for policy than if that seems a remote possibility.
14. For fuller analysis see Colman *et al.* (1991).
15. For details see Batie and Sappington (1986) and Furness *et al.* (1990).
16. NCC was broken into separate national bodies in 1991.
17. The material in this section is covered much more fully in Colman *et al.* (1990).
18. Except in certain designated special areas such as ESAs where the VBs are entitled to the same conservation payments as private owners.

19. See Chapter 4 of this book.
20. The text of the original MacSharry proposals was published in *Agra Europe*, 21 September 1990.

CHAPTER 10

1. The author is grateful to his colleague Dr Bill Slee for helpful comments on a draft, but retains full responsibility for the final content.
2. A substantial commentary on this important statement of Commission thinking has been compiled by the UK House of Lords (1990).

Bibliography

ABARE (1985) *Agricultural Policies in the European Community*, Policy Monograph No. 2 (Canberra: Bureau of Agricultural Economics).

ABARE (1989) *US Grain Policies and the World Market*, Policy Monograph No.4 (Canberra: Australian Bureau of Agriculture and Resource Economics).

Agrawal, P. K. (1990) 'Plant Breeder's Right: Its Relevance in India under Changing Scenario', *Rachis Barley and Wheat Newsletter*, 9: 11–13.

Alexandratos, N. (1988) (ed.) *World Agriculture Toward 2000*, An FAO Study (London: Belhaven Press).

Almanac of China's Commerce Editorial Committee (1990) *Zhongguo Shangye Nianjian, 1990* (Almanac of China's Commerce, 1990) (Beijing: Zhongguo Shangye Nianjianshe).

Almanac of China's Prices Editorial Committee (1989) *Zhongguo Wujia Nianjian 1989* (Almanac of China's Prices, 1989) (Beijing: Zhongguo Wujia Chubanshe).

Alonso, W. (1964) 'Location Theory', in J. Friedmann and W. Alonso (eds) *Regional Development and Planning: A Reader* (Cambridge, Mass.: MIT Press).

Alston, J. (1986) 'An Analysis of Growth of United States Farmland Prices, 1963–82', *American Journal of Agricultural Economics*, 68: 1–9.

Alston, J., Edwards, G. and Freebairn, J. (1988) 'Market Distortions and Benefits from Research', *American Journal of Agricultural Economics*, 70: 281–88.

Anderson, G. and Bishop, R. (1986) 'The Valuation Problem', in Bromley, D. (ed.), *National Resource Economics* (Boston, Mass.: Kluwer).

Anderson, J. R.(1991) 'Agricultural Research in a Variable and Unpredictable World', chapter 4 in P. G. Pardey, J. Roseboom, and J. R. Anderson (eds) *Agricultural Research Policy: International Quantitative Perspectives* (The Hague: International Service for National Agricultural Research).

Anderson, K. (1987) 'On Why Agriculture Declines with Economic Growth', *Agricultural Economics,* 1: 195–207.

Anderson, K. (1989) 'Rent-seeking and price-distorting policies in rich and poor countries', Seminar Paper, No. 428 (Stockholm: Institute for International Economic Studies).

Anderson, K. and Hayami, Y. (1986) *The Political Economy of Agricultural Protection* (Sydney: Allen & Unwin).

Antle, J. M. (1988) *World Agricultural Development and the Future of US Agriculture* (Washington, DC: American Enterprise Institute).

Arndt, T. M. and Ruttan, V. W. (1977) 'Valuing the Productivity of Agricultural Research: Problems and Issues', chapter 1 in T. M. Arndt, D. G.

Dalrymple, and V. W. Ruttan, *Resource Allocation and Productivity in National and International Research* (Minneapolis: University of Minnesota Press).

Askari, H. and Cummings, J. T. (1977) 'Estimating Agricultural Supply Response with the Nerlove Model', *International Economic Review*, 18: 257–92.

Balisacan, A. M. and Roumasset, J. A. (1987) 'Public Choice of Economic Policy: The Growth of Agricultural Protection', *Weltwirtschaftliches Archiv*, 123: 232–47.

Ball, R. (1989) 'What Do We Know About Stock Market Efficiency?', in R. M. Guimaraes *et al.* (eds) *A Reappraisal of the Efficiency of Financial Markets*, NATO, ASI Series (Berlin: Springer-Verlag) 25–55.

Bardhan, Pranab K. (1973) 'Size, Productivity, and Returns to Scale: An Analysis of Farm-level Data for Indian Agriculture', *Journal of Political Economy*, 81(5): 1370–86.

Barker, R. (1988) *Methods for Setting Agricultural Research Priorities: Report of a Bellagio Conference* (Ithaca, NY: Cornell University, Department of Agricultural Economics, Working Paper 88-3).

Barro, R. J. (1990) *Macroeconomics* (3rd edn) (New York: John Wiley).

Bateman, D. (1989) 'Heroes for Present Purposes? – A Look at the Changing Idea of Communal Land Ownership in Britain', *Journal of Agricultural Economics*, 40(3): 269–89.

Batie, S. (1984) 'Alternative Views of Property Rights: Implications for Agricultural Use of Natural Resources', *American Journal of Agricultural Economics*, 66(5): 814–18.

Batie, S. (1989) 'Sustainable Development: Challenges to the Profession of Agricultural Economics', *American Journal of Agricultural Economics*, 71: 1083–101.

Batie, S. S., and Sappington, A. G. (1986) 'Cross-compliance as a Soil Conservation Strategy: A Case Study', *American Journal of Agricultural Economics*, 68(4): 880–5.

Baumol, W. and Oates, W. (1988,) *The Theory of Environmental Policy*, 2nd edn (Cambridge: Cambridge University Press).

Bautista, R. M. (1987) *Production Incentives in Phillipine Agriculture: Effects of Trade and Exchange Rate Policies*, Research Report 59 (Washington, DC: International Food Policy Research Institute).

Bautista, R. M. (1989) 'Development Strategies and Agricultural Incentives', in A. Maunder and A. Valdes (eds) *Agriculture and Governments in an Interdependent World: Proceedings of the 20th International Conference of Agricultural Economists* (Aldershot: Dartmouth).

Bauwens, A. L. G. M. and Douw, L. (1986) 'Rural Development: A Minor Problem in the Netherlands?', *European Review of Agricultural Economics*, 133: 343–66.

Beattie, I. (1988) *Green Money: The Agri-monetary System of the European Community*, Scottish Agricultural Colleges Economic Report, No. 4.

Becker, G. S. (1983) 'A Theory of Competition among Pressure Groups for Political Influence', *Quarterly Journal of Economics*, 98: 371–400.

Begg, D. K. (1982) *The Rational Expectations Revolution in Macroeconomics* (Oxford: Philip Allan).

Beier, F. K., Crespi, R. S. and Straus, J. (1985) *Biotechnology and Patent Protection: An International Review* (Paris: OECD).

Benedictis, M. de (1986) 'Italy: Fragmentation of Policies and Research Effort', *European Review of Agricultural Economics*, 13-3: 327–342.

Berry, R. A. and Cline, W. R. (1979) *Agrarian Structure and Productivity in Developing Countries* (Baltimore, Md.: Johns Hopkins University Press).

Bessler, D. A. (1984) 'Relative Prices and Money: A Vector Autoregression on Brazilian Data', *American Journal of Agricultural Economics*, 66: 25–30.

Binswanger, H. P. and Ruttan, V. W. (1978) *Induced Innovation* (Baltimore, Md.: Johns Hopkins University Press).

Bond, G. E. (1984) 'The Effects of Supply and Interest Rate Shocks in Commodity Futures Markets', *American Journal of Agricultural Economics*, 66: 294–301.

Bosworth, B. P. and Lawrence, R. Z. (1988) 'Managing Macroeconomic Imbalances', *American Journal of Agricultural Economics*, 70: 1006–12.

Braverman A. and Guasch J. L. (1990) 'Agricultural Reform in Developing Countries: Reflections for Eastern Europe', *American Journal of Agricultural Economics*, 72: 1243–51.

Brigham, E. F. and Gapenski, L. G. (1991) *Financial Management – Theory and Practice,* 6th edn (Chicago: Dryden Press).

Brim, C. (1987) *Plant Breeding and Biotechnology in the United States of America: Changing Needs for Protection of Plant Varieties,* paper presented at the Symposium on the Protection of Biotechnological Inventions, Ithaca, NY, 4–5 June.

Bromley, D. W. and Cernea, M. M. (1989) *The Management of Common Property Natural Resources: Some Conceptual and Operational Fallacies,* World Bank Discussion Paper 57 (Washington, DC: World Bank).

Brooks K. (1991) *Decollectivization in East/Central Europe* (Washington, DC: World Bank)

Brooks, K., Guasch, J. L., Braverman, A. and Csaki, Cs. (1991) 'Agriculture and the Transition to the Market', *Journal of Economic Perspectives*, 5: 149–61.

Burniaux, J., Delorme, F., Lienert, I. and Martin, J. P. (1990) 'Walras – A Multisector, Multi-country Applied General Equilibrium Model for Quantifying the Economy-Wide Effects of Agricultural Policies', *OECD Economic Studies*, 13: 69–102.

Burrell, A. (1987) 'E.C. Agricultural Surpluses and Budget Control', *Journal of Agricultural Economics*, 38: 1–14.

Burrell, A. (1989) 'The Demand for Fertilizer in the United Kingdom', *Journal of Agricultural Economics*, 40(1): 1–20.

Burt, O. R. (1986) 'Econometric Modeling of the Capitalization Formula for Farmland Prices', *American Journal of Agricultural Economics*, 68: 10–26.

Butler, L. J. and Marion, B. W. (1983) *Impacts of Patent Protection in the U.S. Seed Industry and Public Plant Breeding,* NC-117 Monograph 16, September (University of Wisconsin).

Capalbo, S. and Antle, J. M. (1989) 'Incorporating Social Costs in the Returns to Agricultural Research', *American Journal of Agricultural Economics*, 71: 458–463.

Capalbo, S. M. and Vo, T. T. (1988) 'A Review of the Evidence on Agricultural Productivity and Aggregate Technology', chapter 3 in S. M. Capalbo and

J. M. Antle (eds) *Agricultural Productivity: Measurement and Explanation* (Washington, DC: Resources for the Future, Inc.).

Carter, Michael R. (1984) 'Identification of the Inverse Relationship between Farm Size and Productivity: An Empirical Analysis of Peasant Agricultural Production', *Oxford Economic Papers*, 36: 131–45.

Cawley, M. (1983) 'Part-time Farming in Rural Development: Evidence from Western Ireland', *Sociol. Ruralis*, 23(1): 63–74.

CCP (1990) 'Decision on Further Improving the Economic Environment, Straightening out the Economic Order, and Deepening the Reforms (excerpts)' (adopted at the fifth plenary session of the 13th Central committee of the CCP on November 9, 1989) *Beijing Review*, 33(7) I–XVI.

Central Rural Policy Research Office Rural Survey Office (1988) 'Nongcun gaige yu nongmin', *Nongye Jing ji Wenti*, 8: 45–51.

Chappell, H. W. (1982) 'Campaign Contributions and Congressional Voting: A Simultaneous Probit–Tobit Model', *Review of Economics and Statistics*, 64: 77–83.

Chen, D. T. (1977) 'The Wharton Agricultural Model: Structural Specification and Some Simulation Results', *American Journal of Agricultural Economics*, 59: 106–16.

Chinese Finance and Banking Studies Association (1988) *Zhongguo jinrong nianjian, 1987* (Almanac of China's Finance and Banking, 1987) (Beijing: Zhongguo Jinrong Chubanshe).

Christiansen, Flemming (1989) 'The Justification and Legalisation of Private Enterprises in China, 1983–1988', *China Information*, 4(2): 78–91.

Christiansen, Flemming (1990) 'Social Division and Peasant Mobility in Mainland China: The Implications of the Hu-k'ou System', *Issues and Studies*, 26(4): 23–42.

Ciriacy-Wantrup, S. V. and Bishop, R. C. (1975) 'Common Property as a Concept in Natural Resources Policy', *Natural Resources Journal*, 15: 713–27.

Cloke, P. J. (1977) 'An Index of Rurality for England and Wales', *Regional Studies*, 11: 31–46.

Coase, R. (1960) 'The Problem of Social Cost', *Journal of Law and Economics*, 3: 1–44.

Colman, D. (1991) 'Land Purchase as a Means of Providing External Benefits from Agriculture' in N. Hanley (ed.), *Farming and the Countryside: An Economic Analysis of External Costs and Benefits* (Oxford: CAB International).

Colman, D. and Young, T. (1989) *Principles of Agricultural Economics* (Cambridge University Press for Wye Studies in Agricultural and Rural Development).

Colman, D., Crabtree, J. R., Froud, J. and O'Carroll, L. (1991) *Comparative Effectiveness of Conservation Instruments* (Report to the Countryside Commission, Dept of Agricultural Economics, University of Manchester).

Commission of the European Communities (1968) *Memorandum on the Reform of Agriculture in the EC*, Com (68) 1000 (Brussels: CEC).

Commission of the European Communities (1973) *Improvement of the Common Agricultural Policy*, Com (73) 1850 (Brussels: CEC).

Commission of the European Communities (1975) *Stocktaking of the Common Agricultural Policy*, Com (75) 100 (Brussels: CEC).

Commission of the European Communities (1979) *Changes in the Common Agricultural Policy to Help Balance the Market and Streamline Expenditure*, Com (79) 710 (Brussels: CEC).

Commission of the European Communities (1981) *Guidelines for European Agriculture*, Com (81) 608 (Brussels: CEC)

Commission of the European Communities (1985) *Perspectives for the Common Agricultural Policy*, Com (85) 333 (Brussels: CEC).

Commission of the European Communities (annual) *The Agricultural Situation in the Community* (Luxembourg: Office of Publications of the European Communities).

Commission of the European Community (1988) *The Future of Rural Society*, COM(88) 501 (Brussels: CEC).

Commission of the European Community (1990) *Farms in Mountainous and Less-Favoured Areas of the Community* (Luxembourg: Office for Official Publications of the ECs).

Copeland, L. S. (1989) *Exchange Rates and International Finance* (Reading, Mass.: Addison-Wesley).

Copeland, T. E. and Weston, J. F. (1983) *Financial Theory and Corporate Policy*, 2nd edn (Reading, Mass.: Addison-Wesley).

Corden, W. M. (1974) *Trade Policy and Economic Welfare* (Oxford University Press).

Corden, W. M. and Neary, J. P. (1982) 'Booming Sector and De-industrialisation in a Small Open Economy', *Economic Journal*, 92: 825–48.

Coursey, D., Hovis, J. and Shulze, W. (1987) 'The Disparity between Willingness to Accept and Willingness to Pay Measures of Value', *Quarterly Journal of Economics*, 102: 679–89.

Cox, C. C. (1976) 'Futures Trading and Market Information', *Journal of Political Economy*, 84: 1215–36.

Crook, Frederick W. (1989a) 'China's Current Household Contract System (Part I)', in US Department of Agriculture, *CPE Agriculture Report*, 2(3): 26–30.

Crook, Frederick W. (1989b) 'China's Current Household Contract System (Part II)', in US Department of Agriculture, *CPE Agriculture Report* 2(4): 27–33.

Csáki Cs. and Gy. Varga (1990) *Agricultural Reform in Eastern Europe in the 90's* (manuscript prepared for the World Bank Conference on Agricultural Transition in Eastern Europe, 29 August–1 September 1990, Budapest, Hungary).

Csáki, Cs. (1983) 'Economic Management and Organization of Hungarian Agriculture', *Journal of Comparative Economics* 7: 317–328.

Csáki, Cs. (1985) 'An Outlook on Food Supply and Demand in CMEA Countries', *Acta Oeconomica* 35: 145–64.

Csáki, Cs. (1989) 'The CMEA Countries and World Trade in Food and Agricultural Products', in A. Maunder and A. Valdes (eds), *Agriculture and Governments in an Interdependent World*, IAAE-Dartmouth.

Csáki, Cs. (1990) 'Agricultural Changes in Eastern Europe at the Beginning of the 1990s', *American Journal of Agricultural Economics*, 72: 1233–42.

Csáki, Cs. (1991) 'Agriculture and Agricultural Policy in Eastern Europe', in K. Burger (ed.), *Agricultural Economics and Policy: International Challenges for the Nineties* (Amsterdam; Oxford: Elsevier).

Dalrymple, D. G. (1990) 'The Excess Burden of Taxation and Public Agricultural Research' in R. G. Echeverria (ed.), *Methods for Diagnosing Research System Constraints and Assessing the Impact of Agricultural Research*, Vol. II (The Hague: International Service for National Agricultural Research) 117–37 .

Davis, J. (1981) 'A Comparison of Procedures for Estimating Returns to Research Using Production Functions', *Australian Journal of Agricultural Economics*, 25: 60–72.

Destler, I. M. and Odell, J. S. (1987) *Anti-protection: Changing Forces in United States Trade Politics* (Washington, DC: Institute for International Economics).

Devadoss, S. and Meyers, W. H. (1987) 'Relative Prices and Money: Further Results for the United States', *American Journal of Agricultural Economics*, 69: 838–42.

Diba, B. T. and Grossman, H. I. (1988) 'Rational Inflationary Bubbles', *Journal of Monetary Economics*, 21: 35–46.

Dixit, A. K. (1990) 'Trade Policy with Imperfect Information', chapter 1 of Jones and Krueger (1990) 9–24.

Dornbusch, R. (1976) 'Expectations and Exchange Rate Dynamics', *Journal of Political Economy*, 84: 1161–76.

Duan, Yingbi (1986) 'Liangshi liutong tizhi bixu da gaige', *Nongye Jing ji Wenti*, 11: 37–40.

Dubgaard, A. (1990) *Danish Policy Measures to Control Agricultural Impacts on the Environment*, Statens Jordbrugsokonomiske Institut, Rappart No. 52, Copenhagen.

Echeverria, R. G. (1990) 'Assessing the Impact of Agricultural Research', in R. G. Echeverria (ed.), *Methods for Diagnosing Research System Constraints and Assessing the Impact of Agricultural Research*, Vol. II (The Hague: International Service for National Agricultural Research) 1–31 .

Echeverria, R. G. (1991) 'Impact of Research and Seed Trade on Maize Productivity', chapter 11 in P. G. Pardey, J. Rosenboom and J. R. Anderson (eds), *Agricultural Research Policy: International Quantitative Perspectives* (Cambridge: Cambridge University Press).

Edwards, G. W. and J. W. Freebairn (1984) 'The Gains from Research into Tradable Commodities', *American Journal of Agricultural Economics*, 66: 41–9.

Engle, R. F. and Grainger, C. W. J. (1987) 'Cointegration and Error Correction: Representation, Estimation and Testing', *Econometrica*, 55: 251–76.

Esty, D. C and Caves, R. E. (1983) 'Market Structure and Political Influence: New Data on Political Expenditures, Activity and Success', *Economic Inquiry*, 21: 24–38.

Evenson, R. E. (1967) 'The Contribution of Agricultural Research to Production', *Journal of Farm Economics*, 49: 1415–25.

Evenson, R. E. (1983) 'Intellectual Property Rights, Agribusiness Research and Development: Implications for the Public Agricultural Research System', *American Journal of Agricultural Economics*, 65: 967–75.

Evenson, R. E., P. E. Waggoner and V. W. Ruttan (1979) 'Economic Benefit from Research: An Example from Agriculture', *Science*, 205: 101–7.

Fama, E. F. (1970) 'Efficient Capital Markets: A Review of Theory and Empirical Work', *Journal of Finance*, 25: 383–425.

Feldstein, M. (1980) 'Inflation, Portfolio Choice and the Prices of Land and Corporate Stock', *American Journal of Agricultural Economics*, 62: 910–16.

Fernandez, R. and Rodrik, D. (1990) *Why is Trade Reform so Unpopular?*, Discussion Paper, No 391 (London: Centre for Economic Policy Research).

Fessenden MacDonald, J. (ed.) (1989) *Bio-Technology and Sustainable Agriculture: Policy Alternatives* (Ithaca, NY: National Agricultural Biotechnology Council, NABA Report 1)

Fessenden MacDonald, J. (ed.) (1990) *Agricultural Biotechnology: Food Safety and Nutritional Quality for the Consumer* (Ithaca, NY: National Agricultural Biotechnology Council, NABA Report 2).

Figlewski, S. (1978) 'Market Efficiency in a Market with Heterogeneous Information', *Journal of Political Economy*, 86: 581–97.

Finger, J. M. (1981) 'Policy Research', *Journal of Political Economy*, 89: 1270–2.

Finger, J. M., Hall, H. K. and Nelson, D. R. (1982) 'The Political Economy of Administered Protection', *American Economic Review*, 72: 452–66.

Food and Agriculture Organisation (quarterly) *Quarterly Bulletin of Statistics* (Rome: FAO).

Fowler, C. and Mooney, P. (1990) *Shattering* (Tucson, Ariz.: University of Arizona Press).

Fox, G. (1985) 'Is the United States Really Underinvesting in Agricultural Research?', *American Journal of Agricultural Economics*, 67: 806–12.

Fox, K. A. (1963) 'The Food and Agriculture Sectors in Advanced Economies', in T. Barna (ed.), *Structural Interdependence and Economic Development* (London: Macmillan)

Francis, C. A. (1988) *Internal Resources for Sustainable Agriculture* (IIED).

Frankel, J. A. (1986) 'Expectations and Commodity Price Dynamics: The Overshooting Model', *American Journal of Agricultural Economics*, 68: 344–8.

Franklin, M. (1988) *Rich Man's Farming: The Crisis in Agriculture* (London: Royal Institute of International Affairs).

Frey, B. (1985) 'The Political Economy of Protection', chapter 9 in D. Greenaway (ed.), *Current Issues in International Trade* (London: Macmillan).

Frydman, R. and Phelps, E. S. (1983) *Individual Forecasting and Aggregate Outcomes* (Cambridge UniversityPress).

Furness, G. W., N. P. Russell and D. R. Colman (1990) *Developing Proposals for Cross-Compliance with Particular Application to the Oilseeds Sector* (Sandy, Beds: Royal Society for the Protection of Birds).

Garcia, G. G. (1989) 'The Impact of Trade and Macroeconomic Policies on the Performance of Agriculture in Latin America', in A. Maunder and A. Valdes (1989) 580–96.

Garcia, P., Leulhold, R. M., Fortenberry, R. and Sarassoro, G. F. (1988) 'Pricing Efficiency in the Live Cattle Futures Market: Further Interpretation and Measurement', *American Agricultural Journal of Agricultural Economics*, 70: 163–9.

Gardner, B. (1987) 'Causes of US Farm Commodity Programs', *Journal of Political Economy*, 95: 290–310.

Gardner, B. L. (1981) 'On the Power of Macroeconomic Linkages to Explain Events in US Agriculture', *American Journal of Agricultural Economics*, 63: 871–8.

Gasson, R. (1988) *The Economics of Part-Time Farming* (London: Longman).

GATT (1986) 'Ministerial Declaration on the Uruguay Round' (Geneva: GATT Focus 41).

Geisow, M. (1991) 'The Proof of the Cloning is in the Eating', *Trends in Biotechnology*, 9: 5–7.

Gelb A. H. and Gray C. W. (1991) *The Transformation of Economies in Central and Eastern Asia*, Policy and Research Series No 17 (Washington, DC: World Bank).

Giessübel, R. and Spitzer, H. (1986) 'Federal Republic of Germany: Rural Development under Federal Government', *European Review of Agricultural Economics*, 13(3): 283–308.

Gordon, H. S. (1954) 'The Economic Theory of a Common Property Resource: The Fishery', *Journal of Political Economy*, 62(2).

Gorter, H. de and D. Zilberman (1990) 'On the Political Economy of Public Goods in Agriculture', *American Journal of Agricultural Economics*, 72: 131–37.

Gorter, H. de, D. Neilson, and G. Rausser (1990) 'Productive and Predatory Public Policies: Research Expenditures and Producer Subsidies in Agriculture', Working Papers in Agricultural Economics, No. 90–17 (Cornell University) December.

Graham-Tomasi, T. (1991) 'Sustainability: Concepts and Applications for Agricultural Research Policy', chapter 3 in P. G. Pardey, J. Roseboom and J. R. Anderson (eds) *Agricultural Research Policy: International Quantitative Perspectives* (The Hague: International Service for National Agricultural Research).

Greenaway, D. (1983) *International Trade Policy* (London: Macmillan).

Greenaway, D. (1985) *Current Issues in International Trade* (London: Macmillan).

Grennes, T. (ed.) (1991) *International Financial Markets and Agricultural Trade* (Boulder, Col.: Westview Press).

Grennes, T. and Lapp, J. S. (1986) 'Neutrality of Inflation in the Agricultural Sector', *Journal of International Money and Finance*, 5: 231–43.

Griliches, Z. (1957 'Hybrid Corn: An Exploration in the Economics of Technological Change', *Econometrica*, 25: 501–22.

Griliches, Z. (1958) 'Research Costs and Social Returns: Hybrid Corn and Related Innovations', *Journal of Political Economy*, 66: 419–31.

Guimaraes, R. M., Kingsman, B. G. and Taylor, S. J. (eds) (1989) *A Reappraisal of the Efficiency of Financial Markets*, NATO, ASI Series (Berlin: Springer-Verlag).

Guither, H. D. (1980) *The Food Lobbyists* (Lexington, Mass.: Lexington Books).

Gutiérrez, M. B. (1991) 'La Legislacion de derechos de obtentor en la Argentina: Una analisis de su funcionamiento y sus efectos', in *Proceedings, Industrial Property Protection of Biotechnological Inventions and Germplasm Use Policies in Latin America and the Caribbean* (San José, Costa Rica: Inter-American Agency for Cooperation on Agriculture).

Hall, P. C. (1991) *The Application of Agricultural Biotechnology in Developing Countries* (Stockholm: Stockholm Environment Institute).

Hallam,D. (1991) 'Cointegration and Error Correction Models: A Beginner's Guide', paper presented at the Annual Conference of the Agricultural Economics Society, Nottingham, April 1991.

Hanley, N. D. (1989) 'Valuing Non-market Goods Using Contingent Valuation', *Journal of Economic Surveys*, 3(3): 235–52.

Hansel, W. (1990) 'Prospective Developments in Animal Agriculture', in W. Lesser (ed.), *Animal Patents: The Legal, Economic, and Social Issues* (New York: Stockton Press) 70–81.

Harrison, G. W., Rutstrom, E. E. and Wigle, R. (1989) 'Costs of Agricultural Trade Wars', chapter 11 in A. B. Stoekel *et al.* (eds), *Macroeconomic Consequences of Farm Support Policies* (Durham and London: Duke University Press).

Harvey, D. R. (1988) 'Research Priorities in Agriculture', *Journal of Agricultural Economics*, 39: 81–97.

Hathaway, D. E. (1987) *Agriculture and the GATT: Rewriting the Rules* (Washington, DC: Institute for International Economics).

Hayami, Y. and Ruttan, V. W. (1985) *Agricultural Development: An International Perspective* (revised edn) (Baltimore, Md.: Johns Hopkins University Press).

He, Kang (1990) 'Seizing the Opportunity for Rich Harvests', *Beijing Review*, 33(3) 25–6.

Heidhues, T. (1979) 'The Gains from Trade: An Applied Political Analysis', chapter 6 of Hillman, J. S. and Schmitz, A. (eds) *International Trade and Agriculture: Theory and Policy* (Boulder, Col.: Westview Press).

Herbst, A. F. (1982) *Capital Budgeting Theory, Quantitative Methods and Applications* (New York: Harper & Row).

Herdt, R. W. and Lynam, J. K. (1992) 'Sustainable Development and the Changing Needs for Impact Assessment of International Agricultural Research' in D. R. Lee (ed.), *Assessment of International Agricultural Research for Sustainable Development* (Ithaca, NY: Cornell International Institute for Food, Agriculture and Development).

Hertford, R. and A. Schmitz (1977) 'Measuring Economic Returns to Agricultural Research' in T. M. Arndt, D. G. Dalrymple, and V. W. Ruttan (eds), *Resource Allocation and Productivity in National and International Research* (Minneapolis: University of Minnesota Press).

Hicks, J. (1974) *The Crisis of Keynesian Economics* (Oxford: Blackwell).

Higgins, J. (1983) *A Study of Part-time Farming in the Republic of Ireland* (Dublin: Agricultural Institute, Socio-Economic Research Series 3).

Hill, B. (1989) *Farm Incomes, Wealth and Agricultural Policy* (Aldershot: Avebury).

Hill, B. E. and Ingersent, K. A. (1977) *An Economic Analysis of Agriculture* (London: Heinemann).

Hillman, A. L. (1988) 'Policy Motives and International Trade Restrictions' in H.-J. Vosgerau, *New Institutional Arrangements for the World Economy* (Berlin: Springer-Verlag).

Hillman, A. L. (1988) *The Political Economy of Protection* (London: Harwood Academic Publishers).

Hillman, J. S. (1991) *Technical Barriers to Agricultural Trade* (Boulder, Col.: Westview Press).

Hillman, J. S. and Rothenberg, R. A. (1988) *Agricultural Trade and Protection in Japan,* Thames Essay No. 52 (London: Gower; Trade Policy Research Centre).

Hine, R. C., Ingersent, K. A. and Rayner, A. J. (1989a) *The Agricultural Negotiations in the Uruguay Round,* CREDIT Research Paper No. 89/3, Department of Economics, University of Nottingham.

Hine, R. C., Ingersent, K. A. and Rayner, A. J. (1989b) 'Agriculture in the Uruguay Round: from the Punta del Este Declaration to the Geneva Accord', *Journal of Agricultural Economics,* 40: 385–96.

HM Treasury (1972) *Forestry in Great Britain: An Interdepartmental Cost-Benefit Study* (London: HMSO).

Hodge, I. D. (1986) 'The Scope and Context of Rural Development', *European Review of Agricultural Economics,* 13–3: 271–282.

Hodge, I. D. (1989) 'Compensation for Nature Conservation', *Environment and Planning A,* 21: 1027–36.

Holden, K., Peel, D. A. and Thompson, J. L. (1985) *Expectations Theory and Evidence* (London: Macmillan).

Holden, K., Peel, D. A. and Thompson, J. L. (1991) *An Introduction to Economic Forecasting* (Cambridge University Press).

Honma, M. and Hayami, Y. (1986) 'Structure of Agricultural Protection in Industrial Countries', *Journal of International Economics,* 20: 115–30.

Hopkins, R. F. (1988) 'Political Calculations in Subsidizing Food', chapter 7 in P. Pinstrup-Anderson (ed.), *Food Subsidies in Developing Countries: Costs, Benefits and Policy Options* (Baltimore, Md.: Johns Hopkins University Press).

Houck, J. P. (1986) *Elements of Agricultural Trade Policy* (New York: Macmillan).

House of Lords (1989) *Nitrate in Water: Report,* Select Committee on the European Communities (London: HMSO).

House of Lords (1990) *The Future of Rural Society,* 24th Report of the Select Committee on the European Communities, HL80 (London: HMSO).

Ingersent, K. A. and Rayner, A. J. (1993) *Agricultural Policy in the US and Western Europe: A Comparative Analysis* (Aldershot: Edward Elgar).

International Monetary Fund (1988) *The Common Agricultural Policy of the European Community* (Washington, DC: IMF).

International Monetary Fund (monthly) *International Financial Statistics* (Washington, DC: IMF).

Jansma D. J., Gamble, H. B., Madden, J. P. and Warland, R. H. (1981) 'Rural Development: A Review of Conceptual and Empirical Studies', in L. R. Martin (ed.), *Economics of Welfare, Rural Development and Natural Resources in Agriculture 1940s to 1970s,* Survey of Agricultural Economic Literature 3 (Minneapolis: University of Minnesota Press).

Jensen, R. C., Manderville T. D. and Karunaratne, N. D. (1977) *Regional Economic Planning* (London: Croom Helm).

Johns, P. M. and Leat, P. M. K. (1986) *An Approach to Regional Economic Modelling,* Economic Report No. 144 (Aberdeen: North of Scotland College of Agriculture).

Johnson, D. G. (1973) *World Agriculture in Disarray* (London: Fontana).

Johnson, D. G. (1975) 'World Agriculture, Commodity Policy and Price Variability', *American Journal of Agricultural Economics,* 57: 823–8.

Johnson, D. G. (1991) *World Agriculture in Disarray*, 2nd edn (London: Macmillan).

Jones, R. W. and Krueger, A. O. (1990) *The Political Economy of International Trade* (Oxford: Blackwell).

Josling, T. E. (1986) 'Agricultural Policies and World Trade: The US and the EC at Bay', in L.Tsoukalis (ed.), *Europe, America and the World Economy* (Oxford: Blackwell).

Josling, T. E., Sanderson, F. H. and Warley, T. K. (1990) 'The Future of International Agricultural Relations: Issues in the GATT Negotiations' in Sanderson, F. H. (ed.), *Agricultural Protectionism in the Industrialised World* (Washington, DC: Resources for the Future).

Kendall, M. (1953) 'The Analysis of Economic Time Series, Part I: Prices', *Journal of the Royal Statistical Society*, 96: 11–25.

Kenney, M. (1986) *Biotechnology: The University–Industrial Complex* (New Haven, Conn.: Yale University Press).

Kloppenburg, J. R. Jr and R. L. Kleinman (1988) 'Seeds of Controversy: National Property versus Common Heritage', chapter 7 in J. R. Kloppenburg, Jr (ed.), *Seeds and Sovereignty* (Durham, NC: Duke University Press).

Knudson, M. K. and Pray, C. E. (1991) 'Plant Variety Protection, Private Funding and Public Sector Research Priorities', paper presented at the annual meeting of the American Economics Assoc., Washington, DC, 28 December.

Kojima, Reeitsu (1988) 'Agricultural Organisation: New Forms, New Contradictions', *China Quarterly*, 116: 706–35.

Krueger, A., Schiff, M. and Valdes, A. (1988) 'Agricultural Incentives in Developing Countries: Measuring the Effect of Sectoral and Economy Wide Policies', *The World Bank Economic Review*, 2: 255–71.

Krugman, P. R. (1989) *Exchange Rate Instability* (Cambridge, Mass. and London: MIT Press).

Lapp, J. (1990) 'Relative Agricultural Prices and Monetary Policy', *American Journal of Agricultural Economics*, 72: 622–30.

Lavergne, R. P. (1983) *The Political Economy of US Tariffs: An Empirical Analysis* (London: Academic Press).

Leblanc, M. and Hrubovcak, J. (1986) 'Dynamic Input Demand – An Application to Agriculture', *Applied Economics*, 18: 807–18.

Lee, D. R. and G. C. Rausser (1992) 'The Structure of Research and Transfer Policies in International Agriculture: Evidence and Implications', in M. Bellamy and B. Greenshields (eds), *Issues in Agricultural Development: Sustainability and Cooperation* (Aldershot: IAAE Occasional Paper No. 6).

Lesser, W. (1991) *Equitable Patent Protection in the Developing World: Issues and Approaches. Tsukubagakuen* (Japan: Eubios Ethics Institute).

Leven, C. (1965) 'Theories of Regional Growth', in *Problems of Chronically Depressed Rural Areas*, North Carolina State University Agricultural Policy Institute API Series 19: 1–12.

Lindner, R. and F. Jarrett (1978) 'Supply Shifts and the Size of Research Results', *American Journal of Agricultural Economics*, 60: 48–58.

Livingstone, I. (1986) 'The Common Property Problem and Pastoralist Economic Behaviour', *Journal of Development Studies*, 23: 5–19.

Lloyd, T. and Rayner, A. J. (1991) 'Land Prices, Rents and Inflation: A Cointegration Analysis', *Oxford Agrarian Studies*, 18: 97–111.

Loomis, J. (1987) 'Expanding Contingent Value Sample Estimates to Aggregate Benefits: Current Practices and Proposed Solutions', *Land Economics*, 63(4): 396–402.

Lowe, P., Marsden T. and Munton, R. (1990) *The Social and Economic Restructuring of Rural Britain: a Position Statement*, ESRC Countryside Change Initiative Working Paper No. 2 (University of Newcastle upon Tyne).

Lynam, J. and R. Herdt (1989) 'Sense and Sustainability: Sustainability as an Objective in International Agricultural Research', *Agricultural Economics*, 3: 381–98.

MacBean, A. I. and D. T. Nguyen (1987) *Commodity Policies: Problems and Prospects* (Beckenham, Kent: Croom Helm).

Malthus, T. R. (1973) *An Essay on the Principle of Population* (London: Dent)

Matthews, A. (1986) 'Ireland: Rural Development in an Agrarian Society', *European Review of Agricultural Economics*, 13–3: 367–90.

Maunder, A. and Valdés, A. (eds) (1989) *Agriculture and Governments in an Interdependent World*, Proceedings of the 20th International Conference of Agricultural Economists (Aldershot: Dartmouth).

Mayer, W. (1984) 'Endogenous Tariff Formation', *American Economic Review*, 74: 970–85.

McCalla, A. F. and Josling, T. E. (1985) *Agricultural Policies and World Markets* (New York: Macmillan).

McCallum, M. (1980) 'Rational Expectations and Macroeconomic Stabilization Policy', *Journal of Money, Credit and Banking*, 12: 716–46.

McClatchy, D. and T. K. Warley (1991) *Agricultural and Trade Policy Reform: Implications for Agricultural Trade*, XXI Congress of the International Association of Agricultural Economists, Tokyo, Japan, 22–29 August.

McInerney, J. P. (1976) 'The Simple Analytics of Natural Resource Economics', *Journal of Agricultural Economics*, 27: 31–52.

McLaughlin, B. (1985) 'Assessing the Extent of Rural Deprivation', *Journal of Agricultural Economics*, 36(1): 77–80.

Messerlin, P. A. (1983) 'Bureaucracies and the Political Economy of Protection, Reflections of a Continental European', *Weltwirtschaftliches Archiv*, 117: 461–96.

Meyer, H. von (1990) 'From Agricultural to Rural Policy in the EC', *Rural Policy Issues* (Enstone, Oxon.: Arkleton Trust).

Midmore, P. (ed.) (1991) *Input–Output Models and the Agricultural Sector* (Aldershot: Avebury).

Miles, H., Lesser, W. and Sears, P. (1991) 'The Economic Implications of Bioengineered Mastitis Control', *Journal of Dairy Science*, 75: 596–605.

Minford, P. and Peel, D. A. (1983) *Rational Expectations and the New Macroeconomics* (Oxford: Martin Robertson).

Ministry of Agriculture Economic Policy Research Centre Rural Cooperative Organisations Task Force (1989) 'Zhongguo nongcun diyu xing hezuo zuzhide shizheng miaosu – quanguo 100 ge xian 1200 ge cun diyu hezuo zuzhi xitong diaocha', *Zhongguo Noncun Jian ji* 1: 5–16.

Moyer, H. W. and Josling, T. E. (1990) *Agricultural Policy Reform: Politics and Process in the EC and USA* (Hemel Hempstead: Harvester Wheatsheaf).

Mueller, D. C. (1989) *Public Choice II* (London: Cambridge University Press).

Muth, J. F. (1961) 'Rational Expectations and the Theory of Price Movements', *Econometrica*, 29: 315–35.

National Economic Development Council (1990) *Understanding Less Favoured Areas: the Importance of Farming to the Rural Economy* (London: NEDC).

National Research Council (1990) *Plant Biotechnology Research for Developing Countries* (Washington, DC: National Academy Press).

Needleman, L. (1968) *Regional Analysis* (London: Penguin).

Nello, Senior S. (1990) 'Agricultural Trade between the EC and Central Europe', unpublished paper (Rome: INEA Seminar, 19 April 1990).

Nerlove, M. (1958) 'Adaptive Expectations and Cobweb Phenomena', *Quarterly Journal of Economics*, 73: 227–40.

New China News Agency Domestic Materials Office (1988) *Shinian Gaige Dashiji, 1978–1987* (Beijing: Xinhua Chubanshe).

Newbery, D. M. G. (1983) 'Futures Trading, Risk Reduction and Price Stabilization', in Streit, M. E. (ed.), *Futures Markets* (Oxford: Blackwell).

Newbery, D. M. G. and Stiglitz, T. E. (1981) *The Theory of Commodity Price Stabilisation: A Study in the Economics of Risk* (Oxford University Press).

Niskanen, W. (1971) *Bureaucracy and Representative Government* (Chicago: Aldine-Atherton).

Norton, G. and Davis, J. (1981) 'Evaluating Returns to Agricultural Research: A Review', *American Journal of Agricultural Economics*, 63: 685–99.

O'Connor, H., Rayner, A. J., Ingersent, K. A. and Hine, R. C. (1991a) *The Agricultural Negotiations in the Uruguay Round: Developments since the Geneva Accord*, University of Nottingham CREDIT Research Paper, No. 91/8.

O'Connor, H., Rayner, A. J., Ingersent, K. A. and Hine, R. C. (1991b) 'Aggregate Measures of Support in the Uruguay Round: Application to the EC Cereals Sector', *Oxford Agrarian Studies*, 19: 91–103.

Obstfeld, M. (1986) 'Overshooting Agricultural Commodity Markets and Public Policy: Discussion', *American Journal of Agricultural Economics*, 68,: 420–1.

OECD (1987) *National Policies and Agricultural Trade* (Paris: Organisation for Economic Cooperation and Development).

OECD (1989) *BioTechnology: Economic and Wider Impacts* (Paris: Organisation for Economic Cooperation and Development).

OECD (1990) *Agricultural Policies, Markets and Trade* (Paris: Organisation for Economic Cooperation and Development).

OECD (1991) *Agricultural Policies, Markets and Trade: Monitoring Outlook, 1991* (Paris: Organisation for Economic Cooperation and Development).

Oehmke, J. (1988) 'The Calculation of Returns to Research in Distorted Markets', *Agricultural Economics*, 2: 291–302.

Office of Technology Assessment (OTA), Congress of the US (1991) *Biotechnology in a Global Economy* (Washington, DC: Government Printing Office, OTA-BA-494).

Oi, Jean C. (1986) 'Peasant Grain Marketing and State Procurement: China's Grain Contracting System', *China Quarterly*, 106: 272–90.

Oi, Jean C. (forthcoming) 'The Fate of the Collective after the Commune', in D. Davis and E. Vogel (eds), *The Social Consequences of Chinese Economic Reforms* (Cambridge, Mass.: Harvard University Press).

Okun, A. (1975) 'Inflation: Its Mechanics and Welfare Costs', *Brookings Papers on Economic Activity*, 2: 351–401.

Oyejide, T. A. (1986) *The Effects of Trade and Exchange Rate Policies on Agriculture in Nigeria* (Washington, DC: International Food Policy Research Institute Research Report 55).

Oyejide, T. A. (1989) 'Macroeconomic Linkages and Agriculture: the African Experience', in Maunder and Valdes, 567–77.

Pardey, P. and G. Craig (1989) 'Causal Relationships between Public Sector Agricultural Research Expenditures and Output', *American Journal of Agricultural Economics*, 71: 9–19.

Pardey, P., Kang, M. and Elliott, H. (1989) 'Structure of Public Support for National Agricultural Research: A Political Economy Perspective', *Agricultural Economics*, 3: 261–78.

Pardey, P. G., Roseboom, J. and Anderson, J. R. (1991) 'Regional Perspectives on National Agricultural Research', chapter 7 in P. G. Pardey, J. Roseboom, and J. R. Anderson (eds), *Agricultural Research Policy: International Quantitative Perspectives* (The Hague: International Service for National Agricultural Research).

Parris, K. P. and Peters, G. H. (1983) 'Agricultural Commodity Trade in a Regime of Floating Exchange Rates', *World Agricultural Economics and Rural Sociology Abstracts*, 25: 241–69.

'"Pay up" call on IOUs to farmers' (1989) *China Daily*, 10 January, 3.

Pearce, D. W. and Turner, R. K. (1990) *Economics of Natural Resources and the Environment* (Hemel Hempstead: Harvester Wheatsheaf).

Pearce, D. W., Markandya, A. and Barbier, E. B. (1989) *Blueprint for a Green Economy* (London: Earthscan Publications).

Penson, J. B. and Talpaz, H. (1988) 'Endogenization of Final Demand and Primary Input Supply in Input–Output Analysis', *Applied Economics*, 20: 739–52.

Perlak, F. J., Deaton, R. W., Armstrong, T. A., Fuchs, R. L., Sims, S. R., Greenplate, J. T. and Fischhoff, D. A. (1990) 'Insect Resistant Cotton Plants', *BioTechnology* 8: 939–43.

Perrin, R. K., Hunnings, K. A. and Ihnen L. A. (1983) *Some Effects of the Plant Variety Protection Act of 1970* (North Carolina State University, Econ. Res. Rpt 46).

Persley, G. J. (1990) 'Beyond Mendel's Garden: Biotechnology in the Service of World Agriculture', *Biotechnology in Agriculture*, No. 1 (Oxford: CAB International).

Pesando, J. E. (1978) 'On the Efficiency of the Bond Market: Some Canadian Evidence', *Journal of Political Economy*, 86: 1057–76.

Peters, G. H. (1991) 'Agriculture and the Macroeconomy', *Journal of Agricultural Economics*, 42: 231–49.

Peterson, W. L. and Hayami, Y. (1977) 'Technical Change in Agriculture', *A Survey of Agricultural Economic Literature*, Vol. 1 (ed. L. R. Martin) (Minneapolis: University of Minnesota Press).

Petit, M. (1981) 'Agriculture and Regional Development in Europe – the Role of Agricultural Economists', *European Review of Agricultural Economics*, 8(2/3): 137–54.

Petit, M. (1985) *Determinants of Agricultural Policies in the United States and the European Community*, Research Report No. 51 (Washington, DC: International Food Policy Research Institute).

Petit, M. *et al.* (1987) *Agricultural Policy Formation in the European Community: The Birth of Milk Quotas and EEC Reform* (Amsterdam: Elsevier).

Potter, C. (1991) *The Diversion of Land: Conservation in a Period of Farming Contraction* (London and New York: Routledge).

Pray, C. E. (1989) 'The Seed Industry and Plant Breeders' Rights: Report of October 4 through 13, 1989 Trip to Argentina and Chile', unpublished report for USAID.

Pray, C. E. and C. F. Neumeyer (1990) 'Problems of Omitting Private Investments in Research when Measuring the Impact of Public Research', in R. G. Echeverria (ed.), *Methods for Diagnosing Research System Constraints and Assessing the Impact of Agricultural Research*, Vol. II (The Hague: International Service for National Agricultural Research) 139–58.

Pray, C. E. and Echeverria, R. G. (1991) 'Private-Sector Agricultural Research in Less-Developed Countries', chapter 10 in P. D. Pardey, J. Rosenboom and J. R. Anderson (eds), *Agricultural Research Policy: International Quantitative Perspectives* (Cambridge: Cambridge University Press).

Rabinowicz, E., Haraldsson, I. and Bolin, O. (1986) 'The Evolution of a Regulation System in Agriculture: the Swedish Case', *Food Policy*, 11: 323–33.

Rausser, G. C. (1982) 'Political Economic Markets: PERTS and PESTS, Food and Agriculture', *American Journal of Agricultural Economics*, 64: 822–33.

Rausser, G. C. (1985) 'Macroeconomics and US Agricultural Policy, in B. L. Gardner (ed.), *US Agricultural Policy: The 1985 Farm Legislation* (Washington, DC: American Enterprise Institute for Public Policy Research) 207–52.

Rausser, G. C., Chalfant, J. A., Love, H. A. and Stamoulis, K. G. (1986) 'Macroeconomic Linkages, Taxes and Subsidies in the US Agricultural Sector', *American Journal of Agricultural Economics*, 68: 399–412.

Rausser, G. C. and Foster, W. (1990) 'Political Preference Functions and Public Policy Reform', *American Journal of Agricultural Economics*, 72: 641–52.

Rayner, A. J. and Reed, G. V. (1979) 'Domestic Price Stabilisation, Trade Restrictions and Buffer Stock Policy: A Theoretical Policy Analysis with Reference to EC Agriculture', *European Review of Agricultural Economics*, 5: 101–18.

Repetto, R. (1985) (ed.) *The Global Possible: Resources, Development and the New Century* (New Haven, Conn. and London: Yale University Press).

Robertson, J. C. and Orden, D. (1990) 'Monetary Impacts on Prices in the Long and Short Run: Some Evidence from New Zealand', *American Journal of Agricultural Economics*, 72: 160–71.

Roe, T. L. and Pardey, P. G. (1991) 'Economic Policy and Investment in Rural Public Goods: A Political Economic Perspective', chapter 1 in P. G. Pardey, J. Roseboom and J. R. Anderson (eds), *Agricultural Research Policy: International Quantitative Perspectives* (The Hague: International Service for National Agricultural Research).

Rogers, P. P. (1985) 'Freshwater', chapter 9 in Repetto, *The Global Possible*.

Roningen, V. and Dixit, P. (1989a) *Economic Implications of Agricultural Policy Reforms in Industrialised Market Economies*, Staff Report No. AGES 89–363 (Washington, DC: Economic Research Service, US Department of Agriculture).

Roningen, V. and Dixit, P. (1989b) *How Level is the Playing Field?: An Economic Analysis of Agricultural Policy Reforms in Industrial Market Economies* (Washington, DC: US Department of Agriculture, Economic Research Service).

Rose, F. (1980) 'Supply Shifts and Research Benefits: Comment', *American Journal of Agricultural Economics*, 62: 834–7.

Runge, C. F. (1981) 'Common Property Externalities: Isolation, Assurance, and Resource Depletion in a Traditional Grazing Context', *American Journal of Agricultural Economics* 63(4): 595–605.

Runge, C. F., Witzke, H. von and Thompson, S. (1987) *Liberal Agricultural Trade as a Public Good: Free Trade versus Free Riding under the GATT* (Minneapolis: University of Minnesota, Center for International Food and Agricultural Policy).

Ruttan, V. W. (1982) *Agricultural Research Policy* (Minneapolis: University of Minnesota Press).

Samuelson, P. A. (1965) 'Proof that Properly Anticipated Prices Fluctuate Randomly', *Industrial Management Review*, 6: 41–9.

Samuelson, P. A. (1972) 'Proof That Properly Anticipated Prices Fluctuate Randomly', in H. Nagatini and K. Crowley (eds), *The Collected Scientific Papers of Paul A. Samuelson*, Vol. 4 (Cambridge, Mass.: MIT Press) 465–70.

Sanderson, F. (ed.) (1990) *Agricultural Protectionism in the Industrialised World* (Washington, DC: Resources for the Future).

Sargent, T. J. (1972) 'Rational Expectations and the Term Structure of Interest Rates', *Journal of Money, Credit and Banking*, 4: 74–97.

Sargent, T. J. (1978) 'Estimation of Dynamic Labour Demand Schedules Under Rational Expectations', *Journal of Political Economy*, 86: 1009–44.

Schmid, A. A. (1985) 'Biotechnology, Plant Variety Protection and Changing Property Institutions in Agriculture', *N. Central Journal of Agricultural Economics*, 7: 130–8.

Schmitz, A. and Seckler, D. (1970) 'Mechanical Agriculture and Social Welfare: The Case of the Tomato Harvester', *American Journal of Agricultural Economics*, 52: 569–78.

Schuh, G. E. (1974) 'The Exchange Rate and US Agriculture', *American Journal of Agricultural Economics*, 56: 1–13.

Schuh, G. E. (1976) 'The New Macroeconomics of Agriculture', *American Journal of Agricultural Economics*, 58: 802–11.

Schuh, G. E. (1989) 'Macro Linkages and Agriculture: the United States Experience', in Maunder and Valdes, *Agriculture and Governments*, 533–9.

Schuh, G. E. and Orden, D. (1988) 'The Macroeconomics of Agriculture and Rural America', in R. J. Hildreth, K. T. Lipton, K. C. Dayton and C. C. O'Connor (eds), *Agriculture and Rural Areas Approaching the 21st Century: Challenges for Agricultural Economics* (Iowa: Iowa State University Press) 347–83.

Schultz, T. W. (1945) *Agriculture in an Unstable Economy* (New York: McGraw-Hill).

Schulze, W. D., d'Arge, R. C. and Brookshire, D. S. (1981) 'Valuing Environmental Commodities: Some Recent Experiments', *Land Economics*, 57(2): 151–72.

Segelken, R. (1990) 'Viral Nucleic Acid Makes Plants Immune to Disease', *Cornell Chronicle*, 13 December, 5.

Senior Nello, S. (1990) *Agricultural Trade between the European Economic Community and Central East Europe*, Seminario INEA, Roma 19 April.

Sheffrin, S. M. (1983) *Rational Expectations* (Cambridge: Cambridge University Press).

Shepsle, K. A. and Weingast, B. R. (1981) 'Political Preferences for the Pork Barrel: A Generalisation', *American Journal of Political Science*, 25: 96–111.

Sherwood, R. M. (1990) *Intellectual Property and Economic Development* (Boulder, Col.: Westview Press).

Shiller, R. J. (1981) 'Do Stock Prices Move Too Much to be Justified by Subsequent Changes in Dividends?', *American Economic Review*, 71: 421–36.

Shucksmith, D. M. and Smith, R. (1991) Farm Household Strategies and Pluriactivity in Upland Scotland, *Journal of Agricultural Economics*, 42(3): 340–53.

Sicular, Terry (1989a) 'China: Food Pricing under Socialism', in T. Sicular (ed.), *Food Price Policy in Asia: A Comparative Study* (Ithaca, NY: Cornell University Press).

Sicular, Terry (1989b) 'Distribution in Rural China: Observations from a Recent Survey in Hubei', unpublished manuscript (Harvard).

Sicular, Terry (1990a) *China's Agricultural Policy during the Reform Period*, Harvard Institute of Economic Research Discussion Paper No. 1522.

Sicular, Terry (1990b) *Ten Years of Reform: Progress and Setbacks in Agricultural Planning and Pricing*, Harvard Institute of Economic Research Discussion Paper No. 1474.

Siebeck, W. E. (ed.) (1990) *Strengthening Protection of Intellectual Property in Developing Countries: A Survey of the Literature*, Discussion Paper 112 (Washington, DC: World Bank).

Simmonds, N. W. (1990) 'The Social Context of Plant Breeding', *Plant Breeding Abstracts*, 60: 337–41.

Smith, A. (1913) *The Wealth of Nations* (London: Routledge).

Snape, R. H. (1989) 'Real Exchange Rates, Real Interest Rates and Agriculture', in Maunder and Valdes, *Agriculture and Governments*, 519–32.

Soderholm, C. G., Otterby, D. E., Ehle, F. R., Linn, J. G., Hansen, W. P. and Annexstad, R. J. (1986, Suppl. 1) 'Effects of Different Doses of Recombinant Bovine Somatotropin (rbSTH) on Milk Production, Body Composition, and Conditions Score in Lactating Cows', *Journal of Dairy Science*, 69:152.

Spears, J. and Ayensu, E. S. (1985) 'Resources, Development and the New Century: Forestry', in R. Repetto (ed.), *The Global Possible: Resources, Development and the New Century* (New Haven, Conn. and London: Yale University Press).

Stallings, D. (1991) 'More on Macroeconomics and Agriculture: International Financial Markets and Agricultural Trade', *Journal of Agricultural Economics Research*, 42: 41–4.

Starleaf, D. R., Meyers, W. H. and Womack, A. W. (1985) 'The Impact of Inflation on the Real Income of US Farmers', *American Journal of Agricultural Economics*, 67: 384–9.

State Statistical Bureau (1986, 1988, 1989, 1990a, 1990b) *Zhongguo Tongji Nianjian* (China Statistical Almanac) (Beijing: Zhongguo Tongji Chubanshe).

State Statistical Bureau Department of Fixed Asset Investment Statistics (1987) *Zhongguo Guding Zichan Touzi Tongji Ziliao, 1950–1985* (Beijing: Zhongguo Tongji Chubanshe).

State Statistical Bureau Department of Rural Socioeconomic Statistics (1985, 1988, 1989) *Zhongguo Nongcun Tongji Nianjian* (Almanac of China's Rural Statistics) (Beijing: Zhongguo Tongji Chubanshe).

Stoeckel, A. B., Vincent, D. and Cuthbertson, S. (1989) *Macroeconomic Consequences of Farm Support Policies* (Durham and London, Duke University Press).

Strange, M. (1988) *Family Farming – A New Economic Vision* (Lincoln, NE: University of Nebraska Press).

Streber, W. R. and Willmitzer, L. (1989) 'Transgenic Tobacco Plants Expressing a Bacterial Detoxifying Enzyme are Resistant to 2, 4-D', *BioTechnology*, 7: 811–16.

Tam, On-Kit (1988) 'Rural Finance in China', *China Quarterly*, 113: 60–76.

Tauer, L. (1989) 'Potential Economic Impacts of Herbicide-resistant Corn', in J. Fessenden MacDonald (ed.), *BioTechnology and Sustainable Agriculture: Policy Alternatives* (Ithaca, NY: National Agricultural Biotechnology Council NABA Report 1) 124–3).

Taylor, S. J. (1982) 'Test of the Random Walk Hypothesis Against a Price-Trend Hypothesis', *Journal of Financial and Quantitative Analysis*, 17: 37–61.

Taylor, S. J. (1983) 'Trading Rules for Investors in Apparently Inefficient Markets', in Streit (ed.), *Futures Markets Modelling* (Oxford: Blackwell) 165–98.

Taylor, S. J. and Tari, A. (1989) 'Further Evidence Against the Efficiency of Futures Markets', in R. M. C. Guimaraes, *et al.* (eds), *A Reappraisal*.

Thomson, K. J. (1981) *Farming in the Fringe*, CCP 142 (Cheltenham: Countryside Commission).

Tracy, M. (1989) *Government and Agriculture in Western Europe, 1880–1988*, 3rd edn (London: Harvester Wheatsheaf).

Tshibaka, T. B. (1986) *The Effects of Trade and Exchange Rate Policies on Agriculture in Zaire* (Washington, DC: International Food Policy Research Institute Research Report 56).

Turnovsky, S. J. (1983) 'The Determination of Spot and Future Prices and Storable Commodities', *Econometrica*, 51: 1363–87.

Tyers, R (1990) 'Trade Reform and Price Risk in Domestic and International Food Markets', *The World Economy*, 13: 212–30.

Tyers, R. and Anderson, K. (1988) 'Liberalising OECD Agricultural Policies in the Uruguay Round: Effects on Trade and Welfare', *Journal of Agricultural Economics*, 39: 192–216.

Tyers, R. and Anderson, K. (1992) *Disarray in World Food Markets: A Quantitative Assessment* (Cambridge: Cambridge University Press).

United Nations (1972) *Guidelines for Project Evaluation* (New York, Project Formulation and Evaluation Series No. 2, IP/SER H/2).

United Nations (1979) *Problems of the Agricultural Development of Less-favoured Areas in Europe*, Proc. Symp. FAO/ECE Committee on Agricultural Problems (Oxford: Pergamon).

United Nations Conference on Trade and Development (UNCTAD) (8 August 1988) *Technology-related Policies and Legislation in a Changing*

Economic and Technological Environment (New York: United Nations, TD/B/C.6/146).

UPOV (1990) *Basic Proposal for a New Act of the International Convention for the Protection of New Variety of Plants* (DC/91/3, Geneva, 9 November).

US Congress (1986) *Technology, Public Policy and the Changing Structure of American Agriculture* (Washington, DC: Office of Technology Assessment).

USDA (1989) *Agricultural-Food Policy Review: US Agricultural Policies in a Changing World* (Washington, DC: US Department of Agriculture, Economic Research Service).

USDA (1990) *China: Agriculture and Trade Report* (Washington, DC: US Department of Agriculture, Economic Research Service).

Variyam, J. N. Jordan, J. L. and Epperson, J. E. (1990) 'Preferences of Citizens for Agricultural Policies: Evidence from a National Survey', *American Journal of Agricultural Economics*, 72: 257–67.

Veeman, T. S. and Fantino, A. A. (1988) 'Productivity in Canadian Agriculture: Empirical Measurement and Growth Trends, 1948–1984', paper presented at XX International Conference of Agricultural Economists, Buenos Aires, Argentina, August.

Vine, A. and Bateman, D. (1981) *Organic Farming Systems in England and Wales: Practice, Performance and Implications* (Aberystwyth: Department of Agricultural Economics, University College of Wales).

Wadekin, K. E (ed.) (1990) *Communist Agriculture: Farming in the Soviet Union and Eastern Europe* (London and New York: Routledge).

Wadekin, K. E. and Brada, J. L. (eds) (1988) *Socialist Agriculture in Transition* (Boulder, Col. and London: Westview Press).

Watson, Andrew (1989) 'Investment Issues in the Chinese Countryside', *Australian Journal of Chinese Affairs*, 22: 85–126.

West, Loraine (1990) 'Rural Credit Markets and the Cost of Capital', mimeo, Stanford University.

Whitby M. C. and Willis, K. G. (1978) *Rural Resource Development: An Economic Approach* (London: Methuen).

Whitby, M., Coggins, G. and Saunders, C. (1990) *Alternative Payment Systems for Management Agreements*, Report Commissioned by the NCC (University of Newcastle upon Tyne).

Wibberley, G. (1981) 'Strong Agricultures but Weak Rural Economies: the Undue Emphasis on Agriculture in European Rural Development', *European Review of Agricultural Economics*, 8(2/3): 155–70.

Wilken, G. C. (1991) *Sustainable Agriculture is the Solution, but What is the Problem?* (Washington, DC: Board for International Food and Agricultural Development and Economic Cooperation, USAID, Occasional Paper No. 14).

Williams, J. (1987) 'Futures Markets: A Consequence of Risk Aversion on Transactions Costs', *Journal of Political Economy*, 95: 1001–23.

Wilson, G. K. (1977) *Special Interests and Policymaking* (London: John Wiley).

Winters, L. A. (1987) 'The Political Economy of Agricultural Policy of Industrial Countries', *European Review of the Agricultural Economics*, 14: 285–304.

Winters, L. A. (1989) 'The So-called Non-Economic Objectives of Agricultural Policy', *OECD Economic Studies*, 13: 237–66.

Winters, L. A. (1990) 'The National Security Argument for Agricultural Protection', *The World Economy*, 13: 170–90.

Wise, W. S. (1984) 'The Shift of Cost Curves and Agricultural Research Benefits', *Journal of Agricultural Economics*, 35: 21–30.

Wise, W. S. (1986) 'The Calculation of Rates of Return on Agricultural Research from Production Functions', *Journal of Agricultural Economics*, 37: 151–62.

Wise, W. S. and Fell, E. (1980) 'Supply Shifts and Research Benefits: Comment', *American Journal of Agricultural Economics*, 62: 838–40.

Wong, Christine (1988) 'Interpreting Rural Industrial Growth in the Post-Mao Period', *Modern China* 14(1): 3–30.

World Bank (1986) *The World Development Report, 1986* (Washington, DC: World Bank).

World Bank (1990) *An Agricultural Strategy for Poland*, report of the Polish European Community (Washington, DC: World Bank, Task Force).

World Commission on Environment and Development (1987) *Our Common Future* (Oxford University Press).

World Intellectual Property Organization (1988) *Existence, Scope and Form of Generally Internationally Accepted and Applied Standards/Norms for the Protection of Intellectual Property* (Geneva, WO/INF 129).

Young, T. and G. Allen (1986) 'Methods for Valuing Countryside Amenity: An Overview', *Journal of Agricultural Economics*, 37(3): 349–64.

Young, T. and M. P. Burton (1991) *Agricultural Sustainability: Definition and Implications for Agricultural Trade Policy* (University of Manchester: Department of Agricultural Economics Working Paper 91/01).

Zou, Jiahua (1990) 'Report on Implementation of the 1989 Plan for National Economic and Social Development and the Draft 1990 Plan (excerpts)', *Beijing Review*, 33(17): I–VIII.

Author Index

Subject Index